Praise for W

"Soulfully conceived, beautifully written, a[...] therapeutic and philosophical knowledge, this book is rich with [...] healing and enhancing our lived experience of the Worlds at all levels, natural, social, and spiritual. McKernan's goal is to guide Heathens, Pagans and Animists into 'a process that leads ever more and more to an experience of wholeness.'... He succeeds admirably; this book is highly recommended. The beauty of its writing and its vision is truly inspirational." —**Winifred Hodge Rose, author of** *Heathen Soul Lore Foundations* **and** *Heathen Soul Lore: A Personal Approach*

"We are living through tough, scary, and disturbing times... *Wyrdcraft* spins a positive web on how to be with it all in a way that grows us, enlightens us, and strengthens the way for us to show up and meet the challenges skillfully... This is an uplifting book but one that does not shy away from facing the dark forces, the shadow. Far from it; Matthew takes us deeper in through practical, experiential exercises [that teach us] to befriend and work with these forces, transforming them into service for the good. Nature wisdom, shamanic wisdom, indigenous wisdom, and magic wisdom are all shared in an entertaining way for attainment of higher states of consciousness... My hope is you take time to read this book and see how it might inspire you to greater awareness and ownership of the transformational powers that are available to us all when we know how to open, look for, and respectfully use them." —**Dr. Tom Pinkson, author of** *The Shamanic Wisdom of the Huichol*

wyrdcraft

About the Author

Matthew Ash McKernan is a licensed psychotherapist (MFT), ecotherapist, bard, and wyrd-worker currently living on the coast of Maine on the mountainous, mythic island of Mount Desert, home of Acadia National Park, sacred ancestral lands of the Wabanaki people. Ash has been attuning to the ways of wyrd since he was a child. He is a walker of worlds, a flametender, a singer, and a dancer, who loves to find, create, share, and hold sacred space-time-consciousness for the exploration and worship of soul in its myriad manifestations. Though he has primarily been a solo practitioner of natural magic for most of his life, he is an initiate of the Sha'can (Shakta Tantra) tradition, and he revels his time spent in community with fellow tantrics, magicians, witches, and mystics within the Reclaiming, Troth, Northeast Heathen, and Wisterian communities. He looks forward to meeting you and yours. You can visit his webpage at www.wyrdwildweb.com. And you can listen to his music at www.mazemorphia.bandcamp.com and www.wildhum .bandcamp.com.

MATTHEW ASH MCKERNAN

wyrdcraft

Healing Self & Nature through the
Mysteries of the Fates

Llewellyn Publications
Woodbury, Minnesota

FIRST EDITION
First Printing, 2023

Book design by Christine Ha
Cover design by Kevin R. Brown
Wyrd sigils by the Llewellyn Art Department (original concepts developed by author)

Llewellyn Publications is a registered trademark of Llewellyn Worldwide Ltd.

Library of Congress Cataloging-in-Publication Data (Pending)
ISBN: 978-0-7387-7177-9

Llewellyn Worldwide Ltd. does not participate in, endorse, or have any authority or responsibility concerning private business transactions between our authors and the public.
    All mail addressed to the author is forwarded but the publisher cannot, unless specifically instructed by the author, give out an address or phone number.
    Any internet references contained in this work are current at publication time, but the publisher cannot guarantee that a specific location will continue to be maintained. Please refer to the publisher's website for links to authors' websites and other sources.

Llewellyn Publications
A Division of Llewellyn Worldwide Ltd.
2143 Wooddale Drive
Woodbury, MN 55125-2989
www.llewellyn.com

Printed in the United States of America

For Koko, Coco, Raven, Freyja, and the Forest

Disclaimer

The use of psychedelic substances and medicines is discussed in this book. Any recreational, medicinal, or ritual use of psychedelics is the sole responsibility and choice of the reader. It is the reader's responsibility to be educated on the legality of these substances, as well as their proper and safe use, which is beyond the scope of this book. The author, the publisher, and their representatives cannot accept any responsibility, legal or otherwise, for any misuse, damage, or harm resulting from the personal choice and judgment of the reader.

In addition, the variety of suggestions, exercises, and practices suggested in this book are in no way a replacement for professional medical and psychological assistance. Rather, they are a supplement to be used in accordance with the reader's own holistic health care regimen. Always consult with trained and accredited professionals when it comes to any physical or psychological disturbance, symptomology, or course of treatment. Neither the author nor the publisher accepts any responsibility for the reader's health or how the reader chooses to use the information contained in this book.

Acknowledgments

First and foremost, I would like to acknowledge and thank Nature—the true author of this book. To the Sun, Moon, stars, trees, waterways, meadows, mountains, and everyone within—you spoke, you sang, you whispered—may your teachings ring true through these pages.

To my parents, brother, sister, and their families; to my extended family; to my grandparents and to their parents and their parents all the way back through time-space—thank you for your hard work, struggles, tears, laughter, song, dance, will, and support. May your enduring love ring true through these pages.

To my teachers—Mildred Dubitzky, James Baraz, Chandra Alexandre, Gieve Patel, Debbie Stone, Renee Beck, Sarah Beth Feley, Judi Noddin, Li Kun Deng, Anthony Guarnieri, Amalia Castonan-Hill, Tom Pinkson, Alan Levin, the sacred plant medicines, and many more—may your teachings ring true through these pages.

To Emily Shurr and Adam Goldman; to Heather Greene, Sami Sherratt, Aundrea Foster, Markus Ironwood, and everyone behind the scenes at Llewellyn Worldwide, thank you for your support and your magical midwifery that helped bring this book into the world.

To all my wise and wily friends with whom I've had the opportunity to play music, get lost in conversation, and traverse many a dimension together. Far too many of you to name, lovers, fools, and warriors on the edge of time, all of you—thank you for the minutes, hours, days, weeks, and years.

May your soul ring true through these pages.

To my spirit guides and to the sacred spots that have brought me comfort, healing, insight, and inspiration while this book came together—to the East Bay Hills, Mount Tamalpais, Emigrant Wilderness, Golden Gate Park, and Mount Desert Island—may your power, guidance, and healing powers ring true through the pages of this book.

To the indigenous peoples—past, present, and future—of these lands I have traversed and inhabited. May your lifeways, stories, song, and dance live on and flourish, and may we heal and transform together as we continue the work of tending this miraculous Web together.

Author's Note

The symbol on the cover (which I refer to as the Web) as well as the other symbols that separate the parts of this book can be used as meditation tools. Consider each of them a window, door, or gateway into wyrd. As you encounter each one, take a moment, relax your body-mind, and spend some minutes focusing—or willing—your awareness on the symbol's center point. Then soften your awareness and spend some minutes taking in the symbol in its entirety. Nothing specific is supposed to happen. Just be with the symbol. Simply let sacred geometry work on you; be open and remain curious. I encourage you to get some colored pencils, markers, or pens and color each symbol in, draw additions to them, and personalize them in creative ways as you go. Let the reading inspire your creations. Have fun! The first symbol in the book, as you will see, is the simplest, composed of three lines, three intersecting threads, each one representing one of the three Fates, or Norns. This symbol is the Seed. Plant this Seed in the void of your imagination with an intention. What intention(s) would you like to bring to your reading? What intention(s) might guide your crafting? May it be so! With each symbol, watch the Seed blossom. Open yourself to that which yearns to come into the world through the fertile void that is psyche. Welcome the Fates and their mysteries into your life. Blessed be!

Contents

Wyrding Ways
Experientials and Exercises

Introduction
Welcome to the Gates of Wyrd

If you are reading this, then fate has brought us together. Somehow, your fate and my fate have led us to this moment. Somehow, you were meant to read these words and contemplate their meaning, just as I was meant to contemplate them and write them down. It's strange how fate connects us across time and space, through words and through meaning.

Something similar might be said about purpose. You are reading this book for a reason. Perhaps your reasons for reading it and my reasons for writing it are in alignment. Perhaps there is an underlying ghost of a song that has called out to us both, drawing us closer to each other in our listening—a shared destiny, if you will, weaving into an even larger song of which and in which we are slowly becoming aware.

Your life is but one thread woven into the tapestry of existence, as is mine. Our life-threads weave together, along with the life-threads of countless other beings and things, near and far. Each thread is composed of countless finer threads, each with its own constellation of elements, raw materials, patterns, and stories, as well as its own purposes playing out within the greater weave and web of life into which we are all woven. You will soon become intimately acquainted with this tapestry, this weave, this web. It is called the Web of Wyrd. Within it, everything is connected to everything else: all plants, all

1

animals, all ecosystems, all matter, all phenomena, all purposes, all meanings, all processes, all possibilities—all interwoven.

If you are reading this book, chances are high that you've already sensed the presence of this Web or already know it intimately. Perhaps you sense that you have a special place and purpose within it. Perhaps you already know what that purpose is, perhaps not. I look forward to exploring this purpose with you throughout the pages of this book.

My personal path to wyrd began when I was around two and half years old. Though I don't have many memories from those very early years of my life, I do have some. I remember the warmth of the sun. I remember the deep blue sky and the long cool green grass as I sat in the shade of an enormous tree in our side yard. I remember playing with a yellow truck. I remember the big red barn, the tall corn bin, and the old textured wood of the outhouse. I remember the strange eyes, horns, and coarse hair of the goats we had. I remember sitting on a low windowsill of a second-story window, laughing, back bouncing against the window screen. I remember the soft, pure, easygoing, and free-flowing bubbling joy of the moment, soon followed by an exhilarating rush and lurch as the window screen popped out and I plummeted downward—everything spinning.

What I don't remember is holding on to my baby blanket as I fell. I don't remember the impact of landing upon it face-first when I hit the bricks below. I don't remember leaving my body, though I do have the somatic memory of it—a memory I later retrieved and processed during a series of mushroom ceremonies in which I took part when I was older. I don't remember my dad picking me up off the ground and rushing me to the emergency room, or the parish priest coming in to read me my last rights. And strangely, I don't remember, merely hours later, playfully running around the hospital that night as if none of it had happened. My parents do, though; it perplexes them to this day.

That fall out the window onto the brick below on that summer day was one of those moments of meaning that shape life and destiny. Though this is certainly not the only moment that shaped my wyrd, who I am today, where I've been, what I've done, what I'm doing, where I'm going, and who I'm becoming can to some extent be traced to that fateful fall. Something happened when my body hit those bricks. The force of the impact was so strong that it sent waves, ripples, and fragments of my soul in every direction at once. My body may have stopped when it hit the ground, but my being kept going, and for a moment, my soul was set free. Of course, I was far too young to understand it as such, but in that moment, I experienced my first initiation into the great beyond.

To try to understand this experience—and to heal from it—I unconsciously did what came naturally: I followed the waves and ripples and began to search for fragments. Thus began the wandering, spiraling, healing soul-journey of my life-thread into wyrd. This journey has led me to many places, people, and experiences. It has made me who I am today—a wounded-healer with a deep fascination for nature, spirituality, mystery, death, psychedelics, and the arts and crafts of the underworld and otherworlds. It led to my obsession with altered states; to my inclinations toward experimental, heavy, trippy music; to raving, ritual, the ecstatic, and the weird. It led me to mysticism, tantra, witchcraft, and seiðr. It also led to me becoming a social worker and psychetherapist. Eventually, this inward and outward expansion led me to all my friends, lovers, teachers, guides, and patrons. It led me from one initiation to the next until it eventually led me to wyrd, to the ways of wyrd, to the beautiful tapestry that is the Web of Wyrd. Eventually, it would lead me to you, reader.

Very early on, the waves and ripples took me deep into the natural world, for it was there where I found the answers to the questions my body was asking; it was there where I began to find healing, and where I felt the push and pull of the beyond most viscerally. It was then and there, as I wandered through the fields and forests of my rural Ohio childhood, where I first began to find the hidden threads—the first pieces of the tapestry. One led me to another; the more I sought, the more I found. Threads were everywhere—buried in the dirt, drifting on the wind, flowing down bubbling streams, meandering up and down sunbaked country roads. Threads rooted in the core of the Earth reached upward and outward through the trees and toward the stars. I held these threads in my hands, mind, and heart as I explored, weaving them together as I went. In this way, I found my way toward healing. In this way, the Web took form.

Over the course of the last four decades, I followed the threads whenever and wherever I found them, down country roads, into cities, down avenues and alleyways, across the country, and around the world. Through the simplest, quietest times, as well as the busiest, wildest times, the strings of the tapestry hummed and danced as I held them in my hands. The years passed, the world changed, I changed. I found myself following threads not only to other people and other places, but to other states of mind and other ways of being—near and far. Some of these threads connected me to people, others to places, others to feelings. Occasionally I would recognize that some threads had stronger vibrations than others. Some even created mesmerizing patterns and songs. To these I paid special attention. I would lose them and find them and lose them and find them again. All the while, the Web was taking form; all the while, I was healing.

About This Book

Wyrd is a multifaceted concept—it is fate, destiny, nature, soul, magic, becoming, and mystery. How can wyrd be all these things at once, you may ask? This is the beauty, magic, and power of wyrd.

This book is about wyrd and the ways of wyrd. The ways of wyrd are the ways of the Fates, and the ways of the Fates are the ways of Nature. This book is a guidebook for attuning to these ways. Wyrdcraft is an experiential practice of attuning to the nature of wyrd and the wyrd of Nature. This attunement—as you will see within these pages, and within the pages of your life—will lead to ecopsychospiritual revelation, healing-transformation, and becoming. This is the beauty, power, and magic of wyrd.

This book is a window into the psychology of animism as it manifests within the pagan, heathen, native, and indigenous mind. Animism is a worldview that experiences everything to be imbued with soul—the oldest of spiritual worldviews. I will use the terms *pagan, paganism, heathen*, and *heathenry* interchangeably throughout this book, but to clarify, *paganism* is a larger umbrella term that covers a wide range of people who self-identify as pagans and practice some form of nature-based spirituality such as druidism, Vodou, ceremonial magick, Hellenic polytheism, and so on. *Heathenry* is another umbrella term that describes those who self-identify as heathens and practice some form of Germanic, Norse, or Anglo-Saxon spiritual path. Some of the most well-known heathen spiritual communities are Ásatrú ("true to the Aesir gods and goddesses"), Vanatrú ("true to the Vanir"), the Troth ("loyal" or "truth"), Forn Siðr ("old ways"), Odinism, and Wodenism ("worship of Odin, Woden," etc.).

Though there are certainly many similarities between these groups as far as who and how they worship, each have their own lenses through which they interpret and practice the surviving, old ways of Northern Europe. Most are inclusive groups that are open to anyone who feels called to them; some, however, including some sects of Odinism, have strong ties to Nazism, are highly exclusive, promote white supremacy, and have been connected to acts of terrorism.

Let me be clear that wyrdcraft is an inclusive approach that is open to anyone who feels called. Wyrdcraft does not discriminate based on spiritual background, race, ethnicity, gender, age, ability, or any other reason. It is not a religion, there are no clergy, and there are no specific rites, rituals, or practices wyrdcraft can call its own. Wyrdcraft is not just for pagans and heathens, though they will be most familiar with many of the concepts and vocabulary found within this book.

Let me also be clear that the practice and process of wyrdcraft is not a historically reconstructed practice. Though wyrd is an ancient concept, wyrdcraft is not an ancient practice, or even an ancient worldview. Rather, it represents a modern synthesis of what I've come to understand through my own life experiences as a pagan, musician, and wounded-healer. Of course, much of what I've come to understand is a result of others' life experiences and teachings as well. I've had many, many teachers—living, dying and dead, human, and other-than-human—on my journey into wyrd. Their teachings will be woven throughout this book.

Though there are some books you can read piecemeal, jumping forward and backward at will, I wouldn't recommend taking that approach with this book. Start with the beginning, end with the ending, then go from there. Wyrd is a complicated concept. Its paradoxical, multifaceted, and mercurial nature makes it quite hard to hold on to. Wyrd is a shapeshifting tapestry of processes, concepts, and phenomena—a kaleidoscopic arabesque of cosmic and psychedelic threads. It can be easy to feel overwhelmed, sidetracked, or lost while exploring them. Fear not, however; getting confused and lost is an important part of the process of coming to understand wyrd and crafting wyrd. Wyrd is, after all, ultimately a mystery that will not and cannot be solved within these pages. This book will not answer all your questions. In fact, it may even generate more.

The most important question we will ask throughout this book is *how?* This is the question of phenomenologists, those interested in exploring and understanding the Nature of things. How—with an emphasis on the here-and-now—is an attuning question. It brings you right into the moment. As you ask this, you attune. How (now) is_____happening? How (now) do I feel? How (now) do I know? How (now) is this process unfolding?

How is the question that will bring you closest to wyrd—as wyrd is first and foremost an existential experience and process that is unfolding in the here-and-now. This is where fate, destiny, nature, magic, soul and becoming are most potent. Yes, *who, what, when,* and *why* will be asked as well, but sometimes they will be asked through the lens of how. The question "Who am I?" for example, can be answered by exploring the question "*How* am I?" Often times, reframing the question through the lens of how (now) shifts one's awareness from the abstract thought realm into the realm of process and of lived experience, into the phenomenological unfolding of consciousness, being and reality in the here-and-now—where wyrd is. For example, the questions "Why is this happening?" and "What is happening?" can also both be answered through the lens of how—"*How* is this happening?" "*How* am I experiencing the phenomenology of the moment?" My guess is that if you are reading this book you are a naturally curious person and you are no stranger to wondering yourself into wonder. If I am correct, then I wish you happy wondering.

In chapter 1 of part 1: What Is Wyrd?, I invite you to look back into wyrd's etymological and historical origins. These subjects will serve as the raw materials from which you can begin to spin your understanding of wyrd. They will be the wool, flax, or cotton, so to speak, that you can spin into usable string and thread, which you can later use for your weaving.

Though the concept of wyrd comes to us via pre-Christian, animist Old Europe, wyrd's shapeshifting presence can be found all around the world. Divine spinners, weavers of fate, and the web—all symbols commonly associated with wyrd—existed all around the globe and still do today. Chapter 2 offers a short mythological survey into several of these trans-spatial and transtemporal cross-cultural manifestations. Hopefully, these explorations will bring some much-needed color to our threads and strings and give us some good ideas for some patterns we might use when we start our weaving.

Chapter 3 will provide you with a loom, so to speak—strong and stable, yet flexible enough to hold the tension of the simultaneous push and pull of wyrd's past, present, and future. Science and the approach of phenomenology will serve the purpose of this loom quite well, as they provide you with a strong and steady yet flexible structure upon which you may begin to weave your understanding and experience of wyrd into a more practical, tangible, and tactile form.

Wyrd can only be known if it is experienced; therefore, you will find several experientials interspersed throughout this book. I refer to these exercises, experiments, and practices as *wyrding ways*. These wyrding ways are just some examples of wyrdcraft in practice. Generally speaking, wyrding is any process by which one attunes to, explores, and affects change to wyrd. One could also call the wyrding ways magic. The wyrding ways presented in this book are designed to help you ground and center the many, sometimes heady, concepts you will encounter as you meander through this misty realm of the Fates. I recommend that you use a specially chosen "wyrd-journal" to record your journeys, thoughts, and experiences to help you make a conceptual map of the territory as you go.

Part 2: The Web of Wyrd is where the weaving will begin. In chapters 4 through 6, I will guide you through a systematic warp-and-weft exploration of the domains—from mind to body to relationship to environment to soul to spirit. I have chosen these domains because they represent the most salient spheres of human experience. Though ultimately, they are all interwoven into one whole, I have chosen to delineate them for the process of digestion. There is a lot of information in this book, and it's best to go thread by thread, step by step, part by part. Each domain is a window, a door, and a path into wyrd. As you explore each domain and engage with the experientials, you will be given several opportunities to locate wyrd within your life. In this way, the tapestry of wyrd will move from abstract to concrete.

As you wander through this book and engage with the wyrding ways, you will all the while be practicing wyrdcraft and developing wyrd consciousness. I first read about wyrd consciousness in scholar and seer Valarie

Wright's *Völuspá: Seiðr as Wyrd Consciousness*, written under the pen name Yngona Desmond. This book offers a riveting retelling and interpretation of the Norse saga *Völuspá* through a mystic lens. It is also a profound revelation into the magical practice of seiðr (to be explored in chapter 12) and the nature of wyrd consciousness (to be explored all throughout this book). In short, wyrd consciousness is the consciousness of Nature and the consciousness of the Fates. This emergent, paradoxical consciousness will not only help you locate wyrd within the domains, but it will also reveal how the domains weave together into the great tapestry known as the Web of Wyrd; it will also reveal your place within it. As such, wyrd consciousness could also be called Web consciousness. Like deep-space and deep-time, the deep-consciousness that is wyrd consciousness is inherently mysterious. You will see this. If you choose to walk through the experiential and existential gates of wyrd consciousness, you will see the veil that occludes the Web and ways of wyrd become ever more transparent, but you will also see that wyrd's mystery goes on and on. Wyrdcraft pushes, pulls and guides one into this mystery.

As the Web arises more into the foreground of your consciousness—as you attune—you will inevitably see that it is wounded and suffering. As you are one with the Web, you will in turn also see how you yourself are wounded and suffering. Wounding and suffering are the result of the natural phenomenon of fragmentation. Chapter 7 will be dedicated to the exploration of the multifaceted nature of this phenomenon through an in-depth inquiry into the symptoms of fragmentation as they manifest within every domain. The psychological, systemic, relational, ecological, and spiritual symptoms of fragmentation are easy to see if you take but a moment or two to look, and a moment or two more to feel. These symptoms have become quite pronounced in our current zeitgeist. Societal fragmentation, climate crisis, systemic oppression, and psychological illness are just a few.

Part 3: Wyrdcraft will shift from the process of fragmentation to the process of integration. Integration has four primary facets: revelation, healing, transformation, and becoming. Each of these facets has a way of reinforcing and encouraging the others. In other words, revelation leads to healing leads to transformation leads to revelation leads to healing leads to transformation leads to revelation—ad infinitum, all in a greater process of becoming. What this magical process of becoming is will become clear as you work through this book and as this book works on you.

In chapter 8, we will begin to delve into the practice of wyrdcraft, just one of many ways to practice integration. As you will see, wyrd—fate, destiny, nature, soul, magic, etc.—can be crafted. This crafting can and will take many forms, depending on who you are, what you are working on, and what you want and need. Your wyrd will determine your wyrdcraft. Your wyrdcraft will develop as you do it—as you attune to, locate, explore, and craft your own wyrd. To better understand how wyrdcraft might constellate within your own unique life-journey, in chapters 9, 10, and 11, I will guide you into a deeper exploration of the wyrdcraftian-triad of psychetherapy, ecotherapy, and magic—into the mysteries of the Well of Wyrd, the Tree of Wyrd, and the Wyrd Three (the Norns, the Fates). Chapter 12 will offer an even deeper dive into the mysteries of the Wyrd Three through an exploration of the ancient and modern Northern magical practice known as seiðr (pronounced *sayth*). Each of these mysteries, and each of these practices—psychetherapy, ecotherapy, and magic—are integrative; each leads to the revelation, healing-transformation, and becoming of the Web.

Wyrd is felt; as such, this book walks you through a firsthand experiential and experimental process of attuning to wyrd and feeling wyrd. This is the only way wyrd, and the ways of wyrd, can truly be known. Wyrdcraft will bring you right to the growing-edge of your being and becoming as a magician, witch, wounded-healer, and human—to the place where your comfort zone and the great unknown overlap. This is a place where powerful alchemy and magic occur, where safety and challenge dance, and where deep revelation, healing-transformation, and becoming happen. It is here where your fate, destiny, nature, soul, and magic will become clearer. As you dance your way through this book, you will uncover memories, wounds, habits, gifts, and potentials that have long been hidden from the light of awareness. Because of wyrdcraft's unearthing tendencies and often uncomfortable alchemical process, I highly recommend you find a licensed therapist, guide, or mentor to process the material that arises as you work through this book. Wyrdcraft is not easy; in fact, it can be an intense process from time to time. Wyrdcraft welcomes change, and change isn't always comfortable. Integration doesn't always feel pleasant. Go gently and go mindfully. Take care of yourself and those around you as you go. Knowing your best methods for self-care and developing new, healthy methods for self-care will be vital as you craft your wyrd. We will cover this important aspect of wyrdcraft in chapter 7.

Before closing the book, chapter 13 will weave it all together, bring things back to the ground, back to center. As wild as this world is, and as complex as the questions can be, the answers are often quite simple and actionable, and much closer than they seem. It all comes back to *how* and *now.* As I've experienced time and time again as a therapist, and as a client of therapy, the answers are already here, within you and within me. All we need is a reminder. All we need to do is remember. I will leave you with this, with practicality, with what can be done, with what can be continued, with the gates of wyrd wide open. But until then, happy reading and blessed becoming.

I am grateful we are meeting here together, at this crossroads, at this gate, in this aching zeitgeist in the ever-potent here-and-now. Beyond this gate, the mysteries of the Fates await exploration and revelation. There is a lot to look forward to from here—so much more than we can know, thanks to wyrd. Wyrd offers us a beautiful kaleidoscopic image of the tapestry of existence, woven and rewoven by the Fates, and by all of us—past, present, and future. All the potential to heal, transform, and become is within us—within me, within you, through and beyond this gate, right here, right now. I invite you to come on through; it's safe-enough, and it's time. Welcome Wyrd!

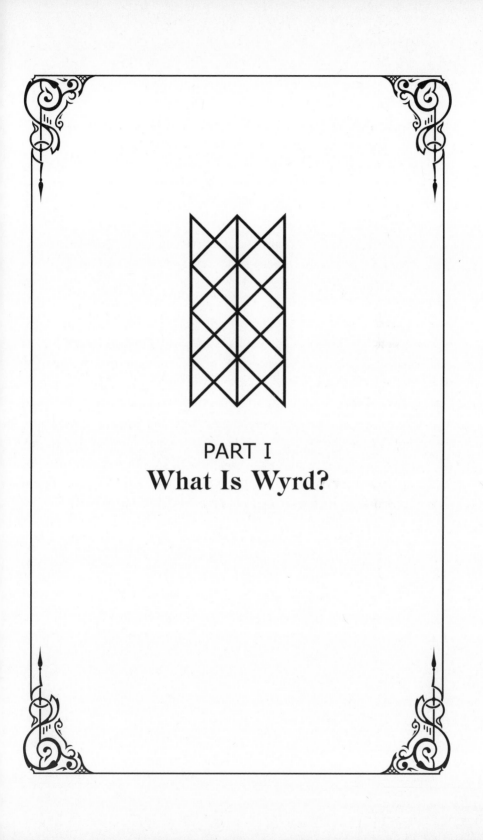

PART I
What Is Wyrd?

Chapter 1
Wyrd History, Etymology, and Culture

Though wyrd is most directly experienced in the present moment, an important part of understanding wyrd's nature is to understand wyrd's past. Wyrd has gone through quite the evolution since its obscure inception in the distant past. The word itself is said to come from the Anglo-Saxons, a conglomeration of indigenous Celtic Britons and heathen Germanic tribes that, in the fifth century, migrated from the European subcontinent to colonize the south and east coast of what we now call England.

Etymologically speaking, the word *wyrd* is said to come from the proto-Indo-European root *wert*, meaning "to turn or wind," and the proto-Germanic word *wurðíz*. It has a number of cognates: in Old Saxon, *wurd*; Old Norse, *urðr* (which is also the name of one of the Norns—the Norse Fates); Old High German, *wurt*; Common Germanic, *wirþ* (which means "to come to pass, to become, to be due"); Dutch, *worden* (meaning "to turn into"); and German, *warden* (meaning "to become"). There was also *weorþ*, which is "origin or worth" in the sense of connotation, price, value and affiliation, identity, esteem, honor, and dignity. In Old English, *wyrd* is a verbal noun formed from the verb *weorþan*, meaning "to come to pass, to become."[1]

---

1. D. Harper, "Weird," *Online Etymology Dictionary*, retrieved August 2019, https://www
.etymonline.com/word/weird#etymonline_v_4898; Max Dashú, *Witches and Pagans:
Women in European Folk Religion, 700–1100* (Richmond, CA: Veleda Press, 2016), 2.

Wyrd was an integral facet of the Germanic, Scandinavian, and Anglo-Saxon worldview and cosmology. Though in Norse culture, the concept of fate was referred to as ørlög (which will be explored in chapter 6), and wyrd and fate were personified by the Norn, Urðr (pronounced *urth*). Taken from Norse scholar, author, and YouTuber Jackson Crawford's translation of the *Poetic Edda* (originally composed by Icelandic historian, poet, and politician Snorri Sturluson), we read:

> Three wise women
> live there,
> by that well
> under that tree.
> Urth is named one,
> another Verthandi,
> the third is named Skuld.
> They carve men's fates
> they determine destiny's laws,
> they choose the lifespan
> of every human child,
> and how each life will end.[2]

Wyrd is also mentioned in Anglo-Saxon lore. From the epic poem *Beowulf*, for example, written sometime between the eight and the tenth centuries, we find the following: *Gæð a wyrd swa hio scel* ("Wyrd goes as she shall") and *Wyrd oft nereð Unfægne eorl, þonne his ellen deah* ("Wyrd often saves a man when his courage avails").[3] In the tenth and eleventh centuries, we can also find examples of *wyrd* in Old English sayings, such as *Wyrd byð swiðost* ("Wyrd is strongest"), *Giet biþ þæt selast, þonne mon him sylf ne mæg Wyrd onwendan, þæt he þonne wel þolige* ("If one may not change Wyrd it is best to suffer it"), and *Seo wyrd and seo hiow hie oft oncyrreð and on oþer hworfeð*

---

2. Jackson Crawford, *The Poetic Edda: Stories of the Norse Gods and Heroes* (Indianapolis, IN: Hacket Publishing Company, 2015), 6.
3. Bartlett Jere Whiting and Helen Wescott Whiting, *Proverbs, Sentences, and Proverbial Phrases: From English Writings Mainly Before 1500* (Cambridge, MA: Belknap Press, 1968), 636.

("Wyrd often changes").[4] In 1445, we find *Deed, weird na fortoun ar nocht for to wyt* ("Death, Weird or Fortune are not to be blamed").[5]

In fourteenth-century Scotland, *wyrd* was used as the verb *to weird* with the connotation "to preordain by decree of fate." In the fifteenth century, it was used in the sense of "having the power to control fate." Women who practiced midwifery, herbalism, healing, and divination were once called weirding women or wise women; eventually they would be deemed witches, and then oppressed and/or murdered for their ways.[6] One well-known early example of wyrd can be found in Shakespeare's *Macbeth*, with the three prophesizing witches known as the Weird Sisters—a transmutation of the earlier Moirai, Nornir, Parcae.[7]

Wyrd continued its evolution through the centuries within the worlds of philosophy, occultism, music, art, and literature. A volume of books could be dedicated to exploring this evolution, but one vibrant thread worth mentioning is the one that connects eighteenth-century Romanticism—in which authors such as Mary Shelley and Edgar Allan Poe devoted their writing to the interweaving of nature, emotion, and the supernatural—to the birth of the late nineteenth- and early twentieth-century subgenre called Weird Fiction, made popular by H. P. Lovecraft, Algernon Blackwood, Robert Bloch, and many others. Weird Fiction, and its offshoots New Weird and Slipstream, are genre-fluid blendings of horror, fantasy, science fiction, folktale, and mythology with sprinklings of the cosmic and the numinous to boot—all things weird.

On a side note, Frank Herbert, author of the science fiction masterpiece *Dune*, gave a shout-out to wyrd with his use of the *weirding way*—a highly secretive and powerful technique of physical, psychological, and psychic mastery perfected by a class of witches known as the Bene Gesserit.[8] Wyrd themes of fate, destiny, ecology, and mysticism weave through the entire *Dune*

---

4. Whiting and Whiting, *Proverbs, Sentences, and Proverbial Phrases*, 636.
5. Whiting and Whiting, *Proverbs, Sentences, and Proverbial Phrases*, 123.
6. Dashú, *Witches and Pagans*, 23; Barbara Ehrenreich and Deirdre English, *Witches, Midwives and Nurses: A History of Women Healers* (New York: The Feminist Press, 2010), 25–59.
7. Ralph Metzner, *The Well of Remembrance: Rediscovering the Earth Wisdom Myths of Northern Europe* (Boulder, CO: Shambhala, 1994), 217.
8. Frank Herbert, *Dune* (New York: ACE, 2005), 359.

series. You will learn a lot about wyrd if you read them. Moreover, I was also pleased to learn that there is a mountain on Venus named Wyrd Mons (Wyrd Mountain).

From Wyrd to Weird

An important aspect of understanding the nature of wyrd has to do with understanding the transformation from *wyrd* to *weird*. Let's begin with the word *weird*. *Weird* is an oft-used word in the English language. It is mostly used as an adjective ("That person is being weird") or a verb ("The sound in the forest weirded him out"). It has dozens of synonyms, some of the most common being *bizarre, eccentric, erratic, far-out, haunting, unusual*… I could go on. As I reflect upon these synonyms, I am struck by their accuracy, in the sense that they are all appropriate ways to describe our world and the nature of reality from time to time. Bizarre, absurd, and strange things happen regularly. I am also struck by the simple fact that they are all feelings. When things get weird, we *feel* weird. Take a moment to reflect. How often have you had an experience that elicited a feeling that resulted in the declaration, "That was weird!"?

Wyrd, too, is a feeling. In fact, wyrd is an experiential phenomenon. Wyrd is first and foremost sensed—it's always been this way. Wyrd is not an abstraction of some bigger-picture being or force that remains ever out of reach; it is a lived experience in the here-and-now. Yes, wyrd can be understood intellectually, but it can only be *known* somatically, emotionally, and relationally—within and through your tender mortal body. The goal of this book, and the goal of wyrdcraft, is quite simply to help you *feel* wyrd, for the more you feel wyrd, the more you will understand the ways of wyrd, and the more you understand the ways of wyrd, the easier it will be to craft wyrd. But I'm getting ahead of myself.

The experience of *weird* describes a wide range of phenomena, experiences, and feelings—perhaps something unexplainable, eerie, or novel just happened; perhaps someone or something has an aura of otherworldliness; perhaps serendipity just knocked at your door—weird! Sometimes weird can be explained, other times it can't. Sometimes it feels meaningful and purposeful, other times not. Sometimes the bizarre can be oddly comforting, sometimes it can feel disconcerting.

Wyrd, too, was felt to be something uncanny, serendipitous, strange. It, too, filled the void of comprehension that came with the seemingly unexplainable happenings and feelings of life and death. Something odd, strange, or mysterious would happen: a synchronicity, a prophetic dream, a metaphysical phenomenon. The crops would be abundant or sparse; hard times would befall in the form of a drought, storm, illness, or epidemic; death would come knocking at the door. Why? Wyrd.

One of the primary things that seems to distinguish the wyrd of yesterday from the weird of today is its association with fate and destiny. To ancient Northern Europeans (as well as to modern heathens and pagans), wyrd was directly associated with fate and attributed to the workings of a goddess—Wyrd. Wyrd entwined people, nature, and events together within a greater, mysterious pattern and process. For the most part, as mainstream society experiences, there is no purpose, destiny, or divine being attributed to weirdness. Although weird experiences can certainly carry some meaning with them, this meaning often stays on the surface. In our secular world, it's easy to let a moment of weirdness pass by without much ado. Depending upon the person and the culture in which the person has been conditioned, weird experiences are usually not perceived as deeply meaningful; they don't carry the same gravitas, they often don't directly refer to the deeper mysteries of life, death, magic, soul, and becoming. They don't speak to us of an underlying pattern or purpose unfolding in the direction of our fate and destiny.

So how did wyrd lose its deeper meaning? Where did we step off the path of wyrd and onto the path of weird? To answer these questions, let's look through the window of anthropology into the consciousness of our ancient ancestors into the worldview of animism.

Looking Through the Lens of Wyrd: Wild Mind and Old Ways

The people of pre-Christian Old Europe, as well as their peers and predecessors all over the globe, were animists and pantheists. Animism is a worldview that sees and feels a universe pervaded by life-force, essence, and sentience—in other words, by soul. To the animists of the past and present, everything was and is imbued with soul. Pantheism has a similar meaning, but with an important caveat. To the pantheist, not only is the universe and everything within it animated by soul, that soul is divinized through an association with specific goddesses, gods, or divine beings.

Ancient animists didn't call themselves animists. The word *animism* didn't exist until a nineteenth-century English anthropologist Sir Edward Tylor used it to describe the worldviews of so-called primitive cultures.[9] For these people, soul was so deeply woven into their felt experience of existence that it was unconsciously unquestioned. It was an experiential fact of life, not merely an intellectual belief.

As author and psychologist Brian Bates describes in his book *The Wisdom of the Wyrd: Teachings for Today from Our Ancient Past*, life was not only imbued with wyrd, but it was structured and directed by wyrd as well. According to Bates, the ways of wyrd described the happenings that took place around, between, and within them. One's birth, death, luck, livelihood, relationships, battles, healing, and survival were all to some extent dependent upon the ways of wyrd.[10]

If wyrd was so important and all pervasive, how could it almost disappear from the world? How could the spiritual experience of wyrd turn into the mundane experience of weird? Though there have been many forces at play in this regard, I'd like to start with the influence of Christianity. Fanatic Christians made it their God-given duty to convert the world to monotheistic Christianity. All over the globe, Christians, as well as other monotheists and polytheists, destroyed, defaced, and built churches on top of or next to sacred pagan and heathen sites. They strategically co-opted and repurposed their deities and festival days, gave them new names, and claimed them as their own. They demonized pagan deities, forbade their worship, outlawed pagan practices and lifeways, and tortured, murdered, and banished countless people in the process.[11]

As monotheism, which represented the new "normal," swept the globe, animism and pantheism—and all that was considered "weird"—were forced

---

9. Alexander Charles Oughter Lonie, "Animism," *In Encyclopædia Britannica*, edited by T. S. Baynes, vol. 2, 9th ed. (New York: Charles Scribner's Sons, 1878), 55–57.

10. Brian Bates, *The Wisdom of the Wyrd: Teachings for Today from Our Ancient Past* (London: Rider, 1996).

11. Edred Thorsson, *Witchdom of the True: A Study of the Vana-Troth and the Roots of Seidr* (Bastrop, TX: Runestar), 12–18.

into hiding. As this happened, psychologically, somatically, and spiritually speaking, the soul and divinity inherent within the natural world, as well as within the psyche-nature connection, was suppressed, repressed, and oppressed. That which was spiritual was made profane and mundane. Soul was essentially taken out of nature, warped, and sequestered to the church, the bible, and the clergy. Soul was extracted from the felt sense and placed far away from the here-and-now, sequestered in heaven above, property of the one true God alone.[12]

In the process, wyrd and the ways of wyrd were suppressed, made illegal, and almost wiped out entirely. Those who practiced pagan and heathen ways (a.k.a. the old ways, which were often healing ways) were oppressed. Wyrd was demonized, its true essence mutated and lost. Eventually, wyrd—as fate, destiny, nature, soul, magic, and mystery—was secularized and turned into the experience of weird, strange, or evil. The spiritual feeling of wyrd became the taboo feeling of weird; the feeling of soulfulness became the feeling of sin.

Of course, it is not solely due to the influence of Christianity that we find ourselves disconnected from soul and wyrd. We also have the changes brought on by the climate, scientism, technologism, hyperrationalism, and more. The forces of so-called progress moved humanity in a very distinct direction: away from nature and natural-wisdom, away from embodiment, sexuality, soul, and the divine union of the god and goddess—away from the wilderness.

If the arc of history has shown us anything, it is that humans are prolific creators of distraction, hierarchy, and technology. For thousands of years, we have endeavored to protect and separate ourselves, our loved ones, and our kin from the dangers of the wilderness (i.e., from death) as much as possible. This protection and separation have taken many forms: clothing, medication, cars, buildings, and so on. While these technologies have certainly improved our quality of life in countless ways, they have inadvertently distanced us from the direct experience of the wilderness and the depth realm of wyrd—from natural wisdom, magic, soul. We will explore the impacts of this throughout this book.

From tribe to village to city to metropolis, the presence and intimacy of the wilderness has gradually faded from human awareness, blocked by

---

12. Metzner, *The Well of Remembrance*, 55–60.

psychological barriers, walls, technology, and the desire for safety, comfort, and hedonistic pleasure. Akin to the dearth between a wooden hut and a skyscraper, the dearth between the human psyche and the psyche of nature has grown exponentially over the millennia. The soul-thread that connects humans and nature has faded from awareness, and the resonance of this thread has grown quiet. We can no longer feel it as we once did. The wild mind has been civilized, and the old ways have been forgotten.

Human beings were already on a steady path of dis-attunement from the wilderness—and thus from wyrd, soul, the goddess, and indigenous wisdom—long before the Anglo-Saxons and Romans entered the scene of Northern Europe. As the so-called civilized, progress-oriented state of mind and way of being spread through the world, so, too, has the decimation of nature-based, soul-based relationality. This erasure happened in the Near East, Africa, and Europe long before it happened in the Americas, East and South Asia, and Australia. The impacts of this soul-loss have been devastating to every domain worldwide.

When pagan Northern European people lost the wilderness, they lost wyrd; they not only lost their connection to nature and soul, they lost their somatic, emotional, and relational intelligence and guidance on how to live in right relationship with the land and with each other. They forgot that humanity is nature. As a result, we also forgot the ways of holistic being and healing. How much of the historical and present suffering in the world can be traced back to the misguided, nature- and soul-disconnected, delusional thoughts, words, and actions of progress-obsessed, hyperrational Northern Europeans? Not all of it, by any means, but a lot of it for certain. We are seeing and feeling the impacts of this right now.

Thankfully, wyrd and its wisdom have not been lost. The ancient animist currents of Northern Europe, as well as of the rest of the world, are still flowing through the collective conscious and unconscious. Many animist, pagan, and indigenous cultures around the world are still alive, still carrying the soul-torch of their ancestors, still seeing and being in wild mind, practicing and sharing the old ways, protecting the wilderness, protecting life, protecting soul—protecting sanity.

Wyrding Ways
Ancestry Meditation

With all this talk of ancestors, take a moment to connect with yours, reader. Let's bring your ancestral wyrd from the abstract realm of thought into the experiential realm of embodiment. Each of us has many long threads of ancestors reaching back into history and pre-history. Let's follow these threads into deep-time, deep-space, and deep-consciousness.

This exercise will help you reconnect with your ancestors, with soul, and with the soul of your ancestors. If you trace your ancestral line backward in time, where do you end up? See how far back you can go. Send love, strength, wisdom, and healing through this line. Imagine: What were your distant ancestors' spiritual beliefs? Before they became monotheists, what type of polytheists and animists were they? What were their lives like? How did their histories unfold? What happened to their worldviews with the passing of time?

You will need:
- Fifteen minutes and a quiet place for meditation
- A meditation cushion, pillow, or chair
- A special candle and incense chosen with your ancestors in mind

1. Set your candle and the incense on the ground in front of you. Light the candle.

2. Sit down in a meditative posture: spine straight, alert and relaxed. Close your eyes, take a few slow, deep belly-breaths in through your nose and out through your mouth. (During a belly-breath, you will first feel your in-breath deep down in your belly, around your belly button. As you breathe in, you will feel your belly expand first, then the expansion and breath will slowly move upward into your chest, up into your neck, culminating in your nostrils. Let your out-breath occur naturally as you relax your body. Breathe out through your mouth or nose, starting at your throat and ending in your deep belly.) Do this at least three times—though more will not hurt—then return to your natural rhythmic breathing.

3. Call to mind your ancestral line. Begin with your siblings, then move on to your parents, grandparents, great-grandparents, great-great-grandparents, and onward. There are threads that connect you all through time-space. Even if you don't know your ancestors or can't picture them, feel into the threads, feel into your DNA—there they are. Breathe into and out of these threads. Feel the energy moving through them.

4. Imagine your ancestors as they lived their lives. Imagine what their lives may have been like, day to day, in the places they lived. Do your best to put yourself in their shoes. Imagine the joys they experienced, the moments of peace, the hopefulness. Imagine their struggles. Imagine their fear, frustration, and grief. What historical events did they live through? Imagine them as they are going through their *dark nights of the soul*.

5. Light the incense you chose specifically for them. As the smoke drifts upward, offer it to them, and with it, send them loving energy. Send them love, strength, courage, compassion. Send them the energy they need to make it through the hard times they are facing. Say to them, "May you have the courage, strength, patience, and compassion to make it through this hard time. It's not easy; I know you can do it. I know because I am here." Imagine the energy moving through the threads to them. Maybe specific people will come to mind, maybe not. Say, "Thank you for all you have done and endured so that one day I might come into the world. Thank you for your blood, sweat, tears, laughter, and joy. Thank you for my life." Send them your love for as long as you can feel it flowing through you.

6. Now, imagine that they—wherever, whenever, and whoever they are in what we call the past—are presently thinking of you and their line of descendants. They sit in meditation, in prayer, and say, "May you, my descendants, have the courage, strength, patience, and compassion to make it through this hard time. I know it's not easy, but I know you can do it. I send you my love and admiration! I send you my blessings. Thank you for your life." Feel their energy and prayers coming to you through the thread. Soak them up, let them feed your inner flame. Send them thanks and love!

7. Still attuned to the thread that connects past-present-future, send your admiration, love, courage, and strength to your descendants,

to future generations, many yet to be born. Say, "Wherever you are, and whatever you may be living through, may you find the courage, strength, patience, and compassion to make it through. I know it's not easy, but I know you can do it. I love you and I shower you with blessings of love and light, healing and joy. Thank you for your life." Exude powerful healing-energy and send it down every thread into their lives. Thank them for their lives and their struggles; send them love!

8. Now, imagine your descendants do the same for you. Know they pray for you. Feel their support, open to their guidance. They, too, thank you for your life. Open yourself to the light, love, healing, courage, and compassion they send you to help you navigate the challenges in your life. Soak in their prayers. Let them feed your inner flame. Send them thanks and love in return!

9. When you feel you are done, take a few slow, deep belly-breaths, stand up, and go about your day with this gratitude and feeling of connection in your heart.

Chapter 2
Weaving and Fate in Myth

Though the concept of wyrd comes from Northern Europe, its presence can be seen globally. The symbols and metaphors associated with wyrd—thread, weaving, magic, spiders, and transformation—can be seen all around the world. Wyrd is fluid, trans-form; it can't be bound or limited by any one form. It wears many different clothes and masks and goes by many different names and genders. Let's explore some of these names and faces. Let's look to the great myths, the great soul-stories, that have survived the scythe of progress and the maze of time; let us take a moment to admire this beautiful patchwork quilt that covers us all—that *is* us all. Let us witness the sheer diversity of form, and in turn, perhaps we may witness its unified essence. As we continue to welcome wyrd back into our lives, let us remember that which once was and, in many ways, still is.

The Fates

We begin our brief and nonchronological mythological remembering of wyrd in Greece with the three Titan weavers and deciders of fates, the Moirai: Clotho (the Spinner), she who spins the thread of a life into being; Lachesis (the Apportioner of Lots), she who measures the length of the thread; and Atropos (the Inevitable), she who cuts the thread. The Moirai were often depicted as three old women wearing golden crowns, each holding their fate-wielding tools and scepters. The Fates were supremely powerful and, because of this, feared. Everything, including the gods and goddesses, were under their sway and dominion. Fate was not set in stone, however; though it was rare, both humans and deities were able to intervene from time to time.

In Roman mythology, we find the equivalent of the Moirai, known as the Parcae. The Parcae, too, were the personification of fate and destiny. Together they attended the birth, controlled the life-thread, and decided the fate of each god, goddess, human, and being. There were many Parcae, though the most powerful and well-known were the three: Nona, she who spins the thread of life on her spindle; Decima, she who measures the thread of life for each being; and Morta, she who decides the method and time of death for all.

To the ancient Norse, the Fates were known as the Norns, or Nornir, whose name derives from the act of twisting and twining. There are three: Urðr (what has become or happened, destiny, or spiritual purpose—also one of the ety-mological roots of wyrd), Verðandi (becoming), and Skuld (should, debt, what ought to happen, or a karmic debt that must be paid). We know very little about the Norns except that they rule over the destiny of all beings in the nine worlds of Norse cosmology. They, just like the Moirai and Parcae, are present at childbirth as birth goddesses. They live in a great hall at the base of the World-Tree, Yggdrasil, the very body of the multiverse, where they lay down the fates of all by carving runes into wood. They protect and water the cosmic Tree, using mud and water from the sacred Well of Urðr (the Well of Wyrd). Though Urðr is the most oft-cited Norn, there were many others besides the three. In fact, it was thought that everybody had their own. They are described at various times as being powerful, scary, harsh, and giving. As you will see, the Norns weave in and out of this entire book.

There are many more fate deities in the world. The Matronae of Ger-mania, Cerridwen of Wales, the scrying goddess Istustaya of Anatolia, and the Annunaki of Sumer are all weavers of life-threads and diviners and purveyors of fate and destiny. During pre-Islamic times on the Arabian Penninsula, we find the goddess Manāt, overseer of time, fate, destiny, and fortune. In Alba-nia, the Fatia decreed the destiny of all newborn children. The Greek goddess Hecate, too, is a goddess of fate, as well as childbirth, magic, and witchcraft. In Hindu mythology, there is the goddess Kali and the god Shiva, both associated with time and cosmic cycles of creation, destruction, and fate. Astrologically speaking, every planet can be said to have an influence over our fates weaving; Saturn and Pluto, however, are often the two planets associated with the mechanics of fate most directly.

There are many more…

Spider Deities

I'd like to give a special mention to a few of the fate-spinning deities that come from the lands known by some as Turtle Island, and by others as the United States of America, as these are the lands on which I live and travel through. There are several native cultures from the southwestern and northwestern United States and southern Canada who share a common cosmological motif—that of a goddess known as Spider Woman or Spider Grandmother.

To the Hopi people, Spider Grandmother was considered an Earth goddess who, along with the Sun god Tawa, brought life into being. It is said that Tawa first imagined life into existence, after which Spider Woman gave birth to it. To each life born, she attaches a thread that ultimately leads back to her as well as to the knowledge of one's origin and destiny. When Spider Woman is called upon, she helps people in many ways, such as giving advice or providing medicinal cures.[13]

The Navajo people have a spider-goddess—a great protector, guide, and teacher—named Na'ashjéii Asdzáá. It is she who wove the web of the multiverse into being, and she who taught the arts of weaving, agriculture, ceremony, and magic to humans. In the Navajo creation myth, it is Spider Woman who told the lost Twins who they are, where to go, and how to survive the dangerous journey to their father, the Sun.[14]

Like most gods and goddesses from around the world, many of these spider deities have both creative and destructive aspects. The Lakota people have a spider-god named Iktomi. Iktomi is a shapeshifter and a trickster. He uses his strings to control humans like puppets. He also has the power to make potions that transform and trick gods and mortals alike. Iktomi has been considered by the Lakota from time immemorial to be the patron of

13. Harold Courlander, *Fourth World of the Hopis* (New York: Crown Publishers, 1970), 17–33.
14. Carol Patterson-Rudolf, *On the Trail of Spider Woman: Petroglyphs, Pictographs, and Myths of the Southwest* (Santa Fe, NM: Ancient City Press, 1997), 83–95.

new technology and invention. There are tales where he comes to the aid of the people to teach them ways to protect themselves from evil and live a better life with technology and to warn them of danger. In other tales, he is a trickster. In either case, Iktomi, like other tricksters, is an awakener and a trickster.[15]

The Pueblo cultures, of which there are many, have spider-goddesses of different names. One is referred to by the name Thought Woman. To the Acoma Pueblo, it was Thought Woman who sang the universe into being and taught her daughters—the mothers of all humans—the ways of growing food, cooking, singing, praying, and ritual so they might then teach these ways to humans. She is so powerful that it is said her real name can only be mentioned within the bounds of sacred ceremony.[16]

Louis Byrd, Omushkego elder and storyteller, tells the story a giant spider, Ehep, who lowered the first two humans onto the Earth using his string and a woven basket. Ehep warned them not to look down at the beauty of the Earth before they reach it, otherwise they would not be able to enjoy their lives on Earth free of suffering. Of course, they looked, thus inviting suffering into the world for future generations to come.[17]

There are many other powerful, respected, and sometimes feared spider-gods and spider-goddesses around the world. From the Akan peoples of Ghana and the Ivory Coast of West Africa, we find the trickster and creator Anansi—the god of all the stories of existence. In ancient Sumer, we find Uttu, spider-goddess and weaver. From the Pacific Micronesian and Polynesian islands of Naura and Kiribati come Areop-Enap and Nareau—both powerful creator spider deities. From Indian Vedic philosophy, we find Indra's Net—an infinite, multidimensional web connecting everything to everything else. There are many more.[18]

15. Richard Erdoes and Alfonso Ortiz, *American Indian Trickster Tales* (New York: Penguin Books, 1999), 91–120.
16. Patterson-Rudolf, *On the Trail of Spider Woman*, 7–30.
17. Louis Byrd, "Native American Spider Mythology: 0024-Our Voices-Ehep Legend," Native Languages of the Americas: Preserving and Promoting American Indian Languages, 1998–2020, http://www.native-languages.org/legends-spider.htm #google_vignette.
18. Marta Weigle, *Spinners & Spinsters: Women and Mythology* (Albuquerque, NM: University of New Mexico Press, 1982).

Worldwide Weaving

To the world's indigenous and pagan peoples, weaving was and still is considered a sacred act, a transmission of divine import, passed from the goddess to the people and from women to girls for centuries. Though spinning and weaving were often considered female-occupied roles, it was not uncommon for men, as well as those of other genders, to be spinners and weavers.

Other than the Fates and Spider, there are many mythological figures and goddesses around the globe known for their weaving. There is the Norse goddess and Queen of Asgard, Frigg, associated with the household, motherhood, fertility, love, marriage, and the domestic arts; wife of the All-Father Odin; and known for her prophetic skills of foreknowledge. Her spinning distaff can be seen in the stars in the constellation of Orion. The Valkyries are also considered the weavers of fate, as they collect the souls of fallen warriors and carry them to Odin's hall, Valhalla, and Freyja's hall, Folkvangr. There are also the Disir—female ancestors—who were described as weavers and decreers of fate.

Back in Greece, we have Athena, goddess of weaving, wisdom, handicraft, and warfare, who wove the multiverse into existence on her loom. The mortal Arachne was famed to have challenged Athena to a weaving contest and won (in some versions of the story) only to be turned into a spider for her hubris. It is from the name Arachne that we derived the scientific classifications of arachnid and Arachnida. There is also Ariadne, wife of Dionysus and goddess of labyrinths, mazes, and paths, whose lifesaving thread helped the hero Theseus find his way into and out of the maze that housed the deadly minotaur, Asterion.

According to the Maori, weaving is a gift from Hine-te-iwaiwa, goddess of weaving, plaiting, the arts, and the moon. In Japan, from the Shinto tradition, there is the cosmic weaver goddess Amaterasu. It is she who created the cosmos, all the other gods, as well as all the clothes they wear. She also gifted humans with the knowledge of weaving hemp and silk. In ancient Mesoamerica, we find the Mayan Moon goddess, Ixchel, whose spiraling drop spindle set the multiverse into motion. In ancient Egypt, there was Nit or Neith, goddess of war and weaving who wove all existence into being on her loom—and continues to do so each new day—as well as the goddess Isis, who taught all weavers how to spin. In Baltic myth, there is Saule, who is said to weave the sunbeams carrying life-energy to all.

And then there's Maya. The concept of Maya has a long and rich symbolic history in India. She is the wondrous and mysterious power of creation, art, and wisdom. She is *that which exists* and *is constantly changing*, with a visual display that is hypnotizing, intoxicating, and mesmerizing. She is often experienced as a distracting force, though she can also paradoxically be a revealer of truth. Maya is the veil of illusion, a woven magic show, the phenomenon of all appearance. Eventually, Maya took on more negative associations with evil and witchcraft.[19]

The peoples of yesteryear saw weaving as a magical and sacred act—many still do. Not only is weaving a process for the creation of important goods, it is also a microcosmic, and magical, activity that mirrors the macrocosmic creation and weaving of the nature of reality itself. The early animist and pantheist cultures all around the world knew this intuitively and wove their own creation myths and stories to describe this experience and to teach others.

It is no coincidence that these mythological and spiritual motifs, such as webs, weaving, spinning, threads, and so on, have been so ubiquitous through time-space. It is a cross-cultural synchronicity. These deities were, and are, archetypal patterns within psyche, within the natural world, and within the fabric of reality itself. The ancient animists of the world sensed this. There are fate, destiny, weaving, and spinning deities the world over. It is worth noting that many of these deities were also Earth, Sun, Moon, Star, Mother, and Creatrix deities. This paints a picture of a world, a solar system, and a multiverse created, animated, and held together by divine weavers, webs, spiders, threads, and strings.

Mythology and the Power of the Imagination

Mythology is an enlightening lens for psychological, relational, and spiritual self-exploration. Myth is open to all sorts of soulful, imaginative interpretations. These interpretations help us see more of ourselves and the world by offering us a chronicle of soul-based, nature-informed living and relating. Myth is a timeless guidebook for a soul-filled life, written by nature through the human psyche. Myth lets you know where you are and where you are going by showing you the underlying patterns and cycles of mind-

---

19. Jules Cashford, *The Moon: Myth and Image* (London: Cassell Illustrated, 2003), 261–262.

body-relationship-environment-soul-spirit as well as the common pitfalls, challenges, gifts, and goals of the human endeavor. In this way, mythology is a high artform that reveals wyrd.

To our ancient ancestors—and to our present-day animist peers—the fabric of reality is held together by stories. These stories, which we now call myth, folktale, and oral tradition, create a complex interweaving of a multiplicity of narratives—or soul-stories. These stories weave human beings, the totality of nature, and the totality of the divine into a larger process, pattern, or greater soul-story. This soul-story has been interpreted and expressed in countless ways since the dawn of humanity's imaginative storytelling capabilities. These stories serve many functions. They paint astounding pictures of the mysteries. They teach, entertain, inspire, awaken, and impart us with an ecopsychospiritual structure that helps us contain our wild and powerful imaginations in healthy, balanced, naturally wise ways.

Far more powerful than humanity likes to admit, the imagination has been and still is one of humanity's defining characteristics. Through our imagination, we have the ability to muse, dream, contemplate, and invent. Anything new that comes into the world—whether it be a theory, a work of art, an invention, or even a child—begins within the cauldron of the imagination, where it simmers and stews and readies itself before taking form. Our thoughts, feelings, and behaviors are so heavily under our imagination's influence that—for better or for worse—our imagination determines much of our wyrd.

As our myths and pagan magics reveal, it is through the imagination that we connect to the archetypal forces that create, mold, preserve, and transform existence. Our soul-stories and old ways help us wield these great imaginal powers through ritual magic, dance, song, and story. Through these wyrding ways, we can learn to contain and guide raw, elemental imagination (i.e., soul) toward its healthy fruition. Our soul-stories and soul-ways reflect aspects of our wyrd back to us and provide us with much-needed guidance, inspiration, and experiential wisdom on our path through life.

As many indigenous wisdom-keepers and ritual elders have said time and time again, our soul-stories preserve the web and weave of life. If we stop telling the stories, singing the songs, and dancing the sacred dances, we will forget them. And if we forget them, we will invite hubris and imbalance into our imaginations, and thus the world, putting the weave of reality at risk of slackening, deteriorating, and falling apart in unnecessarily destructive and painful ways. Is this what we are witnessing in our world right now?

The tales of the world's mythmakers were the glowing efforts of human beings doing their best to make sense of not only the journey of life, but the nature of reality, existence, and being. May the sacred stories, the old ways, and the ritual elders of the world continue to lead us onward and give us guidance. Let them remind us of soul and how to live in relationship with soul—with each other and with the Earth. Let them re-enchant and re-engage our imaginations in loving, naturally wise, and balanced ways. Let them guide our hands as we weave and reweave our own lives in the sacred image of the Web, together. Let their light be there through the darkest of times as we traverse the meandering maze of this great ritual known as life.

Wyrding Ways
The Craft of Storytelling

This exercise is meant to help you reconnect with the natural guidance of soul through your imagination and through soul-story. It is an exercise that asks you take some time to seek out and read at least a few of your ancestors' and/or others' myths and folktales. It asks you to not forget and shows you how not to.

You will need:

- One or two hours of time to dedicate to studying soul-stories (myths)
- Access to a public library or home internet

1. Go to your public library and ask the librarian to point you to the mythology section. Start exploring the rich world of comparative mythology and/or start a search online and/or ask a relative or community elder if they know any stories. You have a long line of ancestors reaching far back into history—that's a lot of stories from which to choose. Have fun as you explore. See just how far back you can go. The farther back, the better. There are a lot of soul-stories out there that are in danger of being forgotten and long to be remembered. The goal is quality, not quantity. Take your time. Don't worry about "consuming" them all.

2. As you read each myth or folktale, contemplate its meaning. Let the imagery work on your imagination. Spend time with it. Let the soul within each story blossom. What are the life- and soul-lessons being taught through them?

3. Learn one of these stories well enough to share it with a friend, a relative, or even a group of consenting strangers (at a storytelling event or gathering of your kindred or coven, for example). Share the stories you love the most. In this way, you can help others remember. Keep the soul that connects past-present-future alive and well.

4. Optional: If you are feeling inspired and creative, develop your own myth or reinterpret an old myth. Retell an old story. Re-paint it. Write a song about it. Act it out.

Chapter 3
Wyrd Science

A s evidenced by the evolution from wyrd into weird over the centuries, it's clear that wyrd has long been in a process of becoming. Human beings the world over have explored and venerated this process since time immemorial. These explorations and venerations eventually led to what pagans, heathens, and indigenous peoples refer to as the old ways. These old ways—relational, magical, devotional, and healing in nature—have been passed down through the ages, through storytelling, craft, song, dance, ceremony, and so on. Though some of these surviving old ways are hundreds, thousands, even tens of thousands of years old, many more of them have been eradicated or forgotten. Their absence has left a massive void in our understanding of self, soul, and nature. For better or for worse, science has both contributed to this void as well as stepped in to try to fill it.

There are some interesting parallels between the old ways and science. Both have, in their own ways, served as vehicles for the observation, measurement, experimentation, and formulation and testing of hypotheses about the nature of existence, life, and being. In a sense, the old ways were the pre-science sciences. Just as science does today, the old ways brought much-needed explanation, containment, and guidance when it came to exploring the mysteries and processes of life.

The spirit of science is an integral part of the human spirit; it is one of curiosity, discovery, and awakening. As we know it today, science has evolved through time-space to successfully delineate much of existence—at least much of *known* existence. Through our scientific endeavors—and earlier ceremonial, astrological, alchemical, and mythological endeavors—we have attempted to put everything in its rightful place in relationship with everything else. We have assigned classifications and delineated systems for almost every process and part of existence imaginable. Science has helped us discern fact from fiction, for the most part. It has helped us figure out how to describe reality physically, mathematically, biologically, chemically, energetically, geologically, astronomically, psychologically, ecologically, and so on.

Though science has certainly committed its fair share of harm to the soul-based imaginal animism, science has also been able to tell us a lot about the nature of wyrd. It is beyond the scope of this book to describe the development and specifics of all the various scientific theories and laws and how they describe the phenomenology of wyrd. Though it would be fascinating, it would also be a brain-frying endeavor, especially for my brain. It is also unnecessary for the purposes of this book. What is necessary, rather, is to propose that each of the domains of science—including all past, present, and future findings, theories, and laws—are all attempts to describe the nature of wyrd and the Web of Wyrd. In other words, the laws, theories, and classifications we have developed through our scientific endeavors are all but descriptions of the structure, pattern, and process of wyrd.

If this is true, then what this means is that we already know a lot about wyrd. Though the word *wyrd* hasn't been used in our scientific discourse yet, at least not to my knowledge, it seems to be only a matter of time before it may be. Wyrd is returning to awareness in ever-novel ways. This can be seen in concepts such as strangeness, strange quarks, and strange attractors, as well as in popular theories like quantum theory, unified field theory, string theory, and systems theory—all intimations of the interweaving of wyrd and science.

Though science has taken us somewhat into the mystery realms, it has only been able to take us so deep. Science is realizing that the void is much deeper and much more mysterious than it was previously thought to be. I think most scientists would agree there are limits to science's reach. Our technologies and theories have, and perhaps can, only bring us so far. It is at this limit, at the alchemical, ever-evolving edge of science's boundary, where animism and spirituality return from scientific exile. In a perfect example of the trickster at play, science is revealing what indigenous people, mystics, and pagans have been saying for millennia. Science is bringing us back to the worldviews of our ancient so-called primitive ancestors—to soul, to nature, and to the divine. One example of this is the development of systems theory.

Systems Theory

Systems theory is the multidisciplinary scientific study of interrelationship, interconnection, interdependence, and wholeness. Physicist and ecologist Fritjof Capra details the evolution of systems theory in his book *The Web of Life: A New Scientific Understanding of Living Systems*. He provides an outline of how, over the last one hundred years, systems thinking has led organismic biologists, quantum physicists, psychologists, and philosophers to create a new scientific paradigm—one that has led to a very important shift in perspective away from the mechanistic, reductionist (soul-less) point of view toward a holistic, integrative (soul-full) point of view.[20]

Systems thinking is exactly what it sounds like; it is a way of thinking, seeing, and studying that considers the collective organization of the system—or network—and the nature of the relationships within it. Systems theory confirms what indigenous wisdom teachings have been saying for thousands of years—that everything is interconnected, interdependent, and interrelated, and that the key to survival and well-being lies in our ability to maintain homeostatic balance within the system. Systems thinking, or ecological consciousness, is foundational to the concept of wyrd.

Gestalt

One of the best ways to understand systems thinking, and thus wyrd, is through the concept of gestalt. A gestalt is a collection of parts that amount to a whole that is greater than the sum of its parts. The study of gestalt—which comes to us via existential philosophy and psychology and has since been applied to science, art, business, therapy, and sociology—is the study of systems, patterns, and phenomenology.

---

20. F. Capra, *The Web of Life: A New Scientific Understanding of Living Systems* (New York: Anchor Books, 1996), 29–50.

I received an in-depth experiential education in gestalt therapy at the California Institute of Integral Studies while working toward my master's degree in counseling psychology. It was at Church Street, a gestalt therapy training center and sliding-scale community counseling center in San Francisco, where I saw my first therapy clients and had the opportunity to put gestalt and systems thinking (and wyrdcraft) into practice.

From the point of view of gestalt therapy, the human being is an organic, dynamic whole composed of a myriad of interrelated parts. These parts work in concert with each other to create the gestalt of one's being. In short, imbalances arise within the gestalt when certain parts within the whole are denied, masked, or given too much or too little power. Using any number of interventions initiated by the trained gestalt therapist, gestalt therapy endeavors to bring the many parts of one's being back into homeostatic balance with each other within the greater organic whole. As such, it tends to the holistic health and well-being of the Web—the whole. We will explore a number of these interventions within the *wyrding ways* offered throughout this book.

The concept of gestalt dovetails nicely with wyrd. Using the language of wyrd, the whole, or the gestalt, is a web, weave, or braid composed of the interweaving of multitudes of threads. Whether traveling toward the macrocosmic or microcosmic, the wyrd-wanderer will find threads within threads within threads, seemingly to no end, all interwoven within the greater tapestry known as the Web of Wyrd. Wyrdcraft is the exploration of these threads and how they interrelate.

The human body is a good example of a gestalt; it is at once a whole as well as a collection of parts: cells, tissues, fluids, organs, systems, and processes. Each of these parts and processes is connected to all the others and serves a function within the greater whole. The health, well-being, and functioning of each part and process play a key role in determining the health, well-being, and functioning of the whole.

Another example of a gestalt is the ecosystem of the Earth. The whole is called the ecosphere. It is composed of a geosphere, hydrosphere, atmosphere, and biosphere. These spheres, or parts, are the threads that weave together to create the gestalt, or wyrd, of the Earth—also known as Gaia. The parts, too, are composed of many other parts or threads. Within each ecosystem—be it tundra, grassland, desert, rainforest, or any other—exists its own array of threads, a.k.a. flora, fauna, geology, climate, and so on. These threads, when woven together, create the weave of that ecosystem. More so, each ecosystem is but a thread woven into a larger braid of an ecosystem.

If you consider the hierarchy of biological structures and systems, you will find different levels of order. At the subatomic level, for example, you will find the elementary particles and how they interact and relate with each other. At the acellular or pre-cellular level, you will find atoms, groups of atoms, molecules, and the biomolecular complex and its processes. Moving onward from there is the subcellular level, which includes organelles and functional groups of biomolecules, biochemical reactions, and interactions. The next level is the level of the cell and all the processes at play there. After that, we find the supercellular level of tissues and functional groupings of cells. Then there is the level of the organs, which is the functional group of tissues. Then the organ system, which is the functional grouping of organs.

All these parts and levels are in relationship with each other, creating the total organism. The organism is a gestalt in and of itself, yet at the same time, it is woven into a larger community (another gestalt), which is then woven into the larger population (another gestalt), which is then woven into the ecosystem, which is then woven into the biome, which is then woven into the ecosphere. Beyond that, we move into the realm of astronomy and the vast orders of the cosmos, from the constituents and processes of the solar system to the galaxy to superclusters of galaxies and so onward and outward to the universal and multiuniversal level. All levels—from micro to macro—are woven together within the great Web of Wyrd. Each level—including all the parts therein—is in relationship with the other levels and the other parts within those levels. Gestalts within gestalts within gestalts; systems within systems within systems. Even though there are emergent processes happening in each of these levels and parts, every process is interwoven into a larger unity in which all is one and there is only one process happening—a great gestalt. What this one process is, is a mystery. Some have called it soul, Tao, One, God, Infinity, or Wyrd. It has many names, and it is nameless.

Whatever this nameless shapeshifting mystery is, it can be explored and experienced firsthand. To experience it, you must first become aware of it, and to become aware of it, you must attune to it. Many of the wyrding ways in this book facilitate this very process. Let's try one now.

Wyrding Ways
Mindfulness and Concentration Meditation

This exercise explores two modes of perception, which also happen to be two forms of meditation: mindfulness meditation and concentration meditation. As you will see, these two modes of meditation play with the polarity of foreground and background; they play with depth-perception (soul-perception/wyrd-perception). The foreground is what is immediately present in awareness, what comes to the fore; the background is what lies behind and beyond the foreground. Usually, the foreground is in focus and the background is slightly out of focus.

You will need:

- A natural place to sit (a park, garden, or wilderness) or a plant or tree with which you can sit
- A blanket, meditation cushion, or camping chair (if you don't have these, you can sit on a stone, a stump, or the ground—or you can stand)
- Note: As with every outdoor exercise suggested in this book, go prepared—educate yourself about ticks, mosquitos, local fauna and flora, poison oak or ivy; bring water and a healthy snack; be mindful of the weather; and try not to get lost or damage anything in your path
- Your journal

1. Find a calm, safe, secluded spot in nature, though you can also do this wherever you are right now. Take a seat, stand, or lie down. Take a minute to settle in; turn off your phone and put it out of sight.

2. Close your eyes and take a few slow, deep belly-breaths in through your nose and out through your mouth. (During a belly-breath, you will first feel your in-breath deep down in your belly, around your belly button. As you breathe in, you will feel your belly expand first, then the expansion and breath will slowly move upward into your chest, up into your neck, culminating in your nostrils. Let your out-breath occur naturally as you relax your body. Breathe out through your mouth or nose, starting at your throat and ending in your deep belly.) Do this at least three times—though more will not hurt.

3. Open your eyes and practice mindfulness meditation. *Mindfulness* is the process of expanding and opening your awareness to whatever is happening in the present moment with a curious, nonjudgmental, and relaxed awareness. Breathe naturally. Be with what is. It is like viewing the whole or large part of a painting, the whole of your body, or the whole of a landscape. Take it all in. Soften your focus and let your awareness open to the spontaneous. Relax and receive. Don't grasp after experience. Don't push it away, either. Allow the experience to be, to come and go in its own time. Let everything have a life of its own. Allow everything its own wyrd. Watch and feel the coming and going of all phenomena within your open and receptive field of awareness. Let the moment flow. Do your best to remain aware of your body-mind as well as your environment. Remember to breathe. Do this for anywhere from ten minutes to an hour or more. When you are done, take notes in your journal. What was the experience like for you? How do you feel?

4. Shift to *concentration* meditation. This is the process of focusing your awareness with a laser-like one-pointedness. The point is to hold your attention on a particular phenomenon for as long as you can. This can be done with the breath as it enters and exits your nose, on a specific place on the body, or an object outside of your body—the Moon, a candleflame, a leaf, a rock, or a symbol, for example. As opposed to opening your awareness to a whole as you would with mindfulness, for this experiment, select one point you can see, near or far, and focus your awareness on that. Do this for ten minutes to an hour. For example: As you lie on the ground, choose one leaf in the canopy above on which to focus. Every time you look away—which will happen again and again—return to the same leaf. As you do this, softly, passively notice what happens to your visual field as a whole. Notice the sensations in your body. When you are done, take notes in your journal. What was the experience like for you? How do you feel?

Note: Whether practicing mindfulness or concentration meditation, you will see the mind's tendency to lose focus, to wander, and to become distracted by thoughts, sensations, memories, or movements in your mind or environment. Your thoughts will wander, your eyes will wander, the point of focus will be lost again and again. Do not be disheartened—this is the nature of the mind. Every time it wanders, all you need to do is gently and compassionately bring your awareness back to the object of meditation. Time after time after time.

The Pattern in All Things

That which is called natural law is simply nature gravitating toward patterns. This is wyrd in action. Wyrd is both the pattern and the movement toward pattern.

Patterns emerge throughout all systems and all domains. The way of wyrd can be witnessed by exploring these patterns. One way patterns manifest is through the phenomenon of fractals. Fractals reveal the design and fabric of the Web. In fact, it is wyrd that makes these fractal patterns look the way they do. Wyrd is fractal. Wyrd is the structural fabric underlying and permeating existence that makes nature take form, behave, and move as it does. There is an underlying pattern throughout the Web, which leads to self-similarity across multiple dimensions. This self-similarity can be seen all throughout the natural world in the presence of fractals.

If you throw a stone into calm water, you will see ripples revealing the structure of wyrd. If you take a photo of the ocean from a mile up, you will see the same structure in the waves and undulations on the water below, albeit much larger. Look at the roots, branches, and leaves of trees; notice the similarities in structure. Then, look at aerial photos of rivers and deltas, look at the palm of your hand and the veins in your arms and eyeballs. Compare them with images of the nervous system, with neurons, with lightning, with mycelium networks, with cosmic superclusters. Compare the geometry of seashells, pinecones, and cacti with feathers, snowflakes, and geological formations. You will see structural similarities between mountains, clouds, canyons, ferns, and DNA—fractals mirroring fractals in a multiplicity of forms, domains, and processes. These are all physical manifestations of the pattern of the Web of Wyrd.

If you want to see wyrd, look anywhere. Look backward, inward, outward, forward; you will see wyrd. You will feel wyrd's pull. Like a moth to flame, the eye, the mind, the heart, body, and soul are all drawn toward the pattern of wyrd. Call it fate, if you will. Wyrd is the pattern in all things known and unknown. Wyrd is the process in all things known and unknown. Wyrd is the fundamental pattern that contains all patterns, the fundamental process that contains all processes, and the path that contains all paths.

Wyrding Ways
Exploring the Pattern in All Things

In this exercise, I invite you to spend some time in the natural world observing the patterns within wyrd. If you can't go into the natural world, go into the human world. Look out your window. Look at your own body. Observe, explore, notice, bring your awareness to reality *as is.* This will help you begin to see bits and pieces of the fabric and pattern of wyrd as it permeates reality. This will be cultivating wyrd consciousness. Ask yourself: Does it make sense to make this a regular practice, or a more regular practice? Note: This can be a great practice to do with a partner. Practice it solo and then practice it together. See what you notice together. Share how each of you feel the Web.

You will need:
- Twenty to sixty minutes or more for walking, sitting, and observing
- Access to a natural landscape—a park, garden, nature preserve (water access would be ideal)

1. After finding your location, the first step is to consciously slow down and open your senses to the natural world around you. Take a few slow, deep breaths in through your nose and out through your mouth. With each out-breath, relax just a little bit more. Return to your natural breathing pattern. Bring your awareness to your body and presence.

2. Begin by just standing naturally, no need to be in a meditative posture. Take a few minutes to soak in your environment. Just stand in place and look around you. Take a relaxed 360-degree turn to view your surroundings. After you make it all the way around, sense into your body and see if it feels called to walk in any particular direction.

3. Choose your direction and go. Let your path meander, follow the natural landscape. Remind yourself why you are there: "I am here to explore the pattern in all things." Begin to walk, slowly and deliberately. As you go, pay particular attention to the forms, colors, textures, lines, patterns, and natural processes you see in the world around you—near and far. Pay attention to every

small and large detail. Take your time. We're going for quality over quantity here. Find the smallest details. How rich is the environment? Find the biggest details. Explore as many things as you can in the environment around you—leaves, stones, sticks, mountains, clouds, and so on. Find the patterns within each of them.

4. Pick up two or three different leaves from different trees and examine the patterns in each of them. Compare the patterns in the leaf with the shape of the tree itself. Notice the similarities between the part and the whole.

5. Select two or three different plants and examine them from top to bottom.

6. Pick up at least two to three different stones of different makes and models. Turn them in your hands and examine the weight, shape, colors, lines, and patterns in each. What are their similarities and differences? You can also do this with shells if they are around. If you are near mountains, compare the stones you hold in your hands with the mountains around you. Notice the similarities in form.

7. Find a water source. If the water is flowing by, calmly watch it for at least five minutes. As you do, breathe slowly, in and out through your nose. Imagine the blood flowing through your veins. If you are by the ocean, calmly watch the waves. Notice the time-space between each wave. See if you can *feel* the frequency at which the waves are coming in. If the water is still, collect a small handful of stones and throw them in one by one. Watch the ripples extending outward from each one. Notice the speed at which they travel. See if you can *feel* the ripples in your body. Throw two at the same time five feet apart. Watch what happens as the ripples cross each other's paths. Then try three, four, a dozen.

8. Optional: With your partner, examine each other's face, eyes, hair, skin, hands, and body. See if you can see any of the same patterns you found in nature on your body. Self-examine your body in front of a mirror.

The Phenomenology of Wyrd

If you wish to have a solid experiential understanding of the nature of wyrd, you must experiment with it and experience it firsthand—you must feel it. The good news is that everybody does. Yes, reader; though you may not be aware of it, you are experiencing wyrd constantly, right now, and in many ways. Just by being, you are being wyrd and experiencing wyrd. This means that it is easy to come to know wyrd. All you need to do is be aware and apply the scientific method to being. You can observe, measure, experiment, and formulate and test hypotheses about the nature of wyrd and the ways of wyrd. You can study it and come to know it practically, functionally, and phenomenologically. In other words, you can come to explore wyrd and feel wyrd in the here-and-now.

Some of the first things that become apparent while beginning to explore the phenomenology of the here-and-now are the senses: sight, hearing, touch, taste, and smell. These five vehicles of experience convey wyrd in their own way: the sight organs relay the nature of wyrd through color, shape, pattern and depth; the hearing organs, through sounds, tones, pitch, intensity, and timbre; the touch organs, through texture, temperature, shape, and weight; the taste organs, through sweetness, sourness, bitterness, saltiness, and spiciness; and the olfactory organs, through smells, pleasant and unpleasant, attractive or repulsive.

Experience does not stop there, for without our highly developed brain and nervous system, our senses and sense experiences would mean nothing. The neural network of our mind-body is one of our prime conveyors of reality, experience, and wyrd. The wyrd of mind-body will be the subject of the next chapter.

There is a range of types of experience. For example, there is physical experience, mental experience, emotional experience, spiritual experience, social experience, virtual experience, subjective experience, objective experience, as well as firsthand, secondhand, and thirdhand experience. Each of these different types of experience is a different vehicle through which to experience distinct facets, or threads, of wyrd. Each can tell you something of your fate, destiny, nature, magic, soul, and becoming.

When one opens to the phenomenology of experience, one simultaneously opens to the phenomenology of wyrd. Awareness and attunement are key.

The more you bring your awareness to your experience in the here-and-now, the more you attune to the moment, the more you bring your awareness to wyrd. The more you bring your awareness to wyrd, the more you develop wyrd consciousness. If you wish to experience wyrd firsthand, bring your awareness to the vast spectrum of your experiences. Every sensory experience in every moment will have something to tell you about the nature of wyrd.

As we finish up this chapter, let's look back on a little of what we've explored together. We have looked at wyrd from many different angles; we've contemplated it historically, etymologically, mythologically, scientifically, and phenomenologically. Just doing this, your practice of wyrdcraft has begun. Hopefully this exploration has helped you start to locate wyrd within the past and bring it into the present—from the abstract to the concrete. Hopefully this has helped you spin some decent threads and build a stable loom upon which you will soon begin your weaving.

Take what you've learned and experienced along with you as you continue to wander and weave through these pages. Feel free to leave behind anything you don't need to carry with you. There still is quite a weird journey ahead. Let's continue onward. I invite you, now, to join me on a warp-and-weft exploration of the domains even deeper into the pattern of wyrd. May your awareness of wyrd blossom in your consciousness.

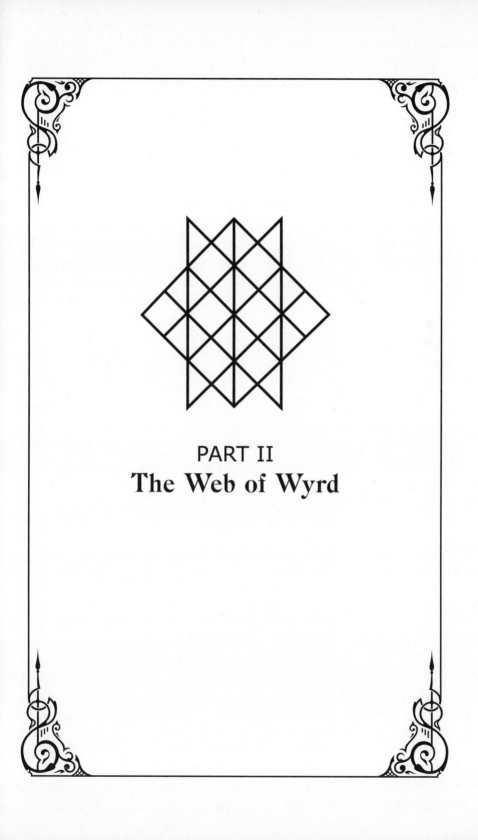

PART II
The Web of Wyrd

Chapter 4
Mind and Body

Thus far, we have explored the nature of wyrd through the vehicles of experience, the senses, the felt sense, phenomenology, history, mythology, etymology, and science. Let us now open the door and take a walk into the domains of mind, body, relationship, environment, soul, and spirit. I have chosen these domains because they represent the major spheres of human experience and existence. Each of them in their own ways could be considered windows, doors, paths, and keys that will lead you into and through a vast maze of life in which you can explore, experience, and understand wyrd—and thus become more wyrd conscious. The delineation of these domains as such is only a temporary, and ultimately illusory, process for exploring the gestalt of Wyrd—both threads and tapestry. There is no true separation between the domains; they are all interwoven in the Web of Wyrd. Hold this in the back of your mind as you proceed through each of them, and remember to *feel* into each of them as you go. We begin with the domain of mind.

The Wyrd of Mind

Though what we call mind and body are inherently interwoven into one mind-body, I would like to create an artificial, temporary separation between the two and take a moment to explore the wyrd of mind. To explore the wyrd of something is to explore the nature or soul of that thing; it is to explore its fabric, weave, composition, behavior, process, purpose, and destiny.

There are many facets of the mind, and these facets have many facets, and these facets have many facets, and so on. The individual mind is woven from many threads. Just to name a few, we have consciousness, imagination, intellect, emotion, language, and memory, as well as all the neurological and biochemical processes that occur within the brain and central nervous system. These threads, as well as many others unnamed, come together to create the weave of the wyrd of mind.

The wyrd of each mind is different, and the wyrd of each mind is the same. This paradoxical coexistence of difference and similarity will be a recurring theme through this entire book, as it is a recurring theme throughout nature. As humans, our brains are composed of the same stuff and generally operate in similar enough ways, and our minds are neurodivergent. No one else experiences my mind like I do, and no one experiences your mind like you do—yet we are all part of (to use Hermetic terminology) the transpersonal Mind of the All.[21] Reality is both a subjective and objective experience. We all exist within the same universe, yet, in a sense, each of us occupies our own little universe that only we can see and travel through. Learning to hold the tension of this paradox—and the many others that are headed your way—is an integral part of the process of wyrdcraft.

There are many ways to attune to the wyrd of the personal and collective mind. Some of these methods—all time-tested and proven to be effective—are contemplation, meditation, psychotherapy, and tarot. If you wish to know the wyrd of mind, dedicate some of your time-space-awareness to engage with these methods.

---

21. Three Initiates, *The Kybalion* (London: Penguin Group, 2008), 6.

Wyrding Ways
An Imaginal Exploration of the Wyrd of Mind

In this wyrding, you will be guided through a simple imaginal exercise in which you will be interviewed by an interstellar traveler. Have fun with it. Loosen up your imagination a little and play. As you engage with this exercise, you will be investigating your mind's wyrd.

You will need:
- Ten minutes of uninterrupted time-space
- A meditation cushion, pillow, or chair

1. Take a seat and a meditative posture: alert, upright, and relaxed. Close your eyes and take a few slow, deep belly-breaths in through your nose and out through your mouth, then return to breathing naturally.

2. Imagine there is a gentle, kind, and weird alien sitting across from you. This alien has come to Earth to learn about the similarities and differences between members of the human species. You are just one of many others the alien will interview. What does this alien look like? How does it, they, she, he, introduce themself?

3. Introduce yourself and begin a dialogue. Imagine what questions the alien may ask and then answer them, one by one. Describe yourself to the alien. Tell them about your personality, your emotionality, your thoughts, wants, and needs. Describe to them your astrological makeup if you know it. Are you an introvert, extrovert, ambivert? Are you an anxious type, a depressive type, an aggressive type? Are you optimistic, pessimistic, realistic? Tell them how you see the world in which you live. Tell them what you love, who you love, what you don't like, who you don't like. What are your interests, hobbies, passions, dreams, and fears? What are your goals? What is life? What is the meaning of life?

4. Now it's your turn to ask the alien to describe her/him/their/ itself to you. How does it describe its personality, hopes, dreams, fears, and goals? Ask them what they love, who they love, what they do and don't like. Is he extraverted or introverted,

optimistic, pessimistic, realistic? How does she see the world in which she lives? Again, have fun with it, relax your imagination, and create. Go with the flow.

5. When you are done, share thank-yous with each other! This information will help you both understand each other, and yourselves, more clearly. Imagine the alien gives you a gift in return for your sharing. What is the gift? Accept it fully in the spirit of gratitude. What do you wish to give to the alien as a way to say thank you?

Other ways to explore wyrd of mind include the following (resources listed in the appendix):

- Unofficially interview a friend over a cup of coffee or tea to get to know their wyrd (ask whatever you'd like—ask some of the questions listed above and see where the answers go)
- Start seeing a licensed psychotherapist and explore your psyche
- Determine your Enneagram Type
- Explore your astrological birth chart
- Determine your Human Design

Psyche

A foundational concept that can be used to understand the nature of wyrd is *psyche*. Psyche is an ancient Greek concept that has been defined as mind, soul, breath, or spirit. In short, according to Greek mythology, Psyche was a beautiful human princess who was transformed into a goddess—the very personification of soul—after her love affair with the god Eros went sideways.

In a shift much like the one that led to wyrd becoming weird, the concept of psyche was transformed from soul into mind—from something spiritual to something materialistic, mundane, and scientific. Over time, soul and mind—which were and are inherently one—were split in twain. Mind became a machine composed of parts, and a blueprint was made. In the process, mind lost its mystery, its depth, its soul.

The mind is a gestalt consisting of many parts that come together to create a whole that is greater than the sum of its parts. This greater whole can also be called psyche. Psyche has many facets; it is part psychological, part relational, part ecological, and part spiritual. Psyche's psychological facet is composed of the same threads as mind: consciousness, language, imagination, cognition, and so on. Psyche is much vaster than this, however; it is also relational. Minds meet and comingle; they adapt to and affect each other. Everybody has a psyche, everybody shares their psyches with each other, and everybody shares a collective psyche together. This even larger psyche, composed of the interweave of multitudes of psyches, is what is known as the collective conscious and collective unconscious. It could also be the collective soul.

As you can see, the terms *psyche*, *soul*, and *mind* can be used interchangeably. Whatever you choose to call this mysterious consciousnessence (consciousness + essence)—psyche, mind, or soul—as you explore it, you will soon come to see that it has many dimensions. Apart from having psychological and relational facets, it also has spiritual and ecological facets as well. In Ancient Latin, *anima* was the word for soul and *anima mundi* was the word for worldsoul. Other names for the world-soul are Mother Earth, Gaia, Nerthus, or Pachamama. Heathens understand Nerthus to be the living spiritual being and soul of the gestalt of the Earth biome. This world-soul, world-psyche, or worldmind has its own animate awareness, consciousness, and intelligence, as do all the parts and processes within it.

Animism is not just the belief, but the feeling and knowing that everything and every process is imbued with soul, psyche, mind. To the animist, every soul has both a way of being and a purpose that weaves it into the larger all-encompassing soul. In other words, each part occupies its own niche within the larger whole. To occupy a niche is to embody a certain type of ecosystemic intelligence. Each intelligence manifests as a way of being, behaving, and relating within the larger intelligence of the greater whole. The intelligence, or niche, as well as the constitution of each thing, is its wyrd. All of this, and more, affects its purpose, destiny, fate, nature, soul, and so on.

Take a raven, for example. A raven occupies its own niche. Raven is what it is and does what it does. It serves a purpose within the gestalt. It relates to the world around it, and the world around it relates to it. As such, the raven has its own wyrd. The same can be said for a tree, gravity, mountain, anger, empathy, and so on. Everything serves an intelligent purpose and occupies a specific niche within the greater whole; everything has its own wyrd. These parts and niches are all *in relationship* with each other. There is a purposeful intelligence and niche to every part and process of existence—every ecosystem, every part of the ecosystem, every body, every part of the body, every cell, every part of the cell, and so on. Each intelligence is a puzzle piece that fits into a larger intelligence, which fits into a larger intelligence—on and on.

These intelligent patterns and processes can be found everywhere—in the growing of a seed into a redwood tree, the formation and behavior of a hurricane or star, the ebb and flow of the tides, the movements of the solar system, the death and decomposition of an organism, the functioning and healing of the body, the evolution of life, the migration patterns of geese, the hunting behaviors of cougars, wolves, orca.

Mind, psyche, or soul reaches through and beyond the mental, psychological, and personal realms into the realm of relationship and beyond into the ecological and spiritual realms. In fact, it is psyche that unites them. Consider for a moment the electromagnetic spectrum, composed of radio waves, microwaves, infrared radiation, visible light, ultraviolet radiation, gamma rays, and X-rays. Human beings can only see a small section of the total spectrum without technological assistance. The same goes for the audio spectrum. The naked human ear can only hear a small part of the total spectrum of sound without the help of hearing technologies. The psyche, too, is a spectrum. Humans can only perceive a small section of the total spectrum of psyche without assistance from psychedelic (soul-revealing) technologies like mythology, meditation, psychedelics, or ritual.

The mind is a doorway that opens into psyche, and the psyche is a doorway that opens into soul. These doors open inward into self and outward into the world, through every domain, integrating all as they go, revealing and reminding us more and more of soul and wyrd in the process; this is what happens as one becomes wyrd conscious. We will follow this inward deepening and outward expansion of psyche, soul, and wyrd as we continue through this book.

<hr/>

Wyrding Ways
Looking into Psyche

I now invite you to take part in a simple meditative exercise that will give you a window into the wyrd of your mind. This is perhaps one of the simplest, oldest, and most effective forms of psychospiritual exploration—breathing meditation.

You will need:
- Fifteen to fifty minutes of undisturbed time-space to meditate
- A meditation cushion or chair or a comfortable place to sit or lie down

1. After you find a suitable place, sit down on your meditation cushion in half-lotus posture (cross-legged with one foot up on the opposite thigh and calf). You can also sit in a chair with your feet flat on the ground and your hands resting on your thighs. Wherever you sit, your spine should be upright, straight, alert, lengthened—but not stiff—and your chin should be slightly tucked. The goal is to find a centered, balanced readiness and relaxedness.

2. Close your eyes. Take three slow, deep belly-breaths in through your nose and out through your mouth. After each out-breath, feel your body relax just a little bit more. Return to your normal breathing pattern.

3. With your eyes closed, bring your awareness to your breath as it flows in and out through your nostrils. Focus your awareness at your philtrum (the midline groove between your upper lip and nostrils). Feel the air pass through this point with each in-breath and out-breath. Notice the subtle coolness of the in-breath and warmth of the out-breath. This is it; this is the practice. Be with the breath. Breathe and be.

4. Each time you realize you are lost in thought, take a mental note of the thought or fantasy in which you were lost. This is the wyrd of your mind; come to know it and see its process momentarily without indulging them, and calmly and lovingly return to your breath, letting the thoughts go. This is the basic practice. Do it as much as you are able—at least once a day, if you can.

5. Optional: You may also wish to experiment with consciously indulging in your thoughts. When you recognize you are thinking, allow yourself to continue your thought process, see where it goes, see how it evolves, see if it resolves. Be curious and open. When you are done with each fantasy, slowly and loving return to the anchor that is your breath at your philtrum.

This practice will tell you a lot about the wyrd of your mind by showing you *how* your mind works. What kind of thoughts and fantasies do you notice emerging through your psyche? Do some thoughts return more often than others? What is it about those thoughts that make them more compelling?

The Wyrd of Body

Though the wyrd of the mind is inextricably interwoven with the wyrd of the body, let's continue with our temporary delineation of the two and focus on the wyrd of body. Like the mind, the human body is a complex interweaving of many threads: circulatory, respiratory, digestive, immune, and so forth. Each of these systems—which work in concert with each other to keep our body functioning, healthy, and alive—is composed of many different organs, tissues, and more.

The wyrd of the body is the soul, nature, fabric, process, purpose, and destiny of the body and the parts of the body. Some of the threads that make up your body's wyrd include your shape and size; your ability; your hair, eye, and skin color; and other genetic factors. Your physical makeup plays a big part in the unfolding of your wyrd.

Wyrding Ways
Exploring the Wyrd of Body

In this exercise, you will be asked to bring awareness and curiosity into an examination of your body. This is just one way to explore the wyrd of your body.

You will need:
- Fifteen to twenty minutes or more of uninterrupted space-time
- A mirror

1. Strip down naked and stand skyclad in front of a mirror. If you don't have access to a mirror, you can still explore most of your body without one.
2. Close your eyes; take a few slow, deep breaths in through your nose and out through your mouth. With each out-breath, relax a little bit more. Return to your regular breathing pattern.
3. Open your eyes and bring your awareness to your body. Notice its shape, coloring, contours, and proportions. Look at the spots, wrinkles, creases, bends, and folds. Bask in the glory that is your body—all your supposed flaws and all. Turn around, lift your arms and legs, explore every hidden nook and cranny. Take your

time with it. Stretch, flex, bend, jump, dance, be silly. Touch your body, squeeze it, rub it. Feel what it is like to feel. This body is the space suit for your ego-consciousness. Do your best not to make any judgments about how you look or feel. Simply examine and observe.

4. If you find any tight, aching, or wounded areas—even healed wounds—give yourself some caring, tender touch and massage. Likewise, if you notice yourself judging any particular aspect of your body, put the palm of your hand on those areas and send yourself love and healing-energy. Say something like, "I see you and feel you—hello," "I love you," "Thank you for your teachings, and for being a part of my wholeness." Notice how your judgments, memories, and emotions *feel* in your body. Don't dwell in the stories. Feel them. Let them have a life of their own; eventually they will pass.

Some of our bodies are very similar, some are very different. Some people love their body, others not so much. Many, if not most, have mixed feelings. There is no one on Earth with a body exactly like yours; your composition is unique. There may be some hard limits to how you can and can't use your body. You may be suffering from a chronic illness or injury. You may live with a disability. It may be hard to accept that this doesn't make your mind-body better or worse than anybody else's, but at some level this is true. This is simply your wyrd, your wholeness; it is all part of your fate, destiny, nature, soul, magic, and process of becoming. Generally speaking, wyrdcraft helps us become aware of our limits, our *supposed* limits, and our limitlessness—all simultaneously while learning how to live as compassionately, fully, wholly, and magically as possible—flaws and all.

The weave of your body's wyrd is yours and yours alone, as the wyrd of your mind is yours and yours alone. Yes, your wyrd is intimately woven with mine and everything else's wyrd, but you are given your own mind-body to use as you will and as you can. You can try to bring awareness to it or not, take care of it or not, love it or not, change it or not, and use it however you like depending on your ability, awareness, intention, and wyrd. You do have a certain degree of free will, no matter how bound by the wheel of Fate you may feel. It's your world and it's your wyrd—and it's our world and it's our wyrd. Everything is in process, becoming, no matter what condition your mind-body is in. *How* you become is the question we are exploring in this book.

Wyrding Ways
Mindfulness of the Senses

Another way to explore the wyrd of body is by embodying the senses. This exercise will consist of bringing mindfulness to the senses. Mindfulness is the art of paying attention and bringing a curious, non-judgmental awareness to the phenomenological experience of whatever is happening in the present moment. In this exercise, you will be bringing mindful awareness to how you are taking in information from the world around you through your senses—right now, wherever you are in this present moment. Focus on one sense at a time. Spend around three to five minutes with each sense.

You will need:
- Twenty to sixty minutes for meditation
- Optional: A meditation cushion, chair, or blanket or a place to sit
- A snack (such as fruit or trail mix)
- Your journal

1. Close your eyes and bring awareness to your sense of hearing. What do you hear right now? What are the qualities of the sounds you hear? How much nuance to each sound can you suss out? Focus on one sound, then focus on all sounds together. What do you notice?

2. Open your eyes and look around. Soak in everything you see right now. Surrender to all that enters your visual field. What do you see? Again, notice the details, colors, textures, motions, and patterns. Shift your perception back and forth from the foreground to the background.

3. Open your mindful awareness to your sense of touch. Feel the contact of your body with the chair, couch, bed, or ground—wherever you are. Feel the elements on your skin—the air, the wind, the heat or cold, the rain, the dryness or humidity, the texture of the objects around you. Use your feet, hands, and body. Lean into things, pick them up, touch them, take your shoes off and walk barefoot. Find the nuance and detail.

4. Bring mindfulness to your sense of taste. Be careful not to poison yourself as you experiment with putting things in your mouth.

Taste your mouth. Taste your tongue. Lick your arm. How does your skin taste? In slow motion, eat the snack you brought with you, paying close attention to the subtleties of the flavors, textures, consistencies. Chew your food with your tongue. Chew it for too long. Dissect the different parts of the food with your tongue.

5. Bring awareness to your sense of smell. What do you smell in this moment? Explore the smell of different rooms, wild spaces, objects, body parts, and substances. Smell—with a nonjudgmental awareness—things that normally smell very bad to you (a public bathroom, for example). Notice the subtleties within the smells of each thing. Smell nice-smelling things, too. Smell flowers, plants, wines, cheeses, chocolates—go wild; smell as many things as you can. Pay attention to the nuance and subtlety of smell.

6. Record your overall impressions in your journal. What was this exercise like for you? What is it like to open to the phenomenology of wyrd in this way?

The Mind-Body Weave

Having introduced mind and body separately, let's now weave them back together and explore the connection between the two. We'll start by addressing the common unconscious misconception that the mind and the body are separate things. This assumption has been around for so long that it has been deeply ingrained into our language, worldview, and lifestyles, and it has deeply affected how we understand healing, medicine, relationships, and reality itself. We will explore this further when we explore the phenomenon of fragmentation in chapter 7.

How do you see things? What is your truth? Do you view the world through a dualistic (fragmenting, separating, and classifying) lens or a nondualistic (integrating, unifying) lens? Perhaps you view the world through both lenses at different times. Dualism states that mind and body exist independently of each other and that they are each doing their own thing. Nondualism states that everything is one—that there is no true separation between anything. According to dualism, the mind is an ephemeral thing, and the body is a corporeal thing; you can touch the body, but you can't touch the mind. It doesn't take too much digging to unearth the flaws within this argument. Minds can certainly touch and be touched. How often has your mind-body been touched by a song, a work of art, or an inspiring idea? How often have you used your mind-body to create something that touched other mind-bodies? How did these moments of inspiration feel in your mind-body? Did you feel excited? Anxious? Joyous? Aroused?

The Felt Sense

As mind and body are interwoven, when you explore the body, you will inherently be exploring the mind, and when you explore the mind, you will inherently be exploring the body. To further illustrate this experience, I would now like to introduce to you the concept of the felt sense.

Defined by philosopher and author Eugene Gendlin in his book *Focusing*, the felt sense is the awareness of one's internal somatic experience.[22] *Somatic* means "relating to the body."

Each somatic experience has its own unique flavor, so to speak, in the felt sense. The weave of the felt sense is composed of a variety of different threads or phenomenological qualities. It can be fluid, airy, hot, cold, electric, heavy, tight, and so on. The felt sense is always changing, as every moment is always changing, as wyrd is always changing. Your felt sense is always here-and-now, waiting for you to bring your awareness to it, waiting for you to attune to it. The more you do, the more you will feel its ever-changing and emergent qualities.

All experiences impact us on the somatic, felt sense level. Every experience has its own unique somatic flavoring, so to speak. For the most part, though not always, positive experiences will elicit a pleasant felt sense and negative experiences will elicit an unpleasant felt sense. Anxiety might be felt in the body as a tightness or restlessness in the belly, chest, or neck. Depression might be felt as a heaviness, as inertia. Loneliness might be felt as physical pain or anxious yearning. Joy is often experienced as a feeling of lightness, exuberance, or excitement. How does love feel? A fantasy or a memory can turn you on. Creativity, curiosity, uncertainty, well-being, wonder, and so on all have a felt sense associated with them. Even the experience of dissociation can have felt sense to it—emptiness, blankness, absence, and so on. All these experiences are part of your mind-body wyrd.

---

22. Eugene Gendlin, *Focusing* (New York: Bantam Dell), 1981.

There are a variety of threads that weave together to create the braid of one's mind-body wyrd. There are emotional threads, cognitive threads, somatic threads, and more. Each thread is a weave unto itself, composed of numerous finer threads. No matter what the experiential thread may be, it can be explored mindfully and phenomenologically. Find, explore, and follow the threads to see the pattern of wyrd.

Wyrding Ways
Meditation on the Felt Sense

This exercise will consist of a meditation and breathing practice that will help you develop your awareness of your felt sense. It is also a form of self-care that can help you manage anxiety, insomnia, and PTSD responses that may arise during the course of your wyrdcraft and life in general.

You will need:
- Ten to thirty minutes of uninterrupted time-space
- A comfortable place to stand, sit, and lie down
- Comfortable clothing
- Your journal

1. Find a comfortable position, whether sitting, standing, or lying down. Close your eyes and take a few slow, deep belly-breaths in through your nose and out through your mouth. With each out-breath, relax just a little bit more. Return to your natural breathing pattern. Notice how you are breathing. Let the air come in and go out naturally—in, out, in, out. Don't try to affect it in any way. Don't force it. In a sense, let your breath breathe you.

2. Bring your awareness to your somatic experience in the moment. In general, how do you feel? Do you notice any tension anywhere? Any aches? Any pleasant sensations? What is your mood and how does that mood feel in your body? What emotions are present, if any? Feel into these questions as you answer them. If there are any tense places in your body, breathe into those places. Relax. Breathe in peace, breathe out tension. Do this for a couple of minutes.

3. Now put your right hand over your heart and your left hand over your belly. Slowly and naturally breathe in through your nose, and then breathe out through your mouth (as if you are breathing through a straw or attempting to cool down a spoonful of hot soup). Count to four on every in-breath and count to eight on every out-breath. Do this for three to five minutes.

4. When you are done with your 4-8 breathing, bring your awareness back to your body and being in general. How do you feel? Do you feel calmer, more excited, or numb, heavy, tense, light, peaceful, restless? Do you notice any sensations—tingling, buzzing, twitching? Spend a few minutes mindfully witnessing.

5. Record the results of your experiments in your journal. You can also practice this with your therapist if you have one. I often practice this with my clients—and therapist.

Do these exercises at different points throughout your day. The more you bring your awareness to your felt sense, the more you will increase your awareness of wyrd. The basic goal is to *be* and to witness your experience with curiosity and without judgment. Just notice, watch, and observe as sensations, thoughts and emotions do their thing. Remember, the goal of wyrdcraft is the cultivation of the awareness of wholeness. Attaining wholeness is an ongoing, lifelong process and practice.

Your mind-body is not an isolated system. Your individual mind-body is a braid that weaves seamlessly into the greater transpersonal mind-body of the Web of Wyrd. You are an integral thread within this Web, as well is every thread within you. Every time you remember this, you are re-membering the soul that is the wholeness of your being—and the Soul that is the All—just a little bit more. You are becoming just a little bit more wyrd conscious. Let us follow this expansion outward into the Web as we shift our focus from the domain of mind-body into the domains of relationship and environment—where mind-bodies are in relationship to other mind-bodies (human as well as other-than-human). Wyrd-soul-psyche is, after all, shared between all people, all places, and all things.

As you move on to the domains of relationship and environment, remember to bring your awareness of mind-body with you. Feel into your experience of everyone and everything you encounter on the way.

Chapter 5
Relationship and Environment

R elationship covers a lot of ground. What comes to mind when you hear the word *relationship*? In many ways, relationship is the foundational experience of being. Because everything is connected to everything else within the Web of Wyrd, during every waking, sleeping, and dreaming moment, you are constantly in relationship with everything else. You are in relationship with the past, present, and future, with the air you breathe, with the ground upon which you walk, with the water that falls from the sky, with the ideas that flow through other peoples' minds. You are in relationship with nature, life, death, sexuality, and the divine. You are in relationship with all these things and more. Everything with which you are in relationship has the potential to affect the course of your fate and destiny.

The Wyrd of Human Relationships

You are a human mind-body, and your mind-body is in relationship with other human mind-bodies. Some of these mind-bodies you know, but many more of them you don't, and many more of them you never will, but don't be fooled by this. Just because you don't know someone or aren't in near proximity to them, that doesn't mean you aren't connected to them and affected by them. There is no escaping the web that connects us. You are woven into it, and it is woven into you. Thoughts, words, and actions are far-travelers as they ripple through the web. Whether you like it or not, we are all in relationship with each other, known and unknown, near and far, seen and unseen, for better or for worse. We all affect each other's wyrd; we are all in a great wyrd dance with each other, cocreating our fate and destiny with every thought, word, and action we bring into the world.

The wyrd of relationship is the soul, nature, fabric, process, purpose, and destiny of the relationship. Like the wyrd of mind-body, the wyrd of relationship is woven from far too many threads to name. It is woven by genetics, culture, values, sexuality, emotion, and more. And just as wyrd varies from person to person and from mind-body to mind-body, relational wyrd varies from relationship to relationship. Each entity brings their own wyrd to the relationship and combines it with the other entity's wyrd to create a new weave or pattern of relational wyrd that is unique to that relationship. There are many types of relationship: family, business, romantic, spiritual, and more. No matter what type of relationship it is, relationship is a co-creative dance; we all do this dance together. When you meet someone new, you consciously and unconsciously attune to the wyrd of that person. When you find yourself attracted to or repelled by a person, you are reacting to his, her, or their wyrd, and his, her, or their wyrd is reacting to yours. Sometimes we may feel very strongly that our wyrd is tightly woven with another's; we might think of this person as our soulmate or nemesis. We are sensitive, empathic, and communicative beings. We are also adaptable and shapeshifting. We change and are changed by each other. All of this is wyrd.

Wyrding Ways
Cultivating Mind-Body-Relationship Awareness

In this exercise, you will be bringing mindfulness to the connection between mind-body-relationship. In the first part, you will examine the mind-body impacts that result from a particular relationship you have with someone in your life. In the second part, you will examine the mind-body impacts that result from your relationship to a particular activity.

1. The next time you are engaged in an engrossing conversation with someone, bring your awareness to your mind-body. Notice what sensations and emotions you are feeling in your body as you interact with this person. How do you feel in relationship with this person? Notice what anxiety, joy, anger, sadness, arousal, boredom, and so on feel like in your body. Later, contemplate the following: How did you meet? What circumstances led to your meeting? How has the arrival of this person changed your life—for better or for worse? Write about this experience in your journal.

2. The next time you are engaged in an engrossing activity, bring awareness to your mind-body. Notice what sensations and emotions arise in your belly, chest, arms, legs, and head as you engage in the activity. Notice what kind of thoughts, mental images, or emotions arise. Why are you engaging in this activity? How will you and/or others benefit from it? How might you and/or others be hurt by it? Be as honest and nonjudgmental toward yourself as you can. Write about this experience in your journal.

The Mirror of Relationship

Our relationships are remarkable mirrors with an uncanny ability to reflect our wyrd back to us. Each relationship—whether it's with a person, place, object, or activity—shows us who we are, what we are about, where we are, and where we are headed. Sometimes a relationship might show us what we want to see; other times it may show us what we don't want to see. Either way, our relationships nevertheless help us see ourselves, our life, our world, and our wyrd more clearly.

As a licensed marriage and family therapist, I work in the realm of relationship. What I have seen is that our relationships have a way of bringing our so-called best and worst selves. In this way, conscious relationship is revelatory. At best, relationships can bring out our loyalty, dedication, integrity, compassion, and so many loving, healing traits and ways of being. At worst, they can bring out our jealously, paranoia, possessiveness, aggression, and other problematic ways of relating. Our relationships are laboratories and playgrounds where we get to experiment and play, make mistakes, learn, reflect, and evolve. Our relational issues and foibles, if explored, can tell us a lot about our wyrd. *How* are you in relationship? Do you have difficulty expressing your wants, needs, and boundaries with people? Does commitment frighten you? There are healthy and unhealthy ways dependence, codependence, and independence manifest. Do you tend to lean too far into one or the other? Can you be manipulative, abusive, distant, ambivalent? Why is that? These are all great questions to ask oneself, and even better to process in individual or couple's therapy. It is good to know what our issues are and from where they come, for then we are given the opportunity to do the work we need to do to craft our destiny in different, and hopefully healthier, more fulfilling directions.

Sexuality is an enlightening and empowering window into one's relational wyrd. By looking at what turns you on and off and where you are at on the sexuality spectrum, you can learn a lot about your nature. How do you express yourself sexually, sensually, and erotically? What do you love to do? What turns you on? Are you monogamous, polyamorous, fluid? Do you have a history of sexual trauma, sex addiction, or porn addiction? Have you done mind-body healing work around your sexuality, past sexual experiences, and current sexual expression? How might processing these things with a skilled sex-positive therapist, peer, or guide affect your life-path? You will see.

Everyone's relationship to sexuality is different and in flux. Sexuality is very much a fluid experience. Some people spend a lot of time thinking about sex and having sex, others not so much. For some, eroticism, sensuality, and sexuality are empowering threads that connect them directly to their lover(s), their world, and their god(s) or goddess(es). For others, these threads are felt to be sinful, or severely triggering.

How much is sexuality a part of your identity and life in general? How much of a growing-edge is sexuality in your life? There is a lot to explore when it comes to the interweaving of wyrd and sexuality. The wonderful, wild, and weird realms of sexuality await your exploration whenever you are ready.

Just as there are large parts of your wyrd that you can come to know within the container of relationship, there are also large parts of your relational wyrd that you might never know if you don't spend extended amounts of time being single or alone now and then—deeply in relationship with yourself. Solitude is an illuminating window into wyrd, as well as a great initiator of meaningful, purposeful change.

Relationship, just like life itself, can be seen through the lens of spiritual process. Conscious relationship can be a deeply spiritual path that leads one directly toward life's great mysteries. The realm of relationship is home to one of life's great paradoxes: you are never alone, and you are always alone. Drop into both sides of this paradox, and you will find yourself engaged in a powerful alchemical process that will have a marked effect on your wyrd.

Relationships are cauldrons cooking up deep magic, deep emotion, and deep transformation. *How* we relate to the thoughts, sensations, and emotions that our relationships generate makes all the difference. This is where magic gets psychological and transformation gets practical. Whether a relationship is amazing or challenging, or amazingly challenging, its wyrd can be crafted. Just toss everything you want to transform into the cauldron of your awareness and let it cook—let it work on you as you work on it.

As a therapist, I get the opportunity to sit at the alchemical crossroads of consciousness, being, and relationship with my clients regularly. There are things they see that I don't, and things I see that they don't, and then there are things we come to see together. With every session, the Web becomes ever more apparent as it reaches through and beyond my clients' lives. It is easy to see how my clients' health and well-being are connected to the health and well-being of the world around them. It's clear that the life and action of one person are connected to the lives and actions of all, that the fate of one person is tied to the fate of all people, and the destiny of one will impact the destiny of all.

At every relational nexus point within this web of relationships, there is another crossroads. It is at these crossroads—these growing-edges—where decisions are made and wyrd is crafted. Should I go this way or that? Do I yell now, or do I take a deep breath and try to talk calmly? Do I break up with my partner or not? Can I try to speak my truth now or not? Do I sit and wait here or continue on? Every crossroads is an opportunity to make a choice—walk the same path, or a different path?

Wyrding Ways
Contemplating Relational Wyrd

This contemplative exercise invites you to take part in an exploration of your relational wyrd. As you contemplate your relational wyrd, you also bring light to your individual wyrd. Write the answers to the questions in your journal or write a summary of your insights from the exercise.

You will need:
- Ten to twenty minutes of uninterrupted time-space
- A comfortable place to sit
- Optional: A journal

1. Call to mind a relationship that is *challenging* for you. (It may be your relationship with a parent, friend, partner, ex, or even a politician or deity.) Ask yourself,
   - What does this relationship, in general, bring up for me emotionally? (Distrust, jealousy, hatred, fear, for example.) Where do I feel these emotions in my body? What do they feel like?
   - What is it about this person/being that I find difficult? What does this person/being do that I find challenging?
   - What are my relational needs that aren't being met by this person/being? (The need to feel safe, heard, respected, understood, etc.) Is it possible to meet these needs by myself or in other ways? What can this person/being do to meet these needs? Can I ask this person if they are able to meet my needs?

2. Now call to mind a relationship that is *easy or easier*—one that makes you feel good. This may even be the same challenging relationship you reflected on (relationships are complicated, after all). Ask yourself,
   - What does this relationship, in general, bring up for me emotionally? (Love, joy, excitement, trust, etc.) Where do I feel these emotions in my body? What do they feel like?
   - What needs does this relationship do a good job of meeting?

– What blessings has this relationship brought into my life?
– In what ways do I, or can I, express gratitude to this person/being for meeting my wants and needs and bringing these blessings into my life?

The answers to these questions will help shine light on the constellation of your relational wyrd—your relational fate and destiny. Reflecting on your relationships can tell you a lot about who you are, how you are, how you feel, and the direction you are headed in life.

The Weaving of Relational Wyrd

Our early childhood relationships play a big part in the formulation of our relational wyrd. Though it is much more complex than "my parents made me this way," it is certainly true that our caregivers, family members, teachers, and early childhood peers have a direct influence on our life-path, fate, and destiny.

We soak in everything we experience; we are sponges. Whether they are good, bad, or neutral, our early relational experiences become internalized into our sense of self and our worldview and become the templates through which we see and understand other relationships throughout our life. Our experiences are woven into our sense of self and then become the narratives or blueprints we use—often unconsciously—to base our expectations and behaviors in subsequent relationships. These templates stay with us as we grow up and direct our lives in predictable ways. We use these templates as models for how relationships *are* or *should be*. If you experience your caregivers, family members, role models, or peers as avoidant, violent, timid, nurturing, and so on, you will to some extent internalize those experiences and ways of being, and they will become woven into your wyrd. As a child, you were almost a completely blank slate. You learned from the people closest to you and developed accordingly.

Because this happens on an unconscious level, the experiences that were woven into your wyrd while younger tend to direct your life from behind the scenes. What triggers you, what bothers you, how you behave with friends and lovers, and even the kinds of lovers you attract are to some extent predetermined by the templates formed by your early relational experiences. Of course, these templates are subject to change.

Some of these templates are passed down transgenerationally. This means that—at the risk of oversimplifying—we learned from our parents, who learned from their parents, who learned from their parents, and so on, all the way back. Past-present-future is interwoven into a braid. Here and now, we are the product of a very long line of past conditioning. And just as we've learned our ways of relating from others, we'll pass on what we've learned to others as well.

Thankfully, these templates and ways of being are not set in stone. Not everything the Fates weave is unchangeable. The Norns carve our fates into wood, not steel or graphene. We can become more aware, learn, evolve, and make different choices at every crossroads we encounter. We can become conscious of our wyrd, of our wounded threads, mend them, and reweave them into the tapestry of our being, snug, well, and whole. We can weave and reweave healthier narratives, new templates, and new ways of being. We can sing new songs and send new vibrations out into the web, thus attracting new people, new experiences, and new energies that are more aligned with our Higher Self. We can all do this together.

Group Identity and Folk-Hood

Another influential player in the weaving of relational wyrd has to do with group identities. Humans naturally tend to place themselves and each other into groups. We do this for many reasons: to feel we belong, to feel a sense of security and stability, to feel the support of community, to learn.

A group is a collection of people with a common identity. Groups tend to collect around shared ethics, values, behavioral norms, dress codes, and so forth. Group identity provides a sense of social, structural, and psychological grounding. It is easier, and generally safer, to understand and relate to the world from within the structure of a group. In a group, you can see who's with you and who's against you, who you can trust and who you can't, who will help you and who won't.

As we age and develop, we learn to which communities we do and don't belong. We learn the walk, talk, dress, and worldview of the group, and we learn to relate to each other in group-specific ways. Group engagement helps us explore and develop our identity and sense of self. As one explores one's identity over the course of one's life, one may very likely experience a number of changes in identity and group affiliation. This is wyrd in process.

We all inherit the DNA of our ancestors. We also inherit worldviews, lifestyles, rituals, and traumas that have been passed down transgenerationally through familial and folk lineages and legacies. All these things, too, are part of our wyrd. We inherit stories of loss, gain, triumph, and hardship from our ancestors and pass them on to our descendants. These stories are rich, full of all the stuff of life, after life, after life. They are the soul-stories of our folk, passed down consciously and unconsciously through genetics, tradition, birthright, and birthplace. Like it or not, our ancestors' wyrd is to some extent our wyrd.

The idea of having a folk is an old one. If someone was considered your folk or kin, they were your people, kindred, tribe, or clan. Theoretically speaking, you could sooner trust your own folk than someone who is not your folk. Folk watch out for each other. Folk share a special bond. In a way, your folk is like your extended family, a unified group of people who share something in common. At its best, to be part of a folk is to be part of a loving and supportive community that reaches deeply into the past, present, and future, and to have a vehicle for the transmission of ancestral wisdom, ritual, and soulful tradition.

There is more to the story of folk, however. Folk-hood has a shadow side— a destructive and self-destructive side. The folk ideal can be used as a rationale to create hierarchies in which some folk are deemed better or worthier than others. This has led to untold suffering and oppression all around the world through the ages. All of this, too, is part of our wyrd, for better or for worse.

The word *folk* comes from the German word *volk*, meaning "people" or "soul of the people." The volk ideal was politicized in the eighteenth and nineteenth centuries in order to uplift and unite the German national identity and spirit. Eventually, the volk ideal was used by the Nazis to privilege ethnic Germans and those of the supposedly superior Aryan race. This type of folkish, or volkisch, pride has persisted into the present day, including within some pagan and heathen sects. Within these groups, the concept of volk is still being used to uphold white supremacist, xenophobic, racist, nationalist, and fascist worldviews and agendas.

It is great to have kin around. Common cultural and ethnic bonds are magical and necessary for many reasons. It is wonderful to love and celebrate your folk, to support each other and honor the traditions, stories, and struggles of your ancestors; there is deep soul-healing to be found in the healing of transgenerational traumas passed through one's folk-line. However, bigoted folkways lead to the creation and perpetuation of artificial divisions and hierarchies, which place some races, cultures, and ideologies above others. This leads to the oppression of some by others—based on skin color, sex, gender, religious affiliation, and so on. Oppression, which can take many forms (racial, class, gender, religious, institutional, systemic, etc.) is traumatizing and leads to a wide range and depth of mind-body-relationship-environment-soul-spirit symptoms. Because everything and everyone is connected, oppression, in any form, is a grievous attack to the health and well-being of all.

Exclusive and oppressive folk-hood and folkways are based on an insidious delusion that occludes one's awareness from the greater Web—that which connects and unifies all beings and all life. As we are all connected at the most fundamental soul-level, this delusion breeds oppression and results in untold suffering for all life. Though bigotry hurts the targets of bigotry most of all, it also hurts the bigots themselves. What goes around comes around. Whatever one puts out into the world (through thought, word, or action) will inevitably return. Hatred, destruction, and divisive thought, word, and action only breed more of the same. The ripple effects from bigoted folk-hood spreads competition, distrust, deceit, violence, and trauma throughout the Web. Putting one's folk above others perpetuates endless cycles of war, violence, anxiety, depression, and a plethora of other mind-body-relationship-environment-soul-spirit symptoms—ad nauseum. Those who oppress others are unconsciously oppressing themselves.

Thankfully, there is a way out of this destructive cycle of oppression. There are ways to heal and transform, together, as one. We can expand the concept of folk and volk to include, and empower, all beings in the web of life. As you practice wyrdcraft and explore your wyrd—as we all explore our wyrd—the threads that connect us will reveal the paradox of our difference, our unity, and our interdependence. Imagine the healing-transformation we could welcome as we turn and face each other and nature as collaborators, family, friends, lovers, and kin. The concept of folk and folk-hood can include all domains as it permeates and reintegrates the human-made world and the natural world. There is a lot of healing to be done, and this may be the only way it is going to get done. Thankfully, as we do this difficult but rewarding work, natural wisdom and soul will come to the foreground, and the fibers, threads, and strings of our common bonds will vibrate and sing a collective song of healing and becoming—together.

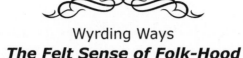

Wyrding Ways
The Felt Sense of Folk-Hood

Personality and folk-identity elicit a felt sense as well. They, too, are threads in one's wyrd. Every aspect of our personality and identity will have its associated felt sense. In this exercise, you will feel into your felt sense of folk-hood.

You will need:

- Ten minutes for undisturbed meditation and contemplation
- A meditation cushion or chair or another comfortable place to sit, lie down, or stand
- Your journal

1. Find a comfortable place to sit, stand, or lie down. Take a few minutes to bring your awareness to your body and breath in the present moment. Just allow yourself to be *as is*. Notice any tension, aches, or other sensations. Close your eyes; take a few slow, deep breaths. After each exhale, relax your body a little bit more. Then return to your natural breathing pattern.

2. Bring your awareness to your felt sense in your body (you may want to focus on your core—your neck, chest, and belly). Make a statement that claims your identity. For example: "I am a woman." "I am trans." "I am queer." "I am old." "I am Black." "I am a Gemini." "I am a nerd." "I am an anarchist." "I am a healer." "I am an alcoholic." "I am a witch." "I am a scientist." "I am Jewish." "I am Muslim." What are your identities? Slowly say each one at a time to yourself silently or out loud. Wait about five seconds, then say it again. Repeat. As you do this, pay close attention to your felt sense. Whatever you affirm, own it. Feel the somatic impression of what it means to you. Notice the thoughts, sensations, and emotions that arise as you embody each statement of identity. Really feel into it as you say it. Soak it in. Try this with at least three to five different identities to which you ascribe.

3. Contemplation: How does your identity determine the decisions you make, the friends you make, and the direction your life takes?

4. Record your experience in your journal.

The Wyrd of Environment

We are not only in relationship with ourselves and the people in our lives, we are also in relationship with the environments in which we live. The wyrd of environment is the nature, fabric, composition, behavior, and inherent processes, purposes, and destinies woven through place. A particular place's wyrd is the constellation of parts, or threads, that create the gestalt, zeitgeist, or soul of that place.

The environment is composed of innumerable threads. The climate is one of these threads, as is the flora and fauna, geography, culture, history, and more. Each separate element or part of a place can be seen as a distinct thread in a larger weave or tapestry that is the place as a whole. Suffice to say, as we become more aware of these threads, we are granted a look-see into the wyrd of place.

The wyrd of each environment—whether natural or human-made—is unique. The wyrd of a swamp is different from the wyrd of a desert. The wyrd of Tokyo is different from the wyrd of Istanbul. The wyrd of Ashland, Ohio, is different from the wyrd of Ashland, Oregon. The wyrd of Rome today is different from the wyrd of Rome two thousand years ago, or even a day ago. The wyrd of a neighborhood, a particular street, house, or room in any given moment is also totally unique.

You don't have to look too deeply to see how the environment in which you live influences who and how you are and where you are headed. If you grew up in a crowded metropolis, you will have had a very different experience than if you grew up in the middle of the wilderness; you will have learned the ways of the city, or you will have learned the ways of the forest. If you grew up in a tribal village in the Amazon, you will have had a very different experience than someone raised in an Amish community in rural Pennsylvania, or in a Sámi community in northern Finland, or in a fifty-story skyscraper in Hong Kong. Of course, there will be similarities between these experiences as well.

No matter where you are, you will learn from and adapt to your physical environment and relational environment. Whether you want to or not, you absorb your environment consciously and unconsciously through osmosis. Whatever experiences you absorb will be woven into your wyrd, thus affecting your fate and destiny moving forward—as well as the fates and destinies of countless others.

As all the domains are connected, if one domain suffers, it will impact all domains. In a general sense, living in a healthy environment will more than likely have a healthy impact on our mind-body-relational-soul-spirit well-being. Living in an unhealthy environment will have the opposite effect. Living in a mixed healthy-unhealthy system will have a mixed healthy-unhealthy effect on mind-body-relational-soul-spirit well-being.

Our governmental systems and institutions are part of our environmental wyrd as well. If our governmental systems are oppressive, delusional, and imbalanced, that will impact our mind-body-relationship wyrd in traumatizing ways. Governments regularly make decisions that don't take into account the importance of holistic health and well-being, thus perpetuating sickness within all domains. An abusive, neglectful, and toxic government is akin to having abusive, neglectful, and toxic parents. In theory, our governments are supposed to protect and support the people. Unfortunately, this is not the case if you look at the majority of governments around the world. They care for some and neglect others. They abuse some and support others. They put some in high esteem and treat others as animals, or worse, as evil. Our systems have been corrupted by the delusion that we are separate, and that the only way is the way of hierarchical existential competition.

The inner and outer landscapes are interwoven. As a therapist, I have found this to be true time and time again. With every session I am given a unique view into the relational interplay between so-called inner and outer, between the individual psyche and the world psyche. What I see is that the common symptoms that bring people to therapy—anxiety, depression, relationship problems, suicidal ideation, and so forth—cannot be extricated from environmental, systemic, and institutional issues and failures.

If you live in an area that suffers the impacts of oppression—i.e., poverty, racism, sexism, religious persecution, war, and environmental degradation—it will certainly impact your physical, psychological, relational, and spiritual well-being. How supportive and safe an environment is, or isn't, definitely matters. Imagine you were born into extreme poverty. What might that experience feel like? Imagine you are gay in a conservative, fundamentalist, homophobic family. How might that experience affect you? Imagine you are the child of a billionaire. How will these different experiences influence the development and life-path of the person? What are the emotional, cognitive, and somatic health implications of living in a highly polluted, poor, war-torn area? What are the implications of living in a clean, calm, safe, resource-abundant environment?

The wyrd of a place will have a direct impact upon the wyrd of every being living in or traveling through that place. In a way, you become the place while you are in the place, wherever you are. You internalize the place and carry it with you into the world wherever you go. The quantity and quality of the threads you weave into your being will depend on the duration and intensity of the experiences you had while there. It is said that "what happens in Vegas stays in Vegas." This is wishful thinking. Whether you want to or not, you will carry your experiences with you—no matter how wild or tame—as long as you walk the Earth, and they will directly and indirectly affect others. Even if you suppress and repress them deep into you unconscious; they will inevitably find their way out.

The wyrd of place can be explored somatically, historically, scientifically, politically, geographically, sociologically, and so on. The wyrd of the domain of environment is constantly shapeshifting—so are you, and so *can* you. The more you feel into your environment, the more fate, destiny, nature, and soul will come into view—craftable. Wyrd can be altered. The templates you've internalized from the people you've met and places you've visited can be transformed with awareness and with mindful crafting and patience.

Wyrding Ways
Walking and Sitting Meditation—Becoming Place

This exercise will consist of a walking and sitting meditation that will help you feel into the wyrd of place. Attuning in this way to your outer landscape simultaneously attunes you to your inner landscape and reveals the threads in the web that connects them to each other.

You will need:
- Twenty minutes to three hours
- A comfortable pair of walking, running, or hiking shoes
- Water and a snack

1. Take a walk around your neighborhood. (If you cannot walk, a bike, bus, car, etc. will do.) As you do, open all your senses to the experience. Be mindful—bring a curious, nonjudgmental awareness to all you see, hear, smell, touch, and taste. Pay attention to what's happening all around you and within you. How does it affect you cognitively, emotionally, somatically?

2. Occasionally, find a good place to sit for at least five minutes, and open your senses to all that is happening in the here-and-now. Be in the experience. When you are ready to move on, thank the place for the experiences it brought into your life.

3. Walk on. Take your walking meditation into new places. Go to different parts of the city, town, or countryside in which you live. Keep your senses open as you go, and stop, and go, and stop, and so on. Each time you stop, soak in the environment and the sensory impacts of each environment.

Practice this often in many different places. Wyrd is not only the natural world; wyrd is the human-made world, too. Wyrd is the city and forest. The ways of wyrd can be seen woven through all. Go into the heart of the wilderness. Go into the heart of the city. Into each, go prepared, go mindfully, and be aware. Don't put yourself in danger unless you are prepared to meet that danger head-on. Compare and contrast your mind-body-relational-environmental experience in each of them. Find somewhere to sit and meditate for a while—feel into the sounds, smells, tastes, sights, and sensations fully. Soak in the place. Become the place. Be the place. Find the threads, follow them and re-member the web. Send gratitude and give offerings to these spaces.

Other potential exercises:

- Bring a journal or sketchbook and sketch something of the environment or write an off-the-cuff, stream-of-consciousness poem.
- Dance. Embody the place in your movements. Experiment creatively. Feel the life around you as you do. Embody the moment. Embody many different environments and feel how different environments move you in different ways. (If you do this in public around strangers, you will most certainly be labeled *weird*. This will be a great opportunity to work with wyrd. How do you limit your movements? How do you hide? How do you express your weirdness?)

- Get to know your neighbors. Talk to strangers. Listen to their stories. Share your stories with them. Form relationships. Nurture and strengthen the threads that connect you.
- Learn the history of the place in which you live. When was it "founded?" What brought people to this place to begin with? Who inhabited this place before you? See how far back in history you can go. Send thanks to the previous stewards of the land.

Sacred Is the Space

As you explore the wyrd of environment, you may just happen upon a sacred place. What exactly makes a space sacred? This is a very personal question that will likely yield different answers depending upon whom you ask. For me, a sacred place is meaningful place, one conducive to inspiration, imagination, meditation, rest, and magic. A sacred space is a liminal space, a place on the edge or beyond consensus-reality time-space-consciousness. A palpable magic can be felt, accessed, and wielded within this liminality. Sacred places are powerful. Their power lies in any number of things: their beauty, their magnitude, their history, their design, or something else. Sacred spaces have an aura that change your aura as you enter them. They fill you with feelings of peace, awe, joy, love, and sometimes even fear and terror. Sacred spaces reveal mystery and divinity through somatic, emotional, relational experience.

In many ways, a sacred space is just a sacred moment, one which can be found or created anywhere—in the middle of the busiest city or in the middle of the most remote wilderness. Some of them have been marked with stone circles, signs, statues, or monuments; others have been marked by nothing and seen by no one. Some of these spaces have been made sacred by a tree, grove of trees, or other natural landmark, energy vortex, ley line, ritual, or event. Some are waiting to be made or found by you. You can create a sacred place just by pausing, appreciating, tending, and spending extended amounts of time there. For many, sacred space feels like home, and often, is home.

This book was in large part written in several sacred spaces I found over the course of my wanderings through the oak, bay, and redwood-covered hills of the San Francisco Bay Area, as well as on the mythical, yet very real, Mount Desert Island, on the rocky coast of Maine. In each of these places, I sat, listened, danced, and sang. I made offerings to this space, and what returned was wyrd. I am filled with gratitude for these and many other naturally revealing, healing, and transformational places in which I had the opportunity to commune with wyrd, including all the cafés, tearooms, occult shops, parks, and bars. The words you read now are the fruits of these fertile places.

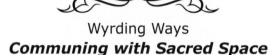

Wyrding Ways
Communing with Sacred Space

There are sacred places in the world waiting to be found. Go find one—go find many. You know a sacred place by how you feel while you are there. It may be a subtle feeling, so go quietly, go respectfully and go aware. Look with your eyes, yes, but look also with your other senses. Look with your heart, your intuition, your curiosity, joy, and wonder. Go open, for you could chance upon the sacred anywhere, in the city or in the wilderness. When you do find the sacred in a place, spend extra time there, return often if you are able, and be prepared to be changed. These spots are places of mystery—*be in* the mystery. Who knows what may come through.

While you are there, take some moments to contemplate what makes this place sacred to you. Its beauty, its location, its history? What do you feel called to do there? Meditate, sing, dance, write, create, cry? Remember, every thing, every place, and every time is imbued with wyrd, which means there are no purely and wholly unsacred places. The sacred, which comes through in the here-and-now, is everywhere. You can connect with this sacredness anywhere.

The blanket of relationship-environment is composed of countless threads and braids, and it is just one part of a larger tapestry. Our remarkable human mind-body can witness, process, and make meaning of this mystery. As we do this, we become more wyrd conscious. This is the work of wyrdcraft, the work of simultaneously healing and remembering, and the work of re-animating and re-enchanting our lives. Let us continue this work together.

As we leave the domains of relationship and environment behind, we find ourselves at the edge of something vast and mysterious, with everything we've gathered on our travels through the other domains in our pack, ready to venture forth—seeking, ever following the call of the Fates—onward into the even weirder dimensions of wyrd consciousness. There is great mystery here, so much to be remembered, in the domains of soul and spirit.

Chapter 6
Soul and Spirit

Let us now enter the wyrd domains of soul and spirit. Just as the sciences have endeavored to describe the nature of reality, so, too, does spirituality. All around the globe, there are spiritual paths and practices that have yielded experiential and testable data about the nature of reality, self, and being. This data may not be quantifiable from a hard science perspective, but don't be fooled by this. Like science, spiritual practices produce direct results that can be verified by firsthand experience—results that will without a doubt change the way you see, understand, and experience yourself, your relationships, your life, and your reality.

There is a plethora of ways to attune to and explore the wyrd of the domains of soul and spirit, as evidenced by the multitude of spiritual paths and spiritual technologies through time-space: meditation, fasting, rites of passage, divination, and so on. If you practice any of these technologies long enough, you will inevitably perceive the emergence of soul and spirit through the veil of delusion, the veil of ego and of mundane life. When this happens, even ordinary activities like going to the grocery store, commuting to work, or using the toilet can become spiritual experiences.

If you really wish to know the wyrd weave of the spiritual domains, firsthand experience is the key. Explore soul-spirit in your own life. Wander, seek, and ye shall find wonder. Experiment, study, play, be mindful, and soul-spirit will bloom in your awareness and in your world.

The Wyrd of Soul

Soul, psyche, and wyrd are synonymous. The soul of a place is akin to the wyrd or psyche of that place. The soul of a person is akin to the wyrd or psyche of the person. The soul of a relationship is akin to the wyrd or psyche of the relationship. The same goes for the environment.

From an animist perspective, everything is imbued with soul and soul-purpose. The soul of something is the nature or essence of that thing. It is the life-force that permeates it and the direction in which that life-force is flowing—its purpose. The experience of soul can be felt as one takes part in a meaningful and purposeful activity. You don't need to be a so-called *spiritual person* to experience this feeling of purpose. Atheists, nihilists, and strict materialists experience soul as well, though they might not label these experiences as such.

One's soul is one's wholeness—as well as one's process of becoming whole. Soul permeates the ego and reveals all its polarities—light and dark, pleasure and pain, pretty and ugly, young and old, health and dis-ease, for example. We experience soul through our ego as it manifests as our personality, identity, and persona (the masks we wear), but soul is also that which resides under and beyond the mask. The more whole a person is, the more soulfulness they exude. The quality of soulfulness develops as a result of time, experience, struggle, courage, love, and wisdom. Because our soul is our wholeness, our purpose becomes clearer as we become more whole.

Soul comes into being and defines itself through the human mind-body-relationship-environment experience in the here-and-now. Soul emerges and speaks to us through images as it flows from the unconscious to the conscious, manifesting as imagination, creativity, dreams, myth, and synchronicity. Soul is the realm of depth *and* soul emerges from depth. As soul moves downward and inward into being, into the unconscious, soul invites us into the core of all cores, into what gestalt therapists call the *fertile void*.[23] Within and from this void, new ideas, new lives, new worlds, and new dimensions are revealed. Like

23. Fritz Perls, *The Gestalt Approach & Eyewitness to Therapy* (Mountain View, CA: Science and Behavior Books, 1973), 99–101.

a seed, soul takes root within these depths and flowers from them in the form of soul's many manifestations. Those people generally considered soulful—i.e., artists, eccentrics, geniuses, so-called crazy people—all know the generative power behind and within this deep experience of soul. For some, soul can be totally overwhelming and scary, as evidenced within some cases of psychosis.

Soul is involved in a mysterious process of becoming. Soul awakens and transmutes the ego as soulfulness arises within and through it. As soul is evoked, invoked, and embodied, it integrates—it heals and transforms—the ego. Though this may mean physical healing as well, it is more so of a deep spiritual healing. Even sick and broken bodies can overflow with soul. Soul is on a transpersonal journey through and beyond ego into the beyond. Soul's process of becoming occurs through mind-body-relationship-environment. Soul becomes conscious through human consciousness—this, too, is wyrd, this, too, is wyrd consciousness in emergence. As soul emerges, one becomes more conscious of soul. Eventually this soul-awareness overflows out of the container of the individual psyche until it connects, or rather reconnects, with the soul-awareness of others and the soul-awareness of the world and cosmos at large. The connective, unitive, and integrative movement of soul-awareness reveals itself the more it is known—the more it speaks and the more one learns to listen. This is the movement of wyrd. Soul consciousness—a.k.a. wyrd consciousness—is revelatory; it illuminates the web that connects everything and helps us re-member all the parts into a whole. It also guides us and helps us tolerate and integrate life's many paradoxical truths.

The Wyrd of Spirit

Spirit is thought to be the infinite, nonlocalized essence of all existence, consciousness, and being. Spirit is a trans-soul—beyond soul. Just as ego awakens into soul, soul awakens into spirit, grows into spirit, or shifts into spirit. Spirit is soul's guide. "Come this way," spirit says to soul. Spirit is soul having undergone a next-level dimensional shift. Like soul, spirit is always calling.

One need not be a self-identified spiritual person to experience spirit. Spirit manifests in the human experience as idealism, hope, freedom, light, and inspiration. Spirit is the breakthrough, again and again, into the next level, into the beyond—through and beyond ego, through and beyond soul, through and beyond the cosmos, even through and beyond spirit.

We are moved by spirit, called by spirit, and guided by spirit as we become spirit.

After ego transmutes into soul and soul transmutes into spirit, we attain the experience of the absolute, of Infinity. This is the domain of spirit—one without boundary. There are no words that can mold it and hold it. Like any other mystery, spirit must be experienced to be understood. As spirit is experienced, spirit transforms both experiencer and experience. In a sense, spirit is the witness, yet spirit also dissolves or devours the witness. Perhaps this is what ceremonial magician Aleister Crowley referred to in his Gnostic Mass when he wrote, "O Lion and O Serpent that destroy the destroyer, be mighty among us."[24] Perhaps he was welcoming spirit.

The ancient Greek word for spirit was *pnuema*, which, interestingly, translates to "breath." Spirit is the breath that gives life to all. Spirit can be found by meditating upon the breath. As Buddha taught humanity, the breath is the door to enlightenment. Like the space between the in- and out-breath, spirit is also emptiness; it is being and non-being, form and formlessness; it is essence, basic, fundamental pure and infinite energy, beyond being, beyond consciousness.

Weaving Soul-Spirit

Soul and spirit are involved in a great spiraling, intertwining dance. A wonderful symbol for this dance is the yin-yang. Imagine that one color is spirit, and the other color is soul. They are distinct, and yet both are dynamic parts of a whole, fluctuating, changing, and adapting to each other as they go. Each contains the other within itself. Soul and spirit have their own wyrd way— their own niche, intelligence, or path to take—but eventually they meet up and morph into one another as they work in concert with each other in the service of Self-Realization, becoming, and unification.

Soul is often associated with the dark, the moon, water, earth, and the body; spirit is often associated with light, sky, sun, wind, fire, and beyond the body. Both spirit and soul guide us up, down, through, and beyond. Together, they dance until their divine union births the new, the infinite. Soul is the experiencer, and spirit, the witness. Spirit without soul is spiritual bypassing;

---

24. Aleister Crowley, *The Equinox: Volume III, Number 10*, ed. Hymenaeus Beta X (Newburyport, MA: Weiser, 1991), 136–137.

soul without spirit is victimhood and depression. Soul-spirit is imminent, here-and-now, and ever present. The goal of life, and of spiritual practice, is to remember this.

Wyrding Ways
Soul-Expression

In this exercise, you will get the opportunity to explore the wyrd of soul-spirit as it moves through your mind-body in the form of a dance. This is the first of a handful of dance experiments offered within this book. With each one, you will learn to explore the active and passive movements of soul-spirit within mind-body.

You will need:
- A device to play music
- A meditation cushion or another place to sit
- A place to dance undisturbed for as long as you wish

1. Find a song or a few that mean a lot to you—ones that inspire you, light you up, or drop you into a deep place. Ready your device, but do not start the music quite yet.

2. Begin by sitting down in a meditative posture—spine straight, relaxed and alert. Close your eyes, take a few slow, deep belly-breaths in through your nose and out through your mouth. With each out-breath, feel your mind-body relax just a little bit more. Return to a normal breathing pattern. Take a minute or two to bring awareness to your body as you sit.

3. Slowly stand, move your cushion aside, and start to move your body. Stretch any tight or sore areas. As you do, breathe slowly, calmly, and deeply into these places. Starting with your feet and moving up to your head, curl your toes, roll your ankles, bend your knees, lift your legs, move your pelvis around in circles, rotate your hips while you stand in place. In a circular motion, arch your spine (forward, sideways right, backward, sideways left, and forward (round and round in a fluid motion); limber up your spine, roll your neck in both directions, roll your shoulders forward and backward, stretch your jaw, open your eyes wide,

stretch your face—take a deep breath. Shake your limbs and bounce up and down. You are ready to start the music.

4. Press play. Tune in to the music: the melodies, rhythms, and lyrics. Feel the music. Let the music decide where to move and how to move. Allow your body to move the way your body wants to move. Attune, become a channel through which the soul-spirit of the music may flow. Don't worry about how the movements look; just focus on the feelings and let them flow. Notice any imagery that arises in your psyche as you dance. Let the imagery have a life of its own. Let the imagery move you as well. Go with the flow, channel the flow, guide the flow. Have fun, be serious, be sensual, be erotic, and allow yourself to experiment.

5. When the dance is done, slowly return to stillness. Feel into the presence of your body. What sensations and emotions do you notice? Give thanks to the soul-spirit of the music. Give thanks to the experience you just had. Take a few deep breaths. Take a seat and meditate for at least a few minutes before you shift from this space. Do your best to carry this energy into the world with you.

6. If you are unable to dance, allow the music to paint a picture within your imagination and dance within the theater of your mind. Let your imagination take over. If you'd like, and if you have the supplies, you can draw or paint whatever you see and feel. As you listen to the flow of soul-spirit through the music, in a stream-of-consciousness fashion, draw the music. Draw whatever comes to your mind. Draw the dance. Don't worry about technique or how it supposedly *should* look. What comes through will not be the definitive and final picture of soul-spirit; it will only be a snapshot of a moment. Have fun!

Meaning and Purpose

One of the most direct ways to experience the wyrd of soul-spirit is through the felt sense of the experiences of meaning and purpose. *Meaning* points to the special significance or definition of a thing, process, or concept. Meaning can be experienced as a resonance within the felt sense when we contemplate, experience, see, or understand the essence of something. *Purpose*, on the other hand, is the felt sense or intuitional affirmation we experience as we do something that is meaningful, important, or aligned with our nature, values, and process of becoming. Purpose denotes a certain degree of determination or intention en route toward the consummation of meaning. What do meaning and purpose mean to you? *How* does meaning and purpose manifest in your life?

Meaning and purpose lend themselves toward finding and fulfilling each other—like soul-spirit, mind-body, and, as we will soon see, fate-destiny—they are intertwined in a mutually supportive and co-creative dance. Spiraling like a double helix, ever on each other's tail, purpose calls meaning into our lives, and meaning calls purpose into our lives.

Meaning and purpose are woven throughout the entirety of our lives, whether we are conscious of it or not. Both bring a spiritual and psychological structure and integrity to our existence; whether they are grand and showy or simple and nuanced, each weaves us tighter into the web of life and the Web of Wyrd.

It is often a prolonged lack of purpose or meaning that leads to many of the symptoms that bring people into therapy: anxiety, depression, confusion, and addiction, for example. There is nothing inherently wrong with a lack of meaning or purpose. In fact, a lack of meaning and purpose are often necessary prerequisites for the realization of deeper meaning and purpose. Adroit tricksters, meaninglessness and purposelessness are often meaning and purpose in disguise. They like to shapeshift, change when we least expect it. They can drop us into a deeper relationship with ourselves, each other, and the world, waking us up to what is more real. Meaninglessness and purposelessness pull us deeper into the fertile void of the soul, the place where the old dies away and the new is born, where newfound or re-found meaning and purpose—i.e., soulfulness and spiritedness—alchemizes and arises.

The void is a scary, deeply misunderstood place. Yes, it is a place of annihilation, however, it is also a place of creation. The void is where the deepest sacrifices and fullest offerings are made. The spiritual compost pile, the inky cauldron in which the deepest transformation occurs, the dark furnace of true sorcery, and the sacrificial fire that is our growing-edge. The void is not a void, it just feels that way to the fearful, grasping, limited ego that has yet to comprehend its greater wholeness. The void is a place of transformation, thus making meaninglessness and purposelessness important catalysts for the alchemy of one's being and becoming. Out with the old, in with the new. Out with that which does not serve the ultimate consummation of love, and in with that which does.

It is from living with a sense of purposefulness that we encounter what fantasy author Erin Morgenstern refers to in her heavily wyrd-themed book *The Starless Sea* as "moments with meaning."[25] Within the hide-and-seek for meaning, we find our purpose, channel our purpose, and explore the route our purpose will take as we journey toward our destiny. The more you do what feels purposeful and meaningful to you, the greater sense of well-being you will find. One word for this fulfilling experience of well-being is *eudaimonia*. A word used by the ancient Greek, *eudaimonia* describes a deep state of well-being that comes from living a life imbued with meaning and purpose. Eudaimonia is often juxtaposed with *hedonia*, which is happiness that issues forth from experiences of pleasure and the absence of pain. Hedonia is a shorter-term, fleeting experience of remembering. Eudaimonia is a deeper, longer-lasting experience of remembering. Both, too, are interwoven to some extent, and are important paths to explore over the course of one's soul-spirit journey homeward.

Wyrding Ways
Contemplation of Purpose and Meaning

The spiritual practice of contemplation is an ancient and helpful one when it comes to exploring one's personal wyrd. Contemplation is the art of combining conscious thought and self-inquiry with meditation. While practicing contemplation, or any other wyrding way for that matter, it is important to work from a relative state of relaxation, for the stiller and more silent you become, the more receptive and perceptive to the subtle movements of soul-spirit you will be.

You will need:
- Twenty minutes or more of undisturbed time to contemplate and write
- A meditation cushion or another place to sit
- Your journal

---

25. Erin Morgenstern, *The Starless Sea: A Novel* (New York: Knopf Doubleday Publishing Group, 2019), 18.

1. Sit down, close your eyes, and take few deep, slow belly-breaths in through your nose and out through your mouth. With each out-breath, relax your body-mind a little bit more.

2. Feel into your body, notice any aches or pains, and breathe into these places. Take a mental note of your emotional state. Are you well, fair-to-middling, not well? Take a mental note of your mental activity. Is your mind busy, calm, tired?

3. Return to your natural breathing pattern in and out through your nose. Bring your awareness to the presence of your mind-body as you sit still and silent. Ask yourself each of these questions. Answer each question in your journal before moving on to the next.
   - What is meaningful to me?
   - What do I care about?
   - What do I love to do?
   - Why do I find _____ meaningful?
   - How do I know _____ is important to me?

4. Take a few slow, deep belly-breaths. Take a minute to pause, relax, and feel into presence before you begin again. Clear your mind to the best of your ability and ask yourself these questions. Again, answer them in your journal.
   - What is my purpose? (If you have an answer, ask yourself how you came to realize this purpose. If you don't have an answer, return to the questions about what is meaningful.)
   - What events led me to realizing this purpose?
   - How can I put what is meaningful to me into practice?

Fate and Ørlög

The experience of meaning and purpose point to two primary facets of wyrd often mentioned throughout this book: fate and destiny. I would be remiss if I did not at least attempt a working definition of these mysterious concepts at some point. What better chance than now, within the mysterious domain of soul-spirit.

It is said that fate is that which we cannot change, and destiny is that which we are meant to do. Some say that fate represents those things that cannot be altered no matter how hard we try. Fate might be thought of as natural law. Something is fated to be when we don't have any control or say over it. The ancient Norse called fate ørlög (pronounced *oerloeg*). Ørlög, which translates as "primal layers, first law, or that which has been laid down first," is decided upon by the Norns.

Your genetic mind-body makeup, the sociopolitical-economic environment into which you were born, and the psychological and relational dynamics of your birth family and caregivers are just a few factors of your ørlög, as are the limitations beset upon you by the laws of nature, biology, physics, and circumstance. Part of your fate or ørlög is thought to be inherited, forged by parents and ancestors and passed down to us transgenerationally—genetically, psychologically, economically, spiritually. Ørlög might even be broadened to include everything you have no control over in your life—the revolution of the Earth around the Sun, the body-mind's requirements for food and water, the inevitability of death. For the most part, once ørlög has been laid down, you can't change it.

In her book *The Astrology of Fate*, psychologist, astrologer, and author Liz Greene paints a beautiful picture of Fate. She describes Fate as the boundary that can't be crossed or the limit that can't be surpassed. The hubris that leads one to belief he/she/they can attempt a crossing of this boundary usually leads to catastrophe. According to Greene, Fate is a powerful, possessive, and authoritarian force. Fate may give you some freedom to live your life how you choose, but only within her structures. Attempt to venture beyond those structural limits, and you invite Fate's wrath, you invite tragedy and death.[26]

There is no moral imperative to wyrd. Fate does not work based on right and wrong or better or worse, but rather on cause and effect, much like the concept of karma. Our choices—whether they are deemed good, bad, or neutral—as well as Fate (Nature) herself, will steer our path toward or away from certain experiences and outcomes. We don't get punished for sinning; rather, we energetically, physically, and psychologically reap what we sow. What you put out into the world will return to you in one form or another—through energetic patterns of cause and effect.

Perhaps this image may help you understand this process. Imagine that every thought, word, or action you put out into the world has a symbolic shape to it (those magically inclined might imagine it as a type of sigil). Now

---

26. Liz Greene, *The Astrology of Fate* (York Beach, ME: Samuel Weiser, 1984), 17–51.

imagine that this shape is created in and issues forth into the world from your solar plexus. It may help to imagine the Care Bears if you are familiar with them. Each Care Bear has a *belly-badge* that represents their soul-quality that they project into the world.

As you create each shape within your center and project it out into the world—through thoughts, words, decisions, and actions—you simultaneously leave an open, receptive space of the same shape in your back, waiting to be filled. You can't see this space in your back, but it is there nonetheless. This means that if you project a heart-shaped thought, word, or action into the world, you will have a heart-shaped absence in your back waiting to be filled by a returning heart-shaped thought, word, or action. If you project anger into the world, you create an opening for anger to return to you into the opening in your back. If you project a violent shape into the world, you create a violent-shaped welcome mat in your back. Like attracts like, a gift for a gift, a curse for a curse—everything you put out into the world travels on an energetic loop that leaves you and returns to you. Life moves in circles and spirals—not straight lines. No matter what the shape is that you put into the world, it will inevitably return. The circle and cycle must be completed. Because it returns into your back from behind, it returns unseen, often as a surprise when you least expect it, or in a different way from how you put it out. You send the shape out into the mystery and from the mystery it returns. Often this happens unconsciously.

I noticed this in an interesting way while riding the bus around San Francisco. Often, if the bus driver was in a good mood and was talkative and kind to the passengers, the passengers would reflect that warmheartedness back. If the bus driver was cold, rude, and unforgiving, the passengers would emanate the same vibrations in return. The whole aura of the bus would change depending on the vibe of the driver and the quality of the ride would be completely different.

Wyrding Ways
Belly-Badge Experiment

In this experiment, you will create your own belly-badge, one aligned with your process of meaning-making and purpose-finding. As you do this, you will not only be developing wyrd consciousness, you will be crafting your wyrd.

You will need:
- Fifteen to thirty minutes or more of undisturbed time-space
- A meditation cushion or place to sit comfortably
- A piece of paper or your journal and a pencil or pen

1. Sit down, close your eyes, and take few slow, deep belly-breaths in through your nose and out through your mouth. With each out-breath relax just a little bit more. Return to your natural breathing pattern.

2. Feel into your body, notice any aches or pains, and breathe into these places. Take a mental note of your emotional state. Are you well, fair-to-middling, not well? Take a mental note of your mental activity. Is your mind busy, calm, tired?

3. Choose one quality that you would like to bring into the world. Perhaps you have already shown an innate propensity for one of these gifts: strength, courage, creativity, love, peace, laughter, gratitude, support, depth, empathy, compassion, joy, pleasure, ecstasy, or another.

4. After you have chosen your quality (or qualities), invoke it into your mind-body. Hold it within the cauldron that is your core—your gut, solar plexus, and heart-center. Imbibe in this feeling. As you do this, let your imagination come alive with spontaneous imagery. For example, the quality of laughter might elicit sparkles, bubbles, or a smiling face. Strength might elicit the Sun, a horse, or a mountain. Do your best to not force an image to come to mind. In fact, do your best not to overthink it. Let your body and your intuitive imagination present you with your image.

5. From this imagery, create a simple composite image of what you imagine—a belly-badge or sigil, if you will. (If you'd like, look

up an image of the Care Bears to get an idea of how this might look.)

6. Imagine placing this composite image within your belly, solar plexus, or heart. Feel the image vibrate deep within your core. This is the soul-quality that you will carry into the world and project into your ever-evolving life-path. Close your eyes and imagine a situation, person, or group of people to which and whom you would like to project this image and energy. Then send it out. Feel the energy flow through the threads that connect you.

7. Draw a composite sketch of this image—this belly-badge. Color it in if you'd like. Don't worry about how good it looks. Belly-badges can be abstract. As you draw and color it, feel into it. Imagine the image is imbued with the qualities you chose. When you are done, put it on your altar or hang it up somewhere special as a reminder.

Destiny

Your destiny could be thought of as that which you are becoming. It is the direction toward which one is headed that lies in the mystery referred to as the future. Our destiny is our destination or *home* where our Higher Self waits to be embodied in the here-and-now. Ceremonial magicians may refer to this as one's reunion with one's Holy Guardian Angel. Your destiny can be thought of as that which you're meant to do; the realization and fulfillment of your life-purpose.

Your fate and destiny can be perceived most intimately when you are closest to your growing-edge of being and becoming, in the place where safety and challenge blend. This is where some of the deepest healing-transformations of being-consciousness-existence occur. As you process your traumas, mistakes, and victories, and as you courageously face your challenges and fears at your growing-edge—again and again over the course of your life—you evolve. This evolution is on a spiraling, meandering path toward your ultimate destiny in a process of becoming.

Fate (ørlög) and destiny have a lot of overlap. Just as mind-body, relationship-environment, soul-spirit, and meaning-purpose are all two sides of the same coin, so are fate and destiny. Fate and destiny, too, are entwined in a magical dance. Fate is "meant to be" in a boundaried, limiting, defined sense; destiny is "meant to be" in a transformative, becoming, defining sense.

Together they interweave to create a single string or braid. In a sense, fate, one thread, describes the law of cause and effect, while destiny, the other thread, describes the law of agency, responsibility, and change. As fate and destiny are woven together, they influence each other and adapt to each other, joining into one path. Even though fate sets certain boundaries on our life-path, we are still involved in a moment-to-moment process of weaving our fate and fulfilling our destiny. This is the alchemical growing-edge where we are shaped and we shape, where we are woven and we weave, the place where Fate and destiny are both in a process of becoming limitless.

The thread that is your destiny and the thread that is your fate are woven together to create a unified life-string. This life-string is your being, woven from all the threads that create the weave of your wyrd that is the totality of all the domains. Your life-string and weave are woven together with the strings, threads, and weaves of everything around you, near and far—mind-body-relationship-environment-soul-spirit—within the great Web of Wyrd. To experience this weave is one of life's greatest gifts. As you practice wyrdcraft and integrate mind-body-relationship-environment-soul-spirit, you can do just that. You can perceive the greater patterns of fate and destiny into which your life is woven and weaving.

When it comes to your wyrd—your fate, destiny, nature, magic soul, and becoming—and your crafting, the more you integrate, the more you see; the more you see, the more you experience; the more you experience, the more you learn; the more you learn, the more you understand; the more you understand, the more embodied you become; the more embodied you become, the more power, guidance, and wisdom you can access; the more power, guidance, and wisdom you can access, the more you can choose to heal, transform, reweave, and weave anew. Your being is a crossroads, an alchemical place where you will meet friends, enemies, and guides alike and work together in an embodied way to make choices that are in alignment with Higher Self—where fate and destiny meet only to continue becoming from there.

We can't change the past of our ancestors, or even our own personal past in this life. However, psychologically speaking, we can change *how* we carry the past into the present and future. This all happens right at the growing-edge. With the help of introspection, contemplation, good therapy, and good magic, we can heal our wounds that direct our life-path from behind the scenes.

We can heal past traumas and other negative yet highly influential experiences that—if left unprocessed—might lead us toward perpetuating unnecessary harm. We can edit our psychological imprinting and conditioning and open new vistas to new opportunities and experiences, create new templates, and re-orient toward the wise, compassionate love of our Higher Self. We can craft our wyrd and move closer to the fulfillment of our destiny. There are a lot of things you can do to affect the course of your fate and destiny, even with the limits set by your ørlög. Wyrdcraft introduces many of these possibilities. As you practice the wyrding ways and engage in crafting your life, you learn, adapt, and evolve. You do this alongside Nature—alongside the Fates. Our soul-therapies can help us forgive those who have wronged us, including ourselves, for all the times we've gotten in our own way of eudaimonic well-being. They can help us heal our inner child, make sense of our emotional and relational wounds, and do the grieving we never got a chance to do in the past. In addition to this, soul-therapies can also help us heal traumas that have been passed down for generations. Believe it or not, wyrdcraft can help you become a lineage healer. You can craft a spell of revelation, healing-transformation, and becoming into the cosmos that affects all—past-present-future.

The Strange Attractor and Psychedelia

The philosopher, ethnobotanist, author, lecturer, and psychenaut Terence McKenna proposed that on a universal scale, there is a great transformative attractor at the end of time pulling life, history, culture, identity, being, and everything else toward it. He called this attractor the "transcendental object at the end of time."[27] According to McKenna, as we draw closer to this attractor, time moves faster and faster, as do change and transformation; novelty increases, and the boundaries, classifications, and ways of being that we have built around ourselves—that which could be illusion or delusion—dissolve. The veil of illusion becomes more and more transparent, and the world becomes realer, weirder, stranger, more magical, and more psychedelic as the essence of reality is unveiled.

---

27. Terence McKenna, "The World Is Far Weirder Than the Maddest Among Us Suppose (1994, Maui, Hawaii)," YouTube, February 6, 2018, https://www.youtube.com/watch?v=flh7O182YlU.

As the attractor pulls us and everything toward it, it pulls everything through a great process of transformation and becoming. What this object is and what it is pulling us toward will be revealed the closer we get to *It*. In other words, our ultimate fate and destiny will be revealed as we get closer to fulfilling them.

Part of the weirdness that occurs as one is pulled toward one's fate and destiny includes an increase in phenomena such as psychedelia, meaningful dreams, visions, déjà vu, and synchronicity. These psychological, psychedelic, magical, metaphysical—and sometimes psychotic—experiences can tell us a lot about wyrd and the nature of wyrd consciousness.

The etymology of the word *psychedelic* translates to "soul-revealing" or "soul-manifesting." Psychedelic substances and experiences render the veil transparent and reveal that which is normally hidden from awareness. As they do this, they expose soul-spirit and magic. These revelations happen more and more as one draws closer to the transcendental object at the end of time—toward our fate and destiny and toward that which lies beyond the pale of consensus reality. Common psychedelic experiences—which can occur not only while under the influence of psychedelic compounds, but also during ritual, for example—include visions of kaleidoscopic patterns, experiences of unity, ego-death, timelessness, synesthesia, contact with other-than-human entities, and more. These psychedelic experiences, which have been a part of human consciousness since time immemorial, are all manifestations of the wyrd of soul-spirit.

As healing as they can be, psychedelic medicines—such as LSD, magic mushrooms, and DMT—are not for everyone. In fact, they are contraindicated for many people for many reasons. There are some people who are already so opened (psychically, empathically, emotionally) that a psychedelic might unleash a deluge of soul that is too much to process all at once, triggering the emergence of preexisting, underlying mental health issues. Psychedelics have a way of dissolving psychological boundaries and structures that many people need to feel psychologically and existentially contained and safe. It is important to have a solid-enough sense of one's core egoic-self—and a certain receptivity to the weirdness of reality—if one is to tolerate its dissolution and reassembly with sanity intact. It will be harder to return to egoic-stability if there is no egoic-stability to begin with.

Note: If you or someone you know is having a psychedelic emergency, call 911 (in the US) or call the Fireside Project's Psychedelic Peer Support Line. You can find the number and web address in the back of this book under resources.

Be mindful and do your research before you open the gates of wyrd in this manner. Though there are currently several medical studies being undertaken to explore the medicinal and therapeutic benefits of psychedelic substances,[28] most are still considered Schedule I substances under the Controlled Substances Act and face the strictest regulations. There are legal, psychological, and physical risks that should be considered if one chooses to use psychedelics for whatever purpose.

As you'd do if you were to take part in a complex and powerful magical ritual of evocation or invocation, ready yourself. Come to know your ego, your worldview, your habits, wants, needs, wounds and traumas. Explore the wyrd of your domains. Study alone and with others, learn to create a sacred ritual space with proper boundaries, learn how to banish. (This will be covered in chapter 11.) Seek out an experienced elder, a trusted guide, a knowledgeable friend, or a therapist trained in psychedelic-assisted psychotherapy to facilitate your journey. Keywords to include in your search for a therapist versed in psychedelics and psychedelic experience and processing are *psychedelic integration therapist*. Though they might not provide trip-sitting services (as this is illegal), they can nonetheless be of great assistance while helping you process and integrate your own psychedelic experiences—an important facet of wyrdcraft.

Synchronicity, Dreams, and Déjà Vu

Soul-spirt often reveals itself through synchronicity, déjà vu, dreams, and visions. If you've ever had any of these experiences, then you've had a psychedelic, soul-revealing experience of wyrd. According to the originator of the term, Swiss psychoanalyst Carl Jung, a *synchronicity* is a "meaningful coincidence" in which events are connected by meaning but aren't necessarily connected by causality.[29] In other words, there may seem to be no apparent reason for the event taking place, yet at the same time, the moment carries

---

28. Multidisciplinary Association for Psychedelic Studies, "Explore Our Research," May 7, 2022, https://maps.org/our-research/.

29. Carl G. Jung, et al., *Man and His Symbols* (New York: Dell, 1968), 226.

with it a felt sense of meaning or purpose. Synchronistic experiences, though especially common while tripping, doing magic, or generally being in the flow, can happen at any time. Déjà vu is one example of this. Déjà vu is the experience of being, seeing, knowing, or feeling that something happening has happened before. Both synchronicity and déjà vu present a unique feeling state when they occur. People often respond to these experiences with the spontaneous declaration, "Weird!" These phenomena certainly elicit a strange, weird felt sense within the body-mind when they occur. This is what wyrd feels like.

Dreams, too, are manifestations of wyrd. As you probably already know, dreams can be prophetic, lucid, nightmarish, surreal, and healing. As they issue forth from the depths of our individual and collective unconscious to grace the lived experience of our daily and nightly lives, they communicate. What our dreams communicate to us, as well as how and why they communicate to us, leaves us with a lot to contemplate and process. Sometimes our dreams can be so impactful that they stay with us for the rest of our life. We tell our friends and family about them. We process them with our therapist. We turn them over and over in our minds as we try to make sense of them—their strangeness, their revelation and power. Dreams can tell us a lot about our personal and collective wyrd. There are many theories about what dreams are and how to interpret them, or even *if* you should interpret them.[30] Whether we understand how to interpret them or not, they inform and influence the way we see and experience reality.

Contact with other-than-human entities is an experience of soul as well. Deities, ghosts, ancestors, nature-spirits, and the like populate the individual, collective, planetary, cosmic, and transpersonal psyche. They offer guidance, warnings, messages, companionship, inspiration, and more. Those who have no conceptual framework for the animist conception of a soul-infused reality tend to label these communications as fantasy, hallucination, or pathology. This is emblematic of a culture that has lost its awareness of soul.

Soul communicates. The images that arise in our dreams, visions, fantasies, and myths, as well as the communications that come to us via nonhuman entities and archetypes, are the healthy, organic communications of soul.

---

30. James Hillman, *The Dream and the Underworld* (New York: Harper & Row, 1979), 91–141.

When a dream, synchronicity, déjà vu, vision, or metaphysical contact elicits a spontaneous "weird," what we are really doing is exclaiming "wyrd!" If but only for a moment, soul has peaked through the illusion. Suddenly we are given a momentary glimpse into the flow. These moments give us a look-see though the veil into the ways of wyrd and the workings of soul's magic that happen every day, right here-and-now in the so-called mundane world. They guide us as they speak to us. "Wake up," they say. "You are on the right path." "You are right where you need to be in your life right now." "Here, take this message, a sign; it will help you get back on track." "Follow me." "Pay special attention to what is happening right now." What a gift! Suddenly, even if only for a moment or two, inner and outer, self and other, self and nature, self and divine, spiritual and mundane, unite, and spiritual purpose—destiny and fate—comes into view.

Wyrding Ways
Wyrd-Journaling

It can be quite an enlivening and awakening experience to realize that synchronicities, dreams, déjà vu, and other strange phenomena are in fact manifestations of wyrd—fate, destiny, nature, soul, magic, and so on. This exercise will help you strengthen your skills at recognizing these experiences when they happen. It will also help you see the larger threads connecting them to your life-purpose.

You will need:
- A journal and a pen or pencil
- Fifteen to thirty minutes or more of undisturbed time-space for journaling

1. Keep a wyrd-journal. In it, keep a record of your dreams, visions, synchronicities, déjà vu, and any psychedelic, metaphysical, or psychic experiences you have. In each instance, describe what happened and what your felt sense of the experience was. Then write down what you think the experience meant. What was it trying to tell you? How does it relate to your purpose?

Other optional exercises:
- Ask your friends and family members about their soul-revealing experiences. What happened to them? What lessons were trying to come through for them?
- Pull a tarot card every morning. Meditate with the card, contemplating its meaning for at least five minutes. Then, throughout your day, take note of synchronistic experiences that correlate with the teachings of the card.

The Domains in Summary

Over the course of the last three chapters, I have guided you through a phenomenological exploration of the domains of mind, body, relationship, environment, soul, and spirit. Though all the domains are ultimately interwoven into one gestalt—the Web of Wyrd—I temporarily delineated them with the hope that in doing so, I might walk you, reader, through a systematic exploration of what wyrd is, and how fate, destiny, soul, and becoming come into play in each of your lives' domains in real time.

I hope you can now see with a little more clarity that the thoughts, perceptions, and fantasies of your mind; the physical makeup and felt sense of your body; the dynamics of your relationships; the effects of your environments; and the movements of soul and spirit all have a direct impact on your personal, as well as our collective, fate, destiny, nature, magic, and becoming. It's time to start reweaving these many threads back together and return them to their rightful place within the greater tapestry. It's time to shift our awareness toward the Web as a whole and further evoke and invoke Web consciousness.

Wyrding Ways
Communing with the Web

This wyrding way will consist of a meditation and guided imagery. The goal of this exercise is not only to conjure an image of the Web within your consciousness, but to invoke it and feel it within your felt sense of being. This exercise offers you an opportunity to digest the material we have covered in this section imaginally and somatically—i.e., soulfully.

You will need:

- Twenty to thirty minutes of undisturbed time-space for meditation
- A meditation cushion or chair or another comfortable place to sit, lie down, or stand

1. Find a place to sit, stand, or lie down. When you are comfortable, close your eyes; take three slow, deep belly-breaths in through your nose and out through your mouth. Feel your mind-body relaxing just a little bit more with each out-breath. Let your breath return to your natural breathing pattern, in and out through your nose.

2. Start with the domains of mind and body. Take a few minutes to visualize the many threads that constitute this domain. Every thought is a thread, as is every fantasy, idea, and memory; as is every sense, sensation, and perception. Curiosity, love, joy, worry, wonder—threads. As you imagine each of these threads and the many others you have explored, weave them together into a long, thick, beautiful braid. See the texture, colors, and pattern of this weave. Feel the energy flowing through it. Give thanks for this braid!

3. Shift to the domains of relationship and environment. Take a few minutes to visualize some of the countless threads of this domain. Every relationship has its own combination of threads, whether it is with your mom, dad, siblings, friends, acquaintances, or strangers. Feel into each of these threads. Hold them in your mind's eye. There is a thread that connects you to the Sun, Moon, and stars. Imagine them all. Feel also the countless threads that connect you to the environments in which you live— the threads of air, fire, water, earth, plant, animal, and mineral. Imagine them all. Imagine the myriad threads in the place you live. As you imagine and feel into each of these threads and the many others you have explored, weave them together into a long, thick, beautiful braid. See the texture, colors, and pattern of this weave. Feel the energy flowing through it. Give thanks for this braid!

4. Now shift to the domains of soul and spirit. What are some of the ways soul and spirit manifest? Every single brushstroke of a painting, every melody and rhythm in a song, every stanza, word, and letter of a poem—all threads of soul and spirit. Every

soulful and spirited laugh, cry, celebration, and struggle, every meaning and every purpose, a thread. Every god, goddess, and archetype, every spiritual practice and every sacred place, also a thread. Imagine these threads and feel the soul-spirit coursing through them, healing and guiding them. Feel into each of them as you weave them together into a long, thick, beautiful braid. See the texture, colors, and pattern of this weave. Feel the energy flowing through it. Give thanks for this braid!

5. You now have three braids before you, each one woven by countless threads. Feel the life-energy and magic pulsing through these threads. Feel them vibrate; hear them sing. Now weave these braids together into one macrocosmic braid. Visualize this great braid that represents your wyrd—your being. Feel the energy pulsing through you; listen to it hum.

6. Now imagine the countless braids of every living being in existence. Look up at the night sky and picture the threads connecting every star with every other star through time-space, including our own. All beings, all domains, and all dimensions, woven together in One endless tapestry of a Web. Feel this Web in its wholeness. Feel its vibrations and listen to its song. Weave your wyrd braid into this great tapestry of the Web of Wyrd. Commune with the Web. Meditate in this immersive experience for as long as you can. Feel the life-energy, the vibrations, the flow. Allow images to come and go through your mind. Listen, through the silence, to the primordial hum of it all. Hum along.

7. When it feels as if your communion is coming to an end, open your eyes. Look at the space around you; notice the colors, shapes, and textures. Listen to the sounds. Feel your body; wiggle your toes and fingers. What you see and feel is the Web; remember this soul-memory. Take three slow, deep belly-breaths, stand up, and shake your body out. Eat a small snack and do your best to hang on to the residual effects of this experience and carry them into the web of life as you go about your day.

Chapter 7
The Fragmentation of the Web

If it's true that things are in fact only going to get weirder and weirder from here on out, then it would benefit all of us to turn toward this weirdness with an open, curious mind, and to venture into it. This is what we have been doing together over the course of this book, but let us continue. Let us venture even further into the weirdness of the Web, that which is all domains interwoven, interdependent, and interrelated. Let's look at what is happening within and to this beautiful, bountiful quilt that comprises all of existence—known and unknown. Let's face the phenomenon of fragmentation. It will not be easy, but it will be worth it.

Fragmentation is the process of separating a larger whole into smaller pieces. Some synonyms of *fragmentation* include *splitting, dismemberment, fracturing,* and *segmentation.* Fragmentation, separation, and division seem to be encoded into the natural evolutionary process of the universe—as well as our larger soul-story. The arc of biological life has evolved from simple to complex, from few to many—forever expanding, adapting, complexifying, diversifying, and specializing. Fragmentation has been a main player in the evolutionary game since time immemorial. It is encoded into the process of life, and it is encoded into our way of seeing and being in the world. It, too, is the way of wyrd.

Classification, analysis, assignment, and differentiation have served as survival mechanisms with the intent to keep us alive and to keep our developing societies operating efficiently. The ways of fragmentation have helped us understand each domain of life in incredibly useful ways over the millennia. They've helped us live longer and become more efficient, as well as kept us engaged and busy with a sense of meaning and purpose. Fragmentation has led to what Taoists call the "myriad of things."[31] Each plant, animal, natural process, object, and piece of technology within the myriad of things has been assigned a name and a purpose. We human beings have created quite a beautiful map of existence together.

It is impossible to demonize fragmentation as it is a natural process that has brought us a lot of good and it has helped us see ourselves more clearly and wholly. However, the story doesn't end there. There is a shadow side to fragmentation; there is an unconscious destructive and self-destructive side to it. Through all our division, demarcation, and analysis, we have inadvertently separated the web of life and the Web of Wyrd into a myriad of pieces and forgotten we've done so. We forgot that everything *was and is* connected, that everything came from a whole and still is a whole. We've scientifically, psychologically, and spiritually delineated and defined everything; we've extracted the pieces from the whole and forgotten that there was a whole to begin with. In short, we've created an illusion and delusion that fragmentation, separation, and difference make up the only true reality.

The Worldview of Fragmentation

Fragmentation is the result of a fragmented worldview. One name for this worldview is dualism. According to dualism, the fundamental duality is composed of two major domains: mind (the inner world in which thoughts, images, and feeling reside) and matter (the outer world in which objects, others, and the world reside). Dualism offers us an either-or, oppositional view of the world—night or day, good or bad, heaven or hell, right or wrong, holy or evil, beautiful or ugly, order or chaos, love or hate, spiritual or mundane, male or female, self or other … I could go on. Duality is the dominant paradigm through which most of our world's cultures experience reality. Except

---

31. Lao Tzu, *Tao Te Ching*, trans. J. C. H. Wu (Boulder, CO: Shambhala, 1990), 64.

for in very rare cases, most of us were likely born and indoctrinated into this paradigm.

Nondualism, on the other hand, is not the opposite of dualism. Nondualism is a different worldview with a different approach toward seeing and being in the world all together. The worldview of nonduality says that there is more to reality than opposites and polarities, and that there is, in fact, a greater whole within which all polarities are integrated. Just as human beings are parts of the whole being of Earth, all perceived and unperceived dualities are parts of the nondual whole—the One, the Tao, the Wyrd, the Nameless. Nonduality acknowledges that even if we do live in a human-constructed, fragmented, dual-world, there is all the while a deeper and more expansive wholeness and unity underlying, overarching, and pervading everything. Nondual teachers like Ramana Maharshi, Gangaji, and Rupert Spira remind us that an embodied awareness of this pervasive wholeness can be experienced firsthand, right here and right now, as illusion is seen for what it is and nondual (wyrd) consciousness awakens.[32]

There are many things that feed the illusion that keeps the nondual experience outside of one's awareness. The unconscious, psychological trick of *splitting* is one such thing. Splitting—also called black-and-white thinking—describes the tendency to see a person, concept, or thing as either all good or all bad. Splitting is the process of taking a thing that has both positive *and* negative qualities, yet only seeing one side while denying the other. Splitting is a product of the dualistic worldview. It points to an inability in a person's thinking to integrate both positive and negative qualities—in one's self, in others, and in the world—into a cohesive, realistic whole. The split mind cannot handle or process the psychological and somatic tension and overwhelm of the nondual experience—it is too overwhelming. The mind that splits cannot face the fear of the perceived death and dissolution of the dualistic ego—a necessary sacrifice that needs to be made (bit by bit) to awaken to the truth that self-other-nature-cosmos is One.

---

32. Ramana Maharshi, *The Spiritual Teachings of Ramana Maharshi* (Boulder, CO: Shambhala, 2004); Gangaji, *You Are That* (Louisville, CO: Sounds True, 2007); Rupert Spira, *The Nature of Consciousness: Essays on the Unity of Mind and Matter* (Oxford, UK: Sahaja, 2017).

There is no gray middle ground in splitting. Often, splitters oscillate between one extreme and the other, depending upon their mood and if the object of their attention is meeting their wants and needs or not. To the splitter, one is either all good or all bad. Splitting does not acknowledge the paradoxical gray area that exists within wholeness, within the nondual. This is unfortunate for many reasons, for it is within this gray area where soul, purpose, meaning, fate, and destiny are waiting to be revealed. There are questions and answers in the gray. Within the tension of opposites that weave together to create the braid of wyrd, there are truths—truths that guide one toward wholeness, revelation, healing, and transformation—within every domain.

Wyrding Ways
Meditation on Fragmentation

To better understand the phenomenon of fragmentation, I'd like to walk you through a thought experiment, contemplation, and meditation. As with every exercise, *feel* into it.

You will need:

- Five to ten minutes of undisturbed time-space for meditation and guided imagery
- A comfortable place to sit, lie down, or stand

1. Start off by getting comfortable; sit or stand. Adopt a meditative posture—spine upright, ready and relaxed. Take a few slow, deep belly-breaths in through your nose and out through your mouth. With each out-breath, relax your diaphragm, belly, chest, and shoulders all the while remaining upright. Return to breathing naturally in and out of your nose.

2. Within your heart-center or solar plexus, imagine a ball of light. Focus on this area as you breathe in and out. Do this until you can feel the presence of energy—perhaps for a few minutes. Just be with this ball of energy and awareness.

3. Imagine you extract this ball of energy from your body and place it out in front of you at arm's length. Return to a meditative posture. Feel the presence of the orb in front of you, floating in space.

4. Next, use your mind's eye and will to separate this sphere into two smaller spheres. See the pair floating in front of you. Now, imagine you have forgotten that you separated them. You now look upon two seemingly separate and independent things. Seeing them this way, unaware that they were once connected, you see one and the other, all the while unaware that each half used to be part of the whole.

5. Now, split each of those parts in two, then forget you have done so, then split each of those parts in two, then forget, then split them again, and forget, and again, and forget, and again. In fact, never stop doing this. This is fragmentation.

6. What do you see in front of you? A multiplicity of parts that used to be One—and still is.

The unity of soul has been forgotten and turned into a myriad of separate and distinct things with no apparent connection to each other. The parts have become so far extracted from Oneness that Oneness has been forgotten and lost to the unconscious, but that doesn't mean we can't remember. This remembering is the process of integration, a process we will explore in the next chapters. With a lack of awareness of the One Tapestry comes an inability to perceive and remember the truth of wholeness—that the many are one, that the halves and pieces are parts of each other, that all threads are interwoven within a great totality of Being. The truth of unity is right before our eyes; it is deep within us, yet all the while it remains hidden by an illusion, a delusion, a psychospiritual blind spot—the shadow.

The Genesis of the Shadow

I mentioned the shadow a few times already, but let's take some time to explore it a little more. The psychological concept of the shadow was developed by transpersonal psychoanalyst Carl Jung. In short, the shadow is the unconscious and everything within it. It is all that is not-conscious. Within this not-conscious is all we can't see, know, or realize—that is, until we do. There are many things hiding in the not-conscious shadow. There are uncomfortable and challenging thoughts, memories, emotions, and impulses—things that have been deemed by you, your family, your cultures and society as ugly, despicable, perverse, and destructive. Thankfully, there is much more to the story of the shadow than this. There is a lot more waiting to be seen. The shadow also houses and hides our magic, power, soul, well-being, and destiny in potentia. The shadow is also home to our unexpressed gifts and unexperienced wholeness.

There is an individual shadow in each of us, and there is a collective shadow that we all share. The individual shadow is an aspect of the individual psyche, and the collective shadow is an aspect of the collective psyche. The shadow is a convenient place to throw away that which we fear, distrust, and don't want to see. In the short term, as we push whatever it is that we don't want to see out of our awareness, it feels as if we are getting rid of it—disappearing it, so to speak. When in reality, it is just added to a massive pile of unconscious material that has been there, and been growing, for a long time.

What happens if this material remains unacknowledged and unprocessed for too long? What will happen if the conscious light of the Sun and Moon are not allowed to illuminate the pile? The material will stagnate, fester, and turn toxic. This is a part of the natural wyrd of the psyche. Eventually, this toxicity will spill out of the individual psyche into the collective and world psyche in the form of symptoms, which, if unaddressed, will lead to a proliferation of more symptoms and perpetuate the fragmentation and suffering of all the domains. This is how the psyche works. It is a natural law of the psyche; it is a natural process. Does this mean that this process is a necessary aspect of the evolution and awakening of soul, being, and consciousness? Perhaps.

Let's return to our thought experiment. Again, imagine the orb of light in front of you—one. Watch as it splits in two; watch as the shadow is born. The shadow is the wound that was created when the part was torn from the whole. As every part used to be part of the whole, every part has this wound, this unconscious blind spot. This painful wound is an ancient wound and a denied wound; thus, it remains largely unseen and unexplored.

When one views the world through the lens of fragmentation—as we are unconsciously habituated to doing—no matter what thing is being perceived, only part of it will ever be seen. The rest of it, its wholeness, will remain hidden from awareness within the shadow—the unconscious. Sadly, wholeness, likeness, and unity will remain unperceived, forgotten. I will look at you, a stranger, unaware that you are part of me. You will look at me, unaware that I am part of you. We will look at nature, unaware that we are one and the same as the forests, bees, waters, sun, and so on. We will not see the layers of truths hidden in the shadow. That is, until we start to explore. Let's continue our exploration together.

When one is torn in two, two wounded parts—both hurting, scared, and guarded—are created. The split and injured parts—unsure why they are in pain—become hesitant, distrustful, defensive, aggressive, and confused. Having been torn apart, each half is left wounded, raw, vulnerable, unsure, and distrustful of the unknown and unseen part in both themselves and in the other. We fear our own shadow as much as we fear others' shadow. We fear that which we cannot see or understand.

Psychologically, spiritually, and relationally speaking, unconscious fragmentation leads to a highly influential existential ambivalence. On one side of this ambivalence, we fear each other (and ourselves), and on the other side, we love each other (and ourselves), while somewhere in the middle, we vacillate uncomfortably, unable to fully trust, stuck in an existential impasse. The love comes from our deep, unconscious awareness of the truth of our underlying unity and wholeness (which is in the background), and the fear comes from the illusion of our separateness (which is in the foreground). Because we are all one and deeply, albeit unconsciously, know ourselves to be, we yearn to remember this. We yearn to spiritually fragment our ego and dissolve into the background—so that we might become whole again. We long for love and re-union, to return to our truest and fullest selves, to come home to Soul, Self, and Source.

Though we deeply long for reunification and magical power and interconnection, at the same time, we fear them. We fear the Fates' call. We fear the weirdness and the necessary loss that comes with transformation and fragmentation of our ego identities and illusions that needs to occur before we can re-member, integrate, and reunite. Learning to trust in the process of sacrifice happens slowly. We identify with our limitations to the extent that we believe they make us who we are. So woven into our sense of self our limitations are that it feels like death whenever they are threatened by the necessities of sacrificial transformation. True freedom—the experience of Infinity—is a terrifying experience to one overidentified with one's egoic-identity, as Infinity devours all that is temporary, false, or delusional. The loss of our identity and the extensions of our identity—our cultures, religions, and the ego-world humans have built—is a terrifying thought, because our ego-identity permeates this world and seems to be the only thing that holds it together.

Also within the shadow hide the thoughts, feelings, and emotions we have long suppressed and repressed as a result of treating each other, our world, and ourselves horrifically. The inward path is a slippery slope at times. The depth of unprocessed guilt, shame, anger, anxiety, and grief that exists within our shadow can easily pull one under. The painful truth about all the hurtful things we've done to each other and to the world under the spell of fragmentation is a lot to bear. These collective truths, memories, emotions, and transgenerational traumas are so overwhelming that we tend to avoid them at all costs, for as long as possible. Unfortunately, the longer we avoid these things, the more our unprocessed shadow material will turn toxic, and the more we perpetuate the self-destructive symptom-cycle of fragmentation and inhibit our potential to self-realize. Left unchecked, this is the path to collective suicide. Thankfully we can process the contents of our shadow and transmute toxicity into health and well-being. This is exactly what wyrdcraft can and does help us do. This is exactly what we are doing right now.

The Symptoms of Fragmentation

As we continue our wyrdcraft, let's take an even deeper look into the shadow together. Let us gaze into it using the bright light of solar consciousness, the soft light of lunar consciousness, and the guiding light of stellar consciousness to see how fragmentation manifests in real time within every domain. Fragmentation can be seen clearly if you look long enough at the world around you and within you; if you cultivate wyrd consciousness, you will see the symptoms of fragmentation, as well as the fate of fragmentation, clearly. Though I will address self-care more fully in the next chapter, it might be a good idea to put it to practice now. As you look and feel into these symptoms—not just glossing them over—it may feel a bit overwhelming. Feel free to practice the breathing exercise suggested within the Meditation on the Felt Sense exercise in chapter 4 before, during, and/or after reading.

Mind-Body Fragmentation

The mind-body split is one of the major sources for unnecessary suffering within the world. The body is constantly communicating its relative well-being and lack of well-being to the mind, and vice versa. Under the influence of fragmentation, that communication becomes confused. Your internal wisdom that speaks to you through your gut, your intuition, and your natural reason becomes fainter and fainter as the mind-body connection is lost. When the mind is isolated from the body, and vice versa, both are left alone, wounded, anxious, and distrustful of the other. When the mind is untethered from the body, when it is unanchored by the body's innate intelligence, it tends to doubt itself and the body. Trust is not possible when communication is not possible. Alone to fend for itself, the split mind-body's primary experience becomes one of distrust, hypervigilance, and delusion; its primary concern becomes maintaining safety, often by any means necessary—even if by destructive, unhealthy means. This can make developing and maintaining healthy, thriving relationships difficult, as anxiety, paranoia, depression, addiction, and other self-destructive behaviors become more problematic.

One of the primary symptoms that results from mind-body fragmentation is a loss of the ability to experience empathy. Out of touch with one's own mind-body wholeness, one has inadvertently lost touch with others' mind-body wholeness. The Web that connects mind-body is the same Web that connects self and other. With this Web hidden from awareness, the empathic threads that connect us to ourselves and each other remain hidden. Without empathy for oneself and for others, humans are more prone to commit acts of violence of all kinds, which in turn lead to increased anxiety, depression, vitriol, guilt, shame, and more. These things can be pushed aside and ignored by the split, unempathetic mind-body for only so long before catastrophe comes knocking at the door.

The fragmented mind-body is also more easily pushed far beyond its healthy limits, worked, partied, abused, and neglected until it becomes sick. Sickness manifests through both physical and psychological symptoms. To split mind and body is to block wise decision-making and full and proper healing and to invite unnecessary suffering. A split mind-body is a system that has lost its orientation, balance, tools, and maps. Without these things to keep mind-body in relative harmony, psyche is at risk of drifting off course from its desired trajectory of health and well-being. Psyche is pulled in a million different directions by mind and a million other directions by body. This often leads to dangerous or unskillful choices, accident, self-harm, sickness, disease, and an inability to fully heal. Instead of the mind-body unit being a source for reflection, healing, deep knowing, and wise decision-making, it will be experienced as a source of confusion, self-doubt, distrust, and anxiety, and a number of other symptoms will arise.

Relational Fragmentation

Mind-bodies are connected to other mind-bodies, therefore, the mind-body split not only impacts our own personal well-being, but the well-being of our family, friends, and extended human and nonhuman family as well. Within a community, one who has lost sense of how to take care of themselves has also lost sense of how to take care of others. Likewise, one who has forgotten how to take care of others has also forgotten how to take care of themselves.

Relational fragmentation makes maintaining healthy relationships very difficult. Again, when there is relational fragmentation, the empathic thread that connects us is forgotten. At best, this leaves us feeling ambivalent about each other. On one side of this ambivalence is a feeling of aloneness, incompleteness, and distrust, while on the other side is a deep, underlying desire to connect and surrender to trust. A wild tension exists between these two polarities that leads to an aching existential confusion that is prone to suppression and repression through various means: social media, addiction, compulsion, and other pathological symptomology. Of course, this leads to severe implications.

The symptoms of relational fragmentation can be seen at all relational levels throughout the web of life, whether it's our relationship with friends, family, society, or the natural world. Some of these symptoms include abuse and oppression, genocide, ecocide, corruption, deceit, murder, rape, manipulation, and so on. What are some others? It is important to acknowledge just how many symptoms there really are within and around us. We must see the wounds if we wish to heal the wounds.

Most of our human-created systems, institutions, and norms were born from the delusional, fragmented worldviews of our unconscious ancestors in power, and many of them are still being perpetuated by our unconscious peers in power today. This unconsciousness is both the result of and the perpetrator of destructive fragmentation. There is a difference between intention and impact. One can have good intentions that inadvertently lead to destructive impacts. This is happening across the world. Unconsciousness works to hide the impacts. The intention to make money and secure the health and well-being for oneself and one's family, for example, can often come at the cost of the health and well-being for other families. It doesn't have to be this way. We can learn to minimize harm by becoming more conscious and making different choices.

Unfortunately, many choices made by our world's governments and institutions do not fully consider the complex ramifications of impact. Because of this, they trend toward perpetuating destructive fragmentation. Our governments operate according to the worldview that we must compete—with each other and with nature—in order to survive. They encourage existential competition rather than existential cooperation. We have been conditioned to assume this paradigm of existential competition is normal. It is woven into capitalism, for example. We have forgotten that we—all parts of the being called Gaia—all share and deserve the same basic needs: to be safe, comfortable, fed, and watered; to live a life with meaning and purpose; to feel aliveness; to love, and to be loved in return—in short, to live in homeostatic balance.

Environmental Fragmentation

The fact that human beings emerged from nature means that human beings *are* nature. Yet somehow, we've created a delusion that we are other than nature, better than nature, and above nature. Nothing could be further from the truth. Unfortunately, as long as we remain psychologically, physically, and spiritually split from our natural environment—as well as our human-made environment—we weave for ourselves a particularly grim fate, not just as individuals, but as a collective. We perpetuate fragmentation through the entirety of the web of life.

As human beings trying to make the most of our lives on Earth, we do ourselves a great disservice when we split nature and put ourselves above nature. We create manifold problems for ourselves and all beings. We invite pathological symptomology into every domain and welcome mind-body illness, relational illness, and spiritual illness. When we separate nature from nature, we separate ourselves from nature's life-giving and healing powers. We poison our food, water, and air, and thus, we poison ourselves. We stand in the way of our own health, well-being, and holistic healing. Psychologically, physically, and emotionally disconnected from nature, we enable the abuse and neglect of our environment, which is the same as unwittingly abusing and neglecting ourselves.

When I open my mind-heart and eyes to the symptoms of environmental fragmentation, I see Covid-19. I see masses of plastics the size of towns, cities, and states floating around the ocean. I see the deforestation of the Amazon rainforest and other forests of the world. I see overpopulation, violence, oppression, and disease. I see environmental protections and human rights laid by the wayside to make room for industrial, corporate, and economic development, growth, and profit. I see the climate crisis unfolding before my very eyes, increased drought and wildfires, increased flooding, and bigger and badder storms. I see the rising and desalinization of the oceans. I see governments waging war on other governments, leaving countless innocent people at risk. I see the widespread death of coral reefs and other sensitive and vital habitats and ecosystems. I see the oppression of native peoples and the stealing of native peoples' lands. I see more…

The fabric of the web of life seems to be coming apart at the seams more and more with every passing month. We have been destroying the diverse flora and fauna of our world's forests, oceans, rivers, and wetlands for too long. We have been poisoning our drinking water, our air, our soils, and each other—the very things we need to survive—for far too long as well. We have been fighting wars for thousands of years. We torture and kill each other. We threaten each other with total nuclear demise. Is it our wyrd to do all these things? Is it meant to happen this way? How much choice do we truly have? Are we meant to make the Earth inhospitable and uninhabitable for ourselves? Why would we do this to ourselves? Why in the wyrd would we self-destruct in this manner?

Spiritual Fragmentation

As we explore the symptoms of spiritual fragmentation, there are two things that must be named. One is that soul-spirit is transpersonal; it imbues and unites all domains—mind-body-relationship-environment—all the time. The other is that soul-spirit and awareness are correlated. In other words, the more awareness one has, the more aware of soul-spirit one will be. Likewise, the less awareness one has, the less aware of soul-spirit one will be.

Soul-spirit exists within every domain and connects every domain, but without awareness, this cannot be seen, experienced, and known. This ultimately makes fragmentation a spiritual illness, and one that results from a transgenerational, systemic crisis of consciousness and a lack of awareness. Not only does fragmentation separate mind from body from relationship from environment from soul from spirit, but fragmentation also separates awareness from the mind-body-relationship-environment-soul-spirit unity. This occludes and fragments the Web. Fragmentation is like a wedge that has been driven between awareness and the Web. A lack of awareness of mind-body will lead to a lack of awareness of soul-spirit within the domain of mind-body, which will lead to pathological symptomology and dis-ease. The same goes for every domain. A lack of awareness in the domain of relationship will lead to a lack of awareness of the spirituality inherent in relationship, which will lead to pathological symptomology and disease; a lack of awareness in the domain of environment will lead to a lack of awareness of the soul-spirit that imbues the environment, which, again, will lead to pathological symptomology, disease, and self-destruction.

Soul-spirit is like a web that connects us to each other; it connects psyche with world-psyche with cosmic-psyche and allows for the free flow of creative and healing life-energy between all. Spiritual fragmentation leads to an inability to experience and access this life-energy. This then leads to a progressive, deleterious deadening of both inner and outer landscapes—a.k.a. nihilism and anhedonia. To be cut off from the web that connects us is to be cut off from our purpose, from healing-transformation, and from deep and meaningful relationships with ourselves, each other, our systems, the world, and the divine.

Wyrding Ways
Symptom Inventory

This exercise will consist of making a symptom inventory of the domains in your life. The more you can bring awareness to the domains and the symptoms within the domains, the better ideas you will have that will lead to healing, and the more whole you will become. This exercise, though difficult, is an important one, as it greatly enhances your chances of bringing revelation and healing-transformation into your life, into your world, and into our collective process of becoming. As you do this exercise, remember to breathe.

You will need:

- Fifteen to thirty minutes or more of uninterrupted time-space
- A journal and a pen
- Your journal
- A meditation cushion or a comfortable place to sit

1. Lie down, stand, or sit in a meditative posture: alert and upright, ready yet relaxed. Take a few slow, deep belly-breaths in through your nose and out through your mouth. With each out-breath, relax your body just a little bit more, especially in your neck, chest, diaphragm, belly, gut, and sphincter. Breathe out and relax. Return to your natural breathing pattern.

2. Begin your symptom inventory of the domains of your life. Give yourself at least three to five minutes with each of these six questions. Be honest with yourself. This exercise is not easy. Be mindful and do your best to not judge or criticize yourself. Take your time; remember to breathe. Take care of yourself. Write your answers in your journal.

    - What are my mind-body symptoms?
    - What are my relational symptoms? (With my partner, friends, family, etc.)
    - What sort of environmental symptoms do I see in the world, near and far? How does my environment impact me?
    - How is my spiritual well-being?
    - What unhealthy behaviors and thought patterns do I engage in?
    - In what ways do I knowingly contribute to or enable fragmentation?

3. Take a few slow, deep belly-breaths in through your nose and out through your mouth. Remind yourself: "I am perfectly imperfect exactly the way I am. I am alive, breathing, and doing my best. As I reveal, heal, transform, and become, my love is growing stronger, deeper, and brighter."

4. Optional: Process what comes up with your therapist, trusted friend, family member, or guide.

Ragnarök: Re-Imagined

If the many symptoms of fragmentation continue to proliferate through all the domains unchecked, we will find ourselves at Ragnarök. Ragnarök—the prophetic *twilight of the gods*—is the Norse apocalypse as foretold by a powerful seeress in the poem known as the Völuspá. Let's take a quick look into how this myth of yore may be manifesting within our zeitgeist. We start with an abridged retelling of the myth:

The story begins with the god Odin journeying to the underworld to consult an unnamed seeress in order to learn about the beginning and end of the multiverse and the fate of his son, Baldr. During their interaction, the seeress tells of the past, present, and future. She speaks of the fate of Baldr and the fate of all the gods. She paints a picture of the beginning, middle, end, and beginning again. She tells of Baldr—god of light, love, and beauty—and his dreams of his death, which his mother, Frigg, also foresees. In an attempt to avert this terrifying fate, Frigg travels through the worlds and asks that each being make a pact not to hurt Baldr. All agree to this pact except for the mistletoe, which Frigg deems harmless. For a time, it seems that Frigg has succeeded, and the crisis has been averted. The gods celebrate in their triumph. It is only a matter of time, however, before Loki—angry at the gods for having imprisoned and excommunicated his children Hel, Fenrir, and Jormungandr—devises a plan for revenge. Loki finds the mistletoe, fashions it into a dart, and tricks Baldr's blind brother, Höd, into throwing the dart at Baldr during a hubristic game, thus killing him and setting Ragnarök in motion.

Three roosters call out—one in the realm of the gods, one in the realm of the giants, and another in the realm of Hel. A terrible three-year winter—called Fimbulwinter—begins, driving humanity headlong into depravity, violence, and chaos. Cosmic wolves devour the Sun and Moon. Hel's guardian wolf, Garm, and the god Tyr kill each other. The wolf Fenrir breaks his magical fetters, kills Odin, and is later killed by Odin's son. Jormungandr, the World-Serpent, breaks free from his ouroborian-knot around Midgard—causing the World-Tree to shudder—before being killed by, and killing, Thor. Loki, also freed from his bonds, leads the giants and inhabitants of Hel into the final battle, where he and the guardian Heimdallr end up killing each other. Many other notable things happen, but in the final act—just as the seeress has foretold—the giant Surtr arrives with his flaming sword, destroying Bifrost (the rainbow bridge that connects the worlds), killing the lord of nature, Freyr, and setting the multiverse aflame. In the end, Surtr's flames burn (almost) all living things until only ash remains. Some unknown amount of time later, a great flood comes and washes all away. Fragmentation has come to its natural end.

This is not the end, though. Just as the phoenix rises from its own ashes, the World-Tree sprouts anew from the great sea and the cycle begins again. Baldr and his brother return from their place in the underworld. The daughter of the Sun takes over her mother's station in the sky. The sons of Thor and Odin, as well as Hoenir and Njord and two humans, Lif and Lifthrasir ("life" and "life-breath"), emerge from their hiding places. And together, they start the whole cycle over again. The prophecy of the seeress ends with a vision of a great eagle swooping down from atop the renewed World-Tree to catch a fish from clean waters flowing through a new, wild, and bountiful world. What life remains continues onward, refreshed, renewed, reborn.

So how does this myth relate to our current day and age? Some people are of the mind that we are currently living through the early stages of Ragnarök, and that things are only going to get worse from here on out. Others say that Ragnarök is cyclical, that it has already happened—as evidenced by previous mass extinctions, world wars, the collapse of civilizations, climatic changes—and it will happen again. Ragnarök, Revelations, the Rapture, the Apocalypse, the End—whatever you call it, there are many who pray for its coming, for to them, it means the return of the Messiah or the dawn of the Golden Age. Some people see Ragnarök as the symptom of a deeper issue and a necessary part of our process of individual and collective awakening. Some see the whole thing as a natural process, a natural law, a great cycle of rebirth-life-death-rebirth, unfolding exactly how it is meant to. What do you think?

I wonder, if Ragnarök is cyclical, or spiral, maybe it need not play out in the same way every time. If we are witnessing the unfolding of Ragnarök yet again, maybe this time around we can do things differently? What if there is an alternative path, an option that the seeress, gods, and giants did not see the last time around? And what if each revolution of the wheel of fire brings with it a r(e)volution of consciousness? What if with each increase of awareness comes the realization of more choices, new options, healthier options? What if there is an unseen path, another way Ragnarök can play out? Maybe there are other ways to look at it. What if even now we have a choice? Let's consider this for a moment. And let's consider the choice to be a simple one: path A (the path of unconsciousness and delusion) or path B (the path of consciousness and revelation).

Path A is the path toward outer apocalypse. The outer apocalypse is the apocalypse that most people imagine when they think about the end of the world. It is the dystopian and violent vision of hell on Earth as depicted in most of our end-of-the-world theories, movies, and series, fully replete with brutality, chaos, starvation, disease, and the death of billions. Path A is the result of hubris unchecked, and of unconscious fragmentation. How many times have you imagined this scenario in your mind? And remember, everything is born and forged in the imagination first before it comes into the world.

Path B, on the other hand, plays out completely differently. Path B is the path toward inner apocalypse. This alternative apocalypse, rather than happening mostly out of our control in the world around us, occurs at a psychological and spiritual level, within us, mostly in our control. On path B, the dissolution and destruction of reality still happen as they do during Ragnarök; however, it begins and ends *within*. Path B is the path of conscious fragmentation.

On path B, the death of the old age and the rebirth of the new age as described in the myth of Ragnarök doesn't need to be a terrifying cataclysmic hell on Earth scenario. Ragnarök can occur as an intentional, conscious alchemical, psychological, and spiritual process. Wyrdcraft is just one of many integrative paths that can facilitate this process. We can choose to avert the unnecessary suffering that would come with the cataclysm of the world around us by consciously facilitating the cataclysm of the delusional worldviews within us, with guidance of course—from people, places, and things, from many sources.

With path B, we can choose to experience and witness the destruction of all that is destroying us—psychetherapeutically—before it actually physically destroys us. Instead of acquiescing to the age-old, unconscious, shadow-possessed, delusional self-destructive habits that will lead us to a living hell on Earth, we can consciously and intentionally process our shadow, destroy our habits and self-destructive patterns as well as our oppressive systems, greed, and fear-based reactivity. On path B, all structures based in delusion—internal and external—will need to be consciously dismantled, burned in the alchemical flame of Surtr's blade. Our self-destructive impulses, worldviews, and lifestyles can be reduced to ash and washed away and reborn within the cleansing waters of soul-awareness and wyrd consciousness. The *I-Me-My-Mine* egoic sense of self can be integrated within the larger *We-Us-Our-Ours* sense of Self.

As discussed in chapter 2, mythology is a mirror into the psyche. It unites the inner and outer landscape. It is prophetic, but it doesn't have to be considered as set in stone. It can be taken metaphorically, psychologically, and spiritually—as an educational soul-story meant to help us get back in homeostatic attunement with nature. The soul-story of Ragnarök can be seen as a warning, foretelling what will happen if we choose path A and play the old-hat game of unconscious existential competition. The soul-story of Ragnarök shows us what will happen if we choose to emulate the ways of the squabbling gods and giants. In the old stories, they, too, are operating from a fragmented worldview of the multiverse. They operate unconsciously; they fight each other, steal from each other, rape, kill, lie, and cheat each other just like humanity. This unconsciousness keeps them stuck in the pattern of existential competition. Our unconsciousness is doing the same. We are living reflections of each other, humans, gods, goddesses, giants, nature.

Imagine if the gods, giants, dwarves, elves, and humans alike awakened to the truth that they were both different and One, all interconnected, all interdependent, all interrelated. Imagine we are all of one mind to consciously and intentionally settle disputes, clarify miscommunication, and heal traumas in healthier ways. Imagine if the gods and giants had access to different options, different paths. What if Odin, Thor, Loki, Tyr, Surtr, and the giants had good therapists, conflict mediators, wise elders, and psychedelic medicines. Imagine each was able to address and heal their inner child, their traumas, and their transgenerational traumas. Imagine if they knew they could avert the bloody and violent apocalypse by doing their own shadow work and integration. Imagine if they could work together to address larger systemic inequities and failures and make sure that everyone's most basic needs were met, and vitriolic annihilation was not necessary. Imagine if they make different choices. Imagine if we do.

When each of us wakes in the morning, we find ourselves at a similar crossroads with a similar choice: Path A or B? Unconsciousness or consciousness? Unintentionality or intentionality? Which path do I want to walk down today? Which path do I want to walk down in this moment? Path A, the path of fear and existential competition, leads to a fragmented soul-mind and the external apocalypse. Path B, the path of love and existential cooperation, leads to one soul-mind, the internal apocalypse, and the rebirth of the golden age within and without.

Path B asks us to re-imagine the apocalypse as an internal process that isn't completely out of our hands. It asks that we consciously and intentionally take responsibility for the impacts of our thoughts, words, and actions; that we make different choices that lead to us becoming more loving of our One Mind and Soul. Path B leads one back to empathy—into body, emotion, and relationship where necessary inner alchemy and integration can and need to occur—to an awakening of Web consciousness. Imagine you and I might turn toward each other, work through our issues, lay down our weapons, reign in and refocus our technologies, and help each other heal and transform both inner and outer worlds in alignment with love and the natural laws of unity, interdependence, interconnectivity, and reciprocity. Imagine the revelation, healing-transformation, and becoming that might be possible. Imagine we might eventually be able to face each other fully, *hug it out*, and heal heart-to-heart, hand-in-hand, side-by-side. Who is to say that this has not been Fate's plan all along?

Fragmentation in Summary

The human mind has taken the whole, separated it into a myriad of parts, and laid each part out on the table to create mind-blowing diagrams and descriptions of what the parts are and how they relate to each other. We have created advanced technologies that have made life easier for countless people and saved the lives of countless more. The subtleties of the Web have come alive. We have learned to procure and create pretty much anything we desire—but at what cost? We have surgically removed and separated all the pieces from the whole to understand how each thing works, yet tragically, we have forgotten how all the pieces fit back together, and remain largely unconscious of the dire necessity to do so. We have separated ourselves from nature, nature from the divine, the divine from us, and ourselves from each other. We have separated mind from body from relationship from environment from soul from spirit. In the process, we have inadvertently and unconsciously lost our center and ground; we have lost awareness of the web and soul. As such, we have diluted, diverted, and dispersed the life-force of the whole.

Our transgenerationally inherited, progress-oriented worldviews and lifestyles have a tendency to perpetuate existential competition, thus giving rise to the proliferation of symptoms throughout the domains. As all is interconnected within the Web, what happens in one domain will eventually impact all domains. This means that symptoms from one domain will affect all domains. The impact of all this fragmentative symptomology has led to a massive eco-spiritual-systemic imbalance that very well might be leading us toward Ragnarök—yet again.

Despite all this, there is still hope. Every day is a new day to remember the Web, remember soul, and realign and rebalance the system as a whole. With every thought, word, and action, we can do our best to return homeostatic balance to all domains—as one. The human species can reintegrate with the soul of the Earth and invite natural healing-energy to return to its natural organismic flow. Human beings are incredibly smart, resilient, and adaptable. We can change internally and externally; we can change ourselves, our ways of relating, and our systems; we can awaken and evolve. Rather than separating ourselves from each other, from nature, and from the divine, we can reintegrate—psychologically, spiritually, and physically.

We can use the natural phenomenon of fragmentation to our collective benefit. We can consciously, intentionally, and therapeutically fragment, dissolve, and transmute all that which does not serve our fullest blossoming and greatest good—internally and externally. We can dismantle our self-destructive economic, social, and governmental systems and rebuild healthier ones in sane ways—in alignment with the natural laws of the Web. We can dismantle our self-destructive psychologies, ideologies, worldviews, and lifestyles and rebuild healthier ones—also in alignment with the wisdom of the Web. We can learn the teachings that fragmentation is offering us. For the more we understand fragmentation, the more we will understand integration.

As we remember soul, we will see through the eyes of soul, feel through the body of soul, and act through the will of soul. This is inherently healing.

As we remember healing, we will see through the eyes of healing, feel through the body of healing, and act through the will of healing. This is inherently transformational. We can reorient toward each other, not as separate entities in eternal competition, but as unique parts of greater complexity, a natural gestalt in eternal collaboration and evolution, with a shared interest in living long, healthy, and meaningful lives. Is the hellish cataclysmic end of the world our only option? Perhaps if we acknowledge that we do have some degree of awareness, agency, and choice, then we can avert the worst of our nightmares we have imagined will come. Perhaps we can avert the self-destructive end of the world by inviting the end of the self-destructive worldview. Perhaps we can craft our wyrd toward healthier, more joyous outcomes. We shall see.

The idea that fragmentation is a natural law, and that we may even need suffering in order to awaken, is a compelling one. Wasn't it through conscious suffering that Christ gave some of his most valuable teachings? Wasn't it living and learning through suffering that led to Buddha's enlightenment? And wasn't it through Odin's conscious self-sacrifices that the mysteries were unveiled? Perhaps we need fragmentation to bring us to rock bottom, to the fertile void, to the place where we are given *the* final choice—path A or path B. Perhaps we need suffering to make us conscious. Or perhaps we can avoid rock bottom by consciously, intentionally, and therapeutically fragmenting, dissolving, and transmuting all that no longer serves our collective health and well-being. Perhaps we can take a proactive, preventative medicine approach.

Do we have any choice as to *how* Ragnarök might unfold? If so, I ask you reader, what is your wyrd in this cosmic drama? What are you meant to do in the face of this ending-beginning? What choices do you have? How can you bring your consciousness and therapeutic intentionality to the situation at hand? How can we limit unnecessary suffering? What other paths might we walk together—heart-to-heart, hand-in-hand, side-by-side? How might we all heal together and come together—humanity, nature, and divinity—as one?

PART III
Wyrdcraft

Chapter 8
Integration and Wyrdcraft

If fragmentation is the separation of the web into a myriad of parts, then integration is the reunification of those parts into a cohesive whole, and if unconscious fragmentation leads to pathological symptomology within every domain, then conscious integration leads to the healing of pathological symptomology within every domain. Integration is a nondual venture; as such, it is not the opposite of fragmentation. In fact, conscious fragmentation *is* integration. Fragmentation is a natural and necessary part of the whole process of becoming. Some things need to go through a natural dissolution—the delusional ego-self, our oppressive systems, for example—so that they may be re-integrated. Integration is a process of revelation, healing-transformation, and becoming that leads to the reunification of both parts and whole, of re-membering mind-body-relationship-environment-soul-spirit into its natural wholeness and unity, and thus, into optimal homeostatic health and well-being. There are many ways to practice integration. Wyrdcraft is just one of them.

Wyrdcraft

What exactly is wyrdcraft? Let's first look at the word itself. The former half of the word, *wyrd*, as you already know, refers to the interweaving of fate, destiny, nature, magic, soul, and becoming. The latter half, *craft*, refers to the skilled, artistic, and manual process of creating or maintaining a good for a specific use. To craft is to intentionally transform resources from one form into another so that the new form may be utilized for a particular purpose. Metalworking, glass blowing, pottery, and woodworking are just a handful of the many different crafts.

Wyrdcraft, then, is the intentional crafting of fate, destiny, nature, magic, soul, and becoming. This crafting takes place in different phases, so to speak:

1. By learning about the concept of wyrd—its etymology, history, mythology, science, and phenomenology. (Covered in chapters 1 through 3.)
2. By exploring and attuning to the phenomenology of wyrd as it manifests within each domain of your life: mind-body-relationship-environment-soul-spirit. (Covered in chapters 4 through 6.)
3. By learning about the concept of fragmentation and exploring and attuning to how fragmentation manifests within the domains of your life. (Covered in chapter 7.)
4. By learning about the concept of integration and intentionally engaging in integrative practices such as psychetherapy, ecotherapy, and magic. (Covered in chapters 8 through 12.)
5. By deepening and expanding consciousness of wyrd through ongoing integration, exploration, and attunement to the ever-flowing, ever-deepening, and ever-expanding mysteries of wyrd.

Wyrdcraft is not a linear process. These phases can happen in any order at any time, as wyrd is *happening* everywhere all the time. What one moment calls for may be different than the moment that came just before. The great ritual dance of existence twists and turns, flows and waves, spirals and shape-shifts. Wyrd wiggles. Wyrdcraft will help you attune to these wiggles.

Wyrdcraft is a process of attuning to wyrd, the ways of wyrd, and wyrd consciousness. Wyrd consciousness—which could also be called ecological consciousness, magical consciousness, spiritual consciousness, or Web consciousness—is the consciousness of Nature, which is one in the same as the consciousness of the Fates. Attuning to and communing with wyrd, therefore, the crafter of wyrd attunes to and communes with the Fates, with Nature. This mystical *attunion* leads to the opening of doors that open to the paths that lead to the mysteries of being, consciousness, existence, and soul.

Though wyrd is an ancient Northern European concept, wyrdcraft is not a historical or ancestral practice. Wyrdcraft is not meant to be a return to some nonexistent idyllic utopian past. Rather, wyrdcraft is meant to be a return to Nature—to that mystical synthesis in which past, present, future, being, consciousness, existence, and soul meld into one in the here-and-now. There is a lot to explore here, and a lot to re-member.

Wyrdcraft is not reserved for those with Northern European ancestry. It is for anyone who feels called to it—anyone. Wyrdcraft is not a religion; it is a way of being and relating. Wyrdcraft is a mystical path and a pathless pass. No matter how young or old your soul might be, no matter what your racial, ethnic, or political background is or what traditions you practice, you are in a process of revelation, healing-transformation, and becoming. Wyrdcraft celebrates this and facilitates this.

You may be wondering what wyrdcraft will look like for you. I wonder, too. I wonder which direction your attuning and communing will take you. You will see as you do it. You will see as the pattern of wyrd emerges around you and within you. Each one of us has our own wyrd; therefore, each one of us will experience wyrd and practice wyrdcraft in our own ways. Your wyrd will determine what your wyrdcraft looks like. The more you come to know how wyrd manifests in the domains of your life, the more your practice will take form.

Your wyrd and your wyrd consciousness will show you where you need to offer your attention. Perhaps relationship challenges will surface—a fallout with an old friend, a fight with a family member, an intense manic elation over a new crush, a breakup. Maybe environmental concerns will arise—the need to relocate, neighborhood crime, pollution, and so on. Perhaps a mind-body concern will pop up—old aches, new pains, or other health challenges. Life has a way of presenting us with challenges, often in a spiral-like and wavelike fashion. Our problems will return again and again until we work through them sufficiently enough to transmute them into health, gnosis, and magic. New and old anxieties, traumas, major life-transitions, and other disturbances of psyche will ask us to dance, sometimes much to our surprise, sometimes much to our chagrin. Shadow-possessed thoughts, words, and actions will spill out, directing us inward to learn of their origin. Spiritual and existential concerns, experiences and yearnings will pull us here and there, awakening us from our sleepwalk, calling us toward ritual, community, truth, devotion, union.

Because wyrdcraft explores the physical, psychological, relational, eco-logical, systemic, spiritual, and magical—the entirety of the Web—it has the potential to be radically transformative and deeply healing in all of life's domains, for all beings, through all time-space-awareness. That's quite a claim, isn't it? Well, I stand by it. If you engage with wyrdcraft wholeheart-edly, if you attune and commune with Nature wholeheartedly, it will without a doubt change you and your world in healing, magical ways.

We have a lot more power to influence our fate and destiny than many of us like to admit. Sure, there are some boundaries that can't be crossed, and for good reason. Some boundaries are necessary, helpful, and healthy. They keep us sane, safe, humble, and humane. There are also many artificial or tempo-rary boundaries that not only can be crossed but also wait for us to do just that. As you come to know your boundaries and limitations on your growing-edge of being and becoming, you can take an honest look at them, feel into them, process them, dance with them for a while, learn their dance, and then decide for yourself how you want to proceed. You can craft your own wyrd; you can affect change to your fate, destiny, nature, soul, and becoming. We can all do this as individuals and as a collective. We can craft our wyrd, and as we do, we can invite balance, harmony, and healing-magic back into every domain—we can invite mystery. This may sound like a tall order, and it may be hard to imagine where to begin, but rest your head and calm thy heart, for the key to beginning is quite simple. All you need to do is be aware.

The Alchemy of Awareness: Turning Toward Wholeness

Wyrdcraft starts and ends with awareness. Awareness is the foundation of attunement, communion, conscious fragmentation, and integration. Aware-ness itself *is* wyrd, in the sense that it is meaningful and purposeful. Awareness is revelatory, healing, and transformative; it will reveal to you all you need to know. It will reveal why and how you, and we, suffer. It will also reveal why and how you and we can be relieved of suffering. Awareness is your link to fate, destiny, nature, magic, soul, becoming, and the Web. Not only is it inter-ested in your survival, but it is also interested in your thriving and becoming. There is an underlying, weird intelligence and purpose to awareness.

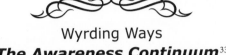

Wyrding Ways
The Awareness Continuum[33]

Let us take a moment to explore the nature of awareness before we continue. This is an experiment I learned and practiced often while at Church Street Counseling Center, the gestalt training center I mentioned earlier. To do this experiment, all you need to do is open your awareness—in other words, pay attention.

According to gestalt therapy, there are three zones of awareness: outer, inner, and middle. The outer zone is everything that is happening around you. The inner zone is everything that is happening internally, somatically—such as sensations, aches, pain, pleasure, emotions, and so on. The middle zone is the zone of the mind, in which fantasies, thought processes, judgments, ruminations, curiosities, and so on occur.

You will need:

- Fifteen to thirty minutes of uninterrupted time-space
- A meditation cushion or chair
- Your journal

1. Take a seat in a meditative posture: spine upright and alert, ready yet relaxed. Close your eyes; take three slow, deep belly-breaths in through your nose and out through your mouth. With each out-breath, relax just a little bit more. Return to your natural breathing.

2. I invite you to bring your awareness to each of the zones. Set a timer and take three to five minutes to devote your awareness to each zone. As you become aware of what is happening in the here-and-now, say to yourself (silently or out loud), "I am aware of _____." You will repeat this phrase many times over the course of this exercise. For example, "I am aware of the sound of cars driving by," (outer zone), "I am aware of a tightness in my chest," (inner zone), "I am aware of curiosity," (middle zone). If you become aware of a fantasy or thought, you don't need to describe the exact fantasy or thought; just say, "I am aware of

---

33. Perls, *The Gestalt Approach & Eyewitness to Therapy*, 64–65.

a fantasy," or, "I am aware of a thought." After each awareness statement, open your awareness again.

3. After you spend two minutes with each zone, open your awareness to all the zones simultaneously. Spend five minutes being aware in this open manner. Attune to being in the moment. Continue to say, aloud or internally, "I am aware of _____." After the minutes are up, take a few more minutes to contemplate the experience. Did anything interesting happen? What was it like for you? Did you favor one zone more than the others?

4. Record your experiences in your journal.

Optional:
- Process with your therapist. This is a great exercise to do with your therapist.
- Practice with a friend. You can either take a few minutes each and then switch, or trade awareness statements back and forth. After you are done, discuss the experience together. What was that like for each of you?
- Take this experiment on the road and into the world. At various points throughout your day, practice the awareness continuum. Try it in as many different places as you can—on the bus, at work, eating lunch, at the bar, and so on.

The Alchemy of Attunement: Becoming Whole

As you open your awareness to your experience of living and being in the moment—as you attune and commune with Nature—you will experience innumerable good, bad, and neutral feeling threads—all vibrating at different frequencies. Some of these threads will vibrate comfortably; others, rather uncomfortably. Maybe you will notice you have a habit of avoiding or grasping the uncomfortable or unpleasant vibrations and threads. Maybe you will notice that sometimes you tend to avoid or grasp the pleasant ones. No matter whether it is the good or the bad that you are avoiding or grasping onto, the goal is to bring awareness to what is happening and what you are feeling in the moment—and to keep your awareness and feeling capacities open when the impulse is to shut both down.

Dealing with change can be hard. I don't need to say it because everyone knows it. Even positive changes can be difficult and uncomfortable. To be successful at wyrdcraft—to re-member more of your wholeness—it will be important to learn how to tolerate discomfort. You need to develop what psychotherapists call *affect tolerance*. Affect tolerance is the ability to handle uncomfortable sensations, memories, emotions, and changes without shutting down or running away. This skill is important when it comes to the processing of life's changes and the healing of psychological wounds. This is what initiatory processes teach the initiate. The growing-edge of being and becoming can be quite uncomfortable at times, to say the least. Do your best to try to see this discomfort as an integral part of your wyrd process of becoming. See discomfort as an invitation or a gift, rather than as something to avoid, or a curse. As you sit with the discomfort of becoming more whole, try to see it as a sacrifice or an offering—a gift for a gift. Do your best to be with your discomfort with a nonjudgmental curiosity and imagine it as an alchemical process. It will not last forever, and it will tell you a lot about your wyrd.

And yes, boundaries are important. A good *no* when a *no* is needed is divine. Saying *no* and walking away from abusive relationships, painful experiences, and (self-)destructive suffering may be the most appropriate, healing, and magically empowering thing to do given the situation at hand. Exploring and expressing your wants, needs, don't wants, and don't needs is an integral part of processing your boundaries at your growing-edge. Boundary is a mystery in and of itself. Important facets of your wyrd become clear as your boundaries become clear. Come to know them. See if you can feel where yes turns into no and no turns into yes, and where ambivalence hangs out in wait.

More often than not, you can look at something while holding it at a distance at first. Attuning can happen slowly. As you become aware of uncomfortable threads and vibrations, know that you just may be able to acclimate yourself and learn to tolerate discomfort and struggle in safe-enough ways. You may find wellsprings of soul, healing, and magic hidden within. Go slowly. As it is said in somatic trauma therapy circles, slower is faster. You can learn to tolerate fear, pain, love, ecstasy, and joy in safe-enough ways. You need not jump heedlessly into the fray at your own detriment. Attune at your own speed. All you need to do is *be*. Mindfully *being* is attuning. Keep this in mind as you heal, transform, and become whole. Be gentle, present, courageous, and mindful. Live life fully; live life soulfully.

Wyrdcraft is a celebration of wholeness. Appreciate the positives and recognize the beauty, joy, love, and light in the world, and remember not to neglect the negatives, the pain, the suffering. They are just as important to open to right now; they are all soul; they are part of your wholeness; they are part of living life purposefully and meaningfully. We must see and feel the wounds if we wish to heal the wounds. Whether you are engaging in psychetherapy, ecotherapy, or magic, remember to do your best to be realistic and look at things *as is*, not as you wish they were or assume them to be. Things are not always as they seem.

Celebrate your successes as well as others'. Do your best to acknowledge the positives, the strengths, the health, and well-being that arise as you craft. Spread good news. Have fun, relax, play. Give and receive good, pleasant, and pleasurable vibrations. This will encourage everyone's crafting. Remember your best methods of self-care, learn new methods, practice them often, practice them more and more, share them with others. One can all too easily get overwhelmed by the plethora of negative vibrations. It is important to balance out the negative and remain realistic—there is also a lot of positive. Don't be an optimist or a pessimist—be a realist … be open to what *is. What is*—as hard as it may be to acknowledge sometimes—will reveal what needs to be done.

You will find, much to your delight, that with awareness and through deep attunement and communion with Nature (the Fates), you have more options and choices than you previously thought. You will be able to make healthier choices, healing choices, and transformative choices. New pathways will reveal themselves. As you do this, you will be practicing magic and welcoming miracles into the world.

The Importance of Self-Care

Self-care is a vital part of wyrdcraft. Here is a list of some different methods of self-care. How many of them have helped you when you have felt stuck, overwhelmed, anxious, or depressed throughout your life? Which ones are your go-to methods? Which methods are new ones you would like to try?

- Exercise (running, swimming, walking, hiking, etc.)
- Playing music, listening to music
- Making art (painting, drawing, sculpting, etc.)
- Crafting

- Eating healthy foods, drinking water, cooking healthy meals
- Meditating
- Yoga, tai chi, qigong
- Dancing
- Sleep, rest, taking naps
- Gardening
- Watching movies
- Spending time with friends, family, pets, and community
- Saying YES and saying NO
- Others? _____

Awareness itself is self-care. Awareness is like a muscle. The more you remember to use it, exercise it, and stretch it, the stronger, more flexible, and more dexterous it becomes. As such, the more awareness you can bring to your present experience of wyrd, the sooner you can recognize if you are straying from balance and some self-care is needed. Perhaps you may even notice that you are overindulging in a specific type of self-care, which can also lead to imbalance. Self-care should theoretically be some combination of enlivening, nourishing, healing, inspiring, and replenishing. In the end, self-care should help you return to the flow and be in the flow. Your self-care practices will help you as you explore wyrd. They will help keep you centered and attuned to the ever-changing fluctuations of homeostatic balance as everything changes within and around you.

Wyrding Ways
Self-Massage as Self-Care

A lot will come up as you craft your wyrd—including potentially overwhelming somatic experiences. This exercise can help you contain and channel the energies flowing through your body-mind-relationship-environment-soul-spirit. It can help you process the revelations of Nature and not be overwhelmed by them. This wyrding way consists of doing a self-massage. This is just one example of self-care you can practice if you are experiencing emotional, psychological, or energetic overload and symptoms of anxiety, insomnia, PTSD, chronic pain, and so on.

You will need:

- Twenty to sixty minutes of uninterrupted time-space
- A comfortable place to stand, sit, and lie down
- Loose-fitting comfortable clothing (you may also choose to do this naked)
- Your journal
- Optional: Body oil for massage

1. Take a seat in a meditative posture: spine upright and alert, ready yet relaxed. Close your eyes, take three slow, deep belly-breaths in through your nose and out through your mouth. With each out-breath, relax just a little bit more. Return to your natural breathing.

2. Before you begin your massage, do a quick body scan and see if you notice any spots that are tense, aching, or wounded. See if you can relax these places. Breathe into them. Do this for a few minutes. Take a mental note; you can give these areas a little more attention during your massage.

3. Begin your massage. Feel free to move around, sit, or lie down as you see fit. Give yourself a lot of room. If you can't give your-self a massage due to an injury or mobility issues, use your awareness to do a self-guided body scan. To do this, imagine a small golden orb filled with the stuff of awareness moving through your body. Start at your toes and very slowly work your way up to your crown and down your arms to your hands. Spend extra time in wounded or aching areas.

4. Whether you do a massage or a scan, go slowly, mindfully, and feel into your process. You are learning how to *feel* and *listen* to your body. Live your education. Spend a little extra time with tight and injured places. Go slow, go deep, and go with care. See if you can find the center of the injury, so to speak—the tight, tender wound. Touch it softly, lovingly; increase pressure if it feels right. Imagine golden, healing energy flowing where it is needed most. Thank your body parts as you go. For example, as you massage your feet, say something like, "Thank you for helping me stand, walk, run, jump, and dance. Without you, I couldn't get here and there." "Thank you, ribs, for protecting my organs." "Thank you, ears, for helping me hear." Go slow. Feel into your gratitude, too.

5. Before you finish, spend some moments sending love to the gestalt of your whole body. Thank your body for all the experiences it brings into your life. For better or for worse, these experiences are the wyrd experiences of your soul—becoming whole, remembering, returning.

6. Drink a big glass of water and some herbal tea. Write about your experience in your journal.

Sacred Reciprocity, the Gift-Cycle, and Frith

In addition to cultivating awareness, attunement, and self-care, another foundational component of wyrdcraft is the ongoing practice of sacred reciprocity. An ancient concept that comes from indigenous, pagan, and heathen worldviews past and present, sacred reciprocity offers guidance on how to maintain healthy, balanced relationships with others, with nature, and with divinity in ways that ensure the health of the Web. In this way, sacred reciprocity is the ultimate form of self-care.

According to the natural law of the Web, everything lives within a dynamic, reciprocal relationship with everything else. This dynamic reciprocity must be mindfully and continually maintained to ensure balance within and between both parts and whole. Every part within the system is engaged in an intimate relationship with every other part—near and far. These parts are constantly giving, taking, receiving, and offering in an ever-fluctuating balancing act of homeostasis. Give and take in balance, and homeostasis will be maintained. Take too much or too little, and you will threaten the balance. If the system becomes too imbalanced, it will collapse.

The healthiest, most balanced relationships are the ones that benefit all parties involved—they are win-win-win scenarios. These relationships have found and learned to maintain the balance between give and take, offering and receiving, sacrifice and boon—not an easy thing to do. The act of giving and the act of receiving are interwoven. Generally speaking, if you wish to receive, then you must give, and if you give, then you will receive. And in a strange paradox, sacred reciprocity affirms that the act of giving *is* receiving, and the act of receiving *is* giving; they are one and the same. As all parts are one within the greater whole, this makes sense.

Sacred reciprocity is referred to as gift-giving or the gift-cycle within heathen culture. The gift-cycle was, and still is, the relational guide and glue that hold social-spiritual life together. The ecospiritual concept of the gift-cycle is different from our concept of gift-giving in the so-called modernized Western world today. Because the truth of interconnection, interdependence, and interrelationship has been largely forgotten, gift-giving usually occurs without the greater social fabric, and the wider ecological web, in mind. Sacred reciprocity and the gift-cycle, on the other hand, acknowledge that we are all connected within the larger Web, and each exchange is an opportunity to strengthen and benefit the Web as a whole.

For the heathen, the gift-cycle was woven into the smallest and largest of exchanges. Humans learned the gift-cycle by observing and living in attunement with nature. They saw that the gift-cycle was a functional way to maintain homeostasis within systems. Upholding sacred giving and sacred receiving benefited everybody and everything. The gift-cycle was applied to the exchange of gifts, goods, services, time, energy, labor, attention, and more. Gift-giving cultivated trust; helped members forge and maintain friendships, alliances, and partnerships; and ensured long-term peace and safety. The gift-cycle was collective agreement woven into the social fabric that kept the community healthy and balanced on a day-to-day basis. Everyone was part of it. If the reciprocity of the gift-cycle was not upheld, not only would the relationship suffer, but the community would also suffer. Gift-giving strengthens the strands that weave everyone and everything together. As such, shame, dishonor, distrust, and ill-ease were placed upon those who neglected to uphold their part of this social-spiritual covenant.

So long as the practice of gift-giving was mutually upheld, it was mutually beneficial and generated what heathens call *frith*. *Frith* is an Old English, Anglo-Saxon term that translates to something like "peace, goodwill, health, or well-being." Frith is a feeling-state of deep spiritual gratitude and eudaimonic contentment. It is the result of living in right relationship within the web and honoring the covenant of sacred reciprocity.

Frith was also cultivated through *grith*. *Grith*, another Old English Anglo-Saxon term, was a temporary period of imposed peace and sanctuary. Periods of grith were instated during special gatherings, known as *Things*. The Thing was a semiregularly occurring community assembly that provided an intentional time and space of truce—in which grith was strictly enforced—to socialize, resolve disputes, hold ceremony, forge alliances, make plans, facilitate trading, and so forth. Nonviolence was strictly enforced at the Thing. Order was kept, and proceedings were overseen by the chieftain and the law-speaker—the one who memorized and recited the laws to the people. The Thing provided an opportunity for a temporary period of grith, in which longer-lasting frith could be cultivated within the greater community.

Maintaining frith and sacred reciprocity is an ongoing process that requires a high degree of awareness, sensitivity, and response-ability, as relationship is constantly in flux. A one-time offense is likely not going to be much of an issue; however, if that offense occurs again and again, what started out as a minute imbalance in a relationship that could have been easily corrected will become larger and impact more relationships. If unchecked for too long, this imbalance will eventually lead to a drastic imbalance and wobble in the system that could lead to collapse.

This is happening as we speak. The gift-cycles that exist between humans, the natural world, the spirits, and the gods have not been upheld. Some parties have taken too much, while other parties have received too little. Sacred reciprocity has been disregarded and forgotten, resulting in an ever-increasing imbalance. The symptoms of this imbalance are manifold. The climate crisis, Covid-19, economic inequality, and systemic oppression are just a few examples.

Human beings have taken too much from each other and from the natural world without giving in return. We have not upheld the sacred covenant that applies to all living beings and systems. We have forgotten the necessity of maintaining the gift-cycle. We have forgotten that self-care is not just about the self. Because we are all connected, true self-care is collective Self-care. Thankfully, the gift-cycle and sacred reciprocity have not been completely lost and left in the past. They are being remembered. Part of the reason for this resurgence is due to the paradigm shift that is accompanying the revival and proliferation of soul—of indigenous wisdom teachings, pagan spirituality and lifeways, psychedelic medicines, and other holistic healing approaches. The old ways are being remembered. Wyrdcraft facilitates this remembering.

Wyrding Ways
Daily Gratitude Practice

The best way to practice sacred reciprocity is to give thanks. This exercise will walk you through a simple gratitude practice that you can do every morning when you awake and every evening before bed. If you can do this outside, great; if not, indoors will be just fine.

You will need:
- Five to ten minutes of undisturbed time-space
- A special incense to burn
- A candle

1. Face the Sun. While standing or sitting in a meditative posture, close your eyes; take a few slow, deep belly-breaths in through your nose and out through your mouth. Take a couple of minutes to breathe, feel into your body, and relax. Light your incense. Slowly and mindfully bow with your hands in prayer mudra at your heart and say, "Greetings Sun! It's so nice to see you again! Thank you for rising today. Thank you for bringing your life, light, warmth, energy, and love into this world. Thank you for reminding me of my own life, light, warmth, energy, and love. Thank you for being a shining example of how to show up—how to be myself. May I carry your sweet medicine into the world with me today and every day, and may I remember to see the light in others. Thank you for your life and thank you for my life! Blessed be!"

2. Bring your awareness to the Earth around and under you and say, "Thank you, Earth. Thank you for your life—for the food I eat, the water I drink, the air I breathe, and the shelter you provide. Thank you for your ever-giving, ever-holding, wise love. Without you, I wouldn't be here—we are interwoven, you and I. Thank you for this body-mind, which is one with you. Thank you for my life; may I remember our oneness as I live it! And may I bring your sweet medicine into the world with me today and every day."

3. Bring your awareness to the Moon. Face it if you can see it. Feel the coming and going of each wave as the moon circles you. Say, "Thank you, Moon, for your life. And thank you *for* life. Without

you, there would be no life on Earth. Thank you for your many teachings of emotionality, change, fluidity, awareness, beauty, and magic. May your soft, moonlight consciousness illuminate the dark places within psyche. May I carry your sweet medicine into the world with me today and every day."

4. Take a few slow, deep breaths and mindfully and deeply bow with your hands together at your heart. Feel into your gratitude for the moment.

5. At the end of your day, before you go to bed, light a candle on your altar, slowly bow, and while standing or sitting down in front of it in a meditative posture, close your eyes; take a few slow, deep belly-breaths in through your nose and out through your mouth. Take a couple of minutes to breathe, feel into your body, and relax. Light your incense and say, "Thank you for this day! Thanks to all the people I've interacted with and all the experiences I've had (give thanks to specific experiences and interactions). Thank you, Sun, Earth, and Moon, for all these opportunities to live my truth, to learn, and to love. May any positive energy that I have accumulated from these interactions and experiences be shared with all beings. May all beings be filled with the light, love, and awareness of self, soul, and wyrd. Thank you for my life. Blessed be!" Slowly, mindfully, and deeply bow with hands together at your heart.

The simple act of centering yourself and bowing is a great way to offer gratitude to any experience or interaction. A slow bow in the spirit of gratitude is a great way to attune and commune, as well as a great way to uphold sacred reciprocity. It can be especially powerful during moments of inspiration or awe, such as witnessing a beautiful sunset or an inspiring tree, a mountain, or a landscape, after a serendipitous experience, and so on. It is easy to honor a sacred moment with a slow, devotional bow—though some may think you are weird to do so. I know you don't need me to tell you, but it's okay to be weird. Try not to let others' judgments of your "weirdness" get in the way of your expression of devotion.

Practical Methods of Integration

Before we delve deeper into the wyrdcraftian-triad of psychetherapy, ecotherapy, and magic, I would like to offer some practical suggestions for how wyrdcraft might be practiced in your everyday life within each of the domains. Keep in mind, the goal of wyrdcraft is not perfection, but wholeness. Wholeness is not just all that is considered beautiful, healthy, and happy, it also includes one's flaws, illnesses, shortcomings, failures, challenges, ugliness, pain, and so on. We are all perfectly imperfect. We are all weird in our own ways. Your wholeness will likely look weird to those who are afraid to be whole. Wholeness is a process. Wholeness is found during and within the process, not just at the supposed end of the process. In fact, you might as well assume there is no end to the process. There is only the ever-flowing and ever-changing here-and-now— the process of awakening to wholeness, of becoming whole.

Your wholeness cannot be blocked by your limitations; on the contrary, they can only add to it. Find your limitations; find those places where your awareness, will, and energy are blocked, stagnant, or in need of attention. Do your best to be with these blocks and wounds mindfully, breathe slowly and deeply, and, if you can, process them with a therapist, guide, or elder. Engage yourself in the alchemical transmutation of lead into gold. See if you can channel that blocked up energy in new, creative, whole-affirming ways. Let the bright solar, soft lunar, and guiding stellar light of your consciousness illuminate each thread and guide you. You may even find that some of your limitations are not true limitations at all, but rather doorways that open to your limitlessness.

As you read through these integrative possibilities, know that they are not conclusive. These options set a high bar and are not easy things to do, so do your best; do what you can, and remember, this life is for learning.

Mind-Body Integration

As you consider these options, see which ones might be doable for you. Which ones will be difficult, or maybe even impossible? Transformation at the growing-edge of being and becoming is not easy, but it is well worth the continual effort.

- *Diet:* Eat whole, healthy, mindfully sourced and prepared foods. Stay away from processed foods and refined sugars as much as possible. Maintain a balanced diet. Bring awareness to how you may use food to soothe anxiety, depression, and so on. Good food is the best medicine you can use for yourself. Supplement your diet and support your health with mindfully sourced medicinal herbs and mushrooms. Drink plenty of water.

- *Exercise:* Develop a diverse, holistic approach to exercise, one that focuses on whole-body health and includes a variety of methods, such as walking, hiking, weight training, running, swimming, climbing, martial arts, and other sports. Always stretch before and after you exercise and be mindful of your body and breath while you exercise. Find your growing-edge. Again, drink plenty of water.

- *Rest and recuperation:* Though sleep needs vary from person to person, try to get anywhere from seven to nine hours of sleep per night. Keep your journal by your bed to record any dreams you may have. Also, remember to rest when you are feeling run-down. Rest is very important. Give yourself some downtime from time to time. The body needs to heal and rejuvenate. Get massages and acupuncture if you can. There are low-fee acupuncture and massage clinics in many cities.

- *Conscious movement:* Holistic mind-body health and wellness can be greatly facilitated by practicing yoga, tai chi, qigong, or any other forms of movement meditation or martial art. Find a class, a teacher, and or videos online. Dance! Take a class, go to the club, find a drum circle, find an ecstatic dance event, or contact an improv event near you; dance as much as you can whenever possible—alone, with friends, in community.

- *Meditation:* There are many meditation exercises mentioned within this book, and many more mentioned in other books, videos, and documentaries. Search out a local Buddhist, Hindu, or nondenominational temple or meditation group and learn from experienced teachers. Practice daily.

- *Breaking addictions:* There are many potential addictions with which we contend as modern, nature- and soul-disconnected peoples and cultures, the most common being drugs (which includes alcohol, caffeine, and nicotine), internet, porn, sugar, junk food, and cellphones. Psychotherapy can help you free yourself of your addictions.

- *Healing process:* If you are able, go see healers: doctors, body workers, energy workers, coaches, therapists, elders, and others. Get professional opinions, guidance, and feedback on your mind-body experience. There are many things we can't see ourselves that others can see. Make use of their education, skills, and gifts.

Relationship-Environment Integration

Again, this list is not conclusive. Because we are constantly in relationship with everything around us all the time, the opportunities to bring mindfulness and intentional healing change to our relationships and our environments will be many. See what makes sense in your life according to your wyrd. These activities are meant to bring you to your growing-edge, and it's definitely not always comfortable out there.

- *Conscious relationship:* Learning to be conscious in relationship is an ongoing process that occurs over the course of one's life. Cultivate healthy communication habits: active listening, learning how to express wants and needs, expressing and maintaining healthy boundaries, nonviolent communication, balancing alone time and social time, being supportive, and allowing yourself to be supported (by friends, family, community). Stay connected. Join or start groups; attend community rituals, events, and gatherings. Spend time learning about different cultures and attending inclusive community events.

- *Community activities:* Community events, meals, rituals, dance, drum circles, and meditation are all great ways to heal the wounds of relationship-environment, as are volunteering and service. Offer your time, energy, and resources to those in need and to causes you feel are important. Give back, maintain sacred reciprocity, remember the gift-cycle.

- *Conscious employment:* Take a good look at your work situation. Does your work perpetuate harm to others or the planet? Does your work leave you feeling fulfilled? Is it meaningful? If not, what kind of work does sound meaningful and purposeful to you? Strive to shift your line of work toward something that does less harm to self, other, world. Let go of that which does not serve you or others; work to learn new skills and network in the direction you wish to go. Volunteer, engage in community service.

- *Ecological restoration:* When you go on nature walks, pick up any trash you see. Plant trees, grow plants in your home, create and maintain a garden, or find a community garden in which you can work. Find an organization that does ecological restoration—donate your time, energy, and money, or apply to join full-time.

- *Mindful consumption:* Be mindful of what you buy, how much you buy, and where you buy. Do your best to support products and organizations that minimize harm to the Earth and the Earth's communities—human or otherwise. Try to avoid buying unnecessary products that use plastics—recyclable or not. Move toward cleaner energy, less waste, reuse, and sharing. Do your best to do least harm.

- *Political organizing and action:* Many of the changes you or I might wish to see in the world cannot occur if our governments and institutions are not actively transforming themselves. Collective organizing and political action are powerful ways to affect change to the wyrd of all domains. Stay informed about current issues, read, learn history, political theory. Use your mind-body-voice to speak out and take action. Offer your time, energy, support and resources to support systemic change. Show up, engage, fight oppression in the ways you see best fit. Connect with others, engage in productive dialogue and be a part of the collective process of systemic healing and institutional change. Speak out now!

Soul-Spirit Integration

There are myriad ways to practice soul-spirit integration. I've listed just some of the most basic, general practices—each is a path you can follow. You will see which paths make sense for you. Mix and match, try them all, focus on one or two—see where they go. The name of the game is experimentation and exploration. Find your growing-edge and do your best to stay engaged with the dance of soul-spirit on the ritual dance floor that is your life.

- *Meditation:* This is perhaps *the* foundational integrative practice as it increases one's awareness. If you do not already have one, start a daily meditation practice. Begin with five minutes a day and work your way up to forty minutes to an hour or more. There are many ways to practice meditation. A good place to start is with Buddhist meditation—mindfulness, for example. If you can, learn from an experienced teacher—in person or online.

- *Conscious movement:* Practices like tai chi, qigong, ecstatic dance, contact improv, martial arts, and others will help you attune to the subtle energies of soul-spirit within body-mind-relationship-environment. Try to maintain a daily practice; if possible, combine multiple methods. This can also include exercise.

- *Study:* Read spiritual books from a variety of traditions from around the world. Watch documentaries and other educational videos. Attend community rituals; connect with elders and spiritual community. Every spiritual path has a formal or informal code of ethics and values that can be applied to right living (the Noble Eight-Fold Path of Buddhism, for example). Do your best to live what you learn in integrity.

- *Pilgrimage:* Take pilgrimages to sacred sites. Spend time in holy places in meditation, prayer, devotion, and ritual—alone and with others. Heed the call.

- *Ritual:* There are countless ways in which ritual may take form. Many of them are aligned with the seasons, equinoxes, solstices, and phases of the Moon. Learn ritual by connecting with an Earth-based spiritual community to which you feel drawn. I will include some resources in the appendix. Learn from elders, practice with peers, and practice solo.

This is just a small selection of integrative practices with which you can engage as you explore and craft your wyrd. Consider these options to be some of the basic practices of mundane magic. Holistic mind-body-relationship-environment-soul-spirit integration takes time, research, education, dedication, and persistence. This book is not your one-stop shop for wyrdcraft. There are countless threads reaching inward and outward from here. There are resources of love and light waiting for you to reach out and connect.

Don't be surprised if you encounter several psychological, physical, or systemic roadblocks on your path. Integration is difficult. Do your best. If you fail, or rather, when you fail—when you forget about awareness, attunement, self-care, and reciprocity—take a deep breath, center yourself, and get back up and start again. Reach out to friends, family, and those in your community. We are here to help each other. Again, the goal is not perfection, but rather to be in a process that leads ever more and more to the experience of wholeness. There is a great love that can contain all flaws, all wounds, all gifts, all potentials—in all beings and places. We can cultivate this love and explore the weirdness of becoming together.

Wyrdcraft is a path woven from many paths. It is a syncretic theory and practice that resonates with many cosmologies, worldviews, and practices. The foundation of wyrdcraft—or any holistic path of integration, for that matter—rests upon awareness, attunement, self-care, choice, and sacred reciprocity. It also rests on patience, persistence, heartiness, and compassion. Just do your best and take good care of yourself and others. The path that is your life will unfold as you live it and experiment with it. Create your own craft; weave your own wyrd. I will craft and weave my own.

In summary, the integrative practice of wyrdcraft is a process designed to help one locate wyrd, attune to wyrd, heal wyrd, and reweave wyrd. Wyrdcraft is a practical, natural, magical path that leads to the development of wyrd consciousness and the holistic healing-transformation of all the domains. Wyrdcraft is informal and loose because, like nature, like you, it is bound to fluctuate and evolve. Work with what life throws at you. Work with what Nature reveals. Be aware, be receptive, follow the call whenever and wherever you hear it, follow your symptoms and wounds, follow your bliss, and go with the flow. Surrender when surrender is needed, act when action is needed, show up, say yes, say no, and never give up; no matter how many times you fail, start again. Do least harm, take care of yourself, and do your best—I know you will. I will, too.

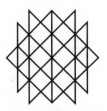

Chapter 9

The Mysteries of
the Well: Psychetherapy

At the base of the World-Tree, Yggdrasil, where the Norns, Urðr, Verðandi, and Skuld abide in their hall, there is an unfathomable well called Urðr-brunnr, the Well of Urðr, the Well of Wyrd. According to ancient Norse heathen cosmology the sacred water within this cosmic womb of a Well is said to be so pure that it turns everything within it white, including its mud, which the Norns—loyal tenders of the Tree—rub on Yggdrasil's bark as a means of preserving and protecting it from the harts, dragons, and serpents that incessantly gnaw on it.

The waters and mud within the Well help keep the Tree—the totality of the nine-worlds—alive. Two white swans live in the Well, which is also sometimes described as a vast body of water. Every day the Norns water Yggdrasil using the Well's sacred waters, ensuring the preservation of the multiverse, and every night, dew falls off the leaves and branches of the Tree back into the Well, replenishing its waters once again; thus, the gift-cycle of life spirals on.

The Wells of Wyrd

There are two other wells from which Yggdrasil draws sustenance. One is called Mímisbrunnr (The Well of Mimir). This well, located in Jötunheim, the realm of the giants, is said to be the source of all wisdom-memory, as Mimir is said to be the wisest of all beings in the nine-worlds. Odin plucked out one of his own eyes and offered it to the omniscient giant Mimir in order to take a drink from this well so that he might apprehend the mysteries of existence—and so he did. The third well, Hvergelmir, which translates to something akin to "boiling spring," is home to the underworld dragon Níðhöggr, who incessantly chews on the great Tree's roots. This third well is located deep within the primordial ice realm of Niflheim, the underworld realm ruled by the half-living, half-dead goddess Hel.

Each of these wells serves up a different draught, and each draught quenches the soul in different ways, for within their animated, potent depths flows the holy waters of awakening and remembrance. Approach each well humbly, bearing gifts, gaze upon the surface, gaze into the depths, and drink deeply.

Wyrding Ways
Communing with the Well of Wyrd

In this exercise, you will be communing with the Well of Wyrd through meditation and guided imagery. While there, you may also encounter the Wyrd Tree and the Wyrd Three. If you would like to take a moment with them, go for it; however, remember to return your focus to the Well itself. You will have opportunities to commune directly with the Tree and the Three in the next two chapters.

You will need:
- Fifteen to sixty minutes (or more) of undisturbed time-space
- A meditation cushion or chair
- Incense that has been chosen intentionally as an offering to the Well
- Your journal

1. Stand or sit in a meditative position with spine upright, chest open, belly relaxed. Close your eyes, take three slow, deep belly-breaths in through your nose and out through your mouth. Return to your natural breathing pattern. Bring your awareness to your body as whole.

2. Focus your awareness on your center (your heart-space or solar plexus). Imagine you are breathing into this space and filling it with light and energy. Do this for a couple of minutes.

3. Imagine there is a spinning spindle of energetic raw material in your core. From this spindle of prima materia, draw a thread up your spine and out the crown of your head. Guide it upward to the Sun and weave it into its core. Feel the energy of the Sun flow down the thread into your core. Then, from the spindle, pull a thread of prima materia down your spine into the Earth. Weave it into the Earth's core. Feel the energy from the Earth's core flow through the thread up into your core. Now imagine the thread in its entirety, reaching all the way from the core of the Earth, through the core of you, to the core of the Sun. Feel the energy circulating up and down through this thread. This sacred pillar is what the Anglo-Saxons called Irminsul—the World-Axis. Feel the energy flowing up and down through this pillar.

4. Now imagine that the pillar grows roots from its base. These roots are huge and expansive. Imagine as they sink deeply into the depths of soul, from which they draw sustenance and energy up into its thick, strong, yet flexible trunk. Feel this energy moving upward into your being. As it rises to the top of the pillar, you notice it begins to sprout into innumerable branches, each strong and flexible, sprouting innumerable leaves, all of which reach into the expanses of the spirit-sky, where they soak in sustenance and energy.

5. Somewhere at the base of the Tree is the Well. You feel its deep liquid magic before you see it. Move closer to it. Take a few moments and let it materialize before you as it comes into view. Does it look like a well? A large body of water? A void? Let it take form.

6. Relax your core; feel the ambient energy or aura of this well. This is the Well of Psyche, the Well of Soul. This is the well of your unconscious. There is mystery here, and magic. Use your mind's eye to gaze softly upon the water's surface. Look into its depths; feel how deep it is—immeasurable. What do you see? Allow images, sensations, and thoughts to float to the surface from the depths below. Be with these images. Feel them as they arise. What do they say? *How* do they say? Through thought, image, sensation, memory, knowing? Whatever arises, let it

work on you. Let it have a life of its own. No need to force anything. Let the waters flow as they want to flow.

7. Light your incense, which you have chosen specifically to offer
   to the Well, to Psyche, to Soul, to your unconscious. Say, "Thank
   you for your existence; thank you for your depths and expanse.
   Thank you for your mysteries. Thank you for your teachings.
   I will return again, with gifts. Until then, blessed be."

8. Take a few slow, deep belly-breaths, open your eyes, look at the
   space around you, notice the colors, textures, and shapes. Begin
   to move your body; shake if you need to. Stand up, give the
   experience you just had a slow, deep bow of gratitude. Carry this
   energy into the world with you as you go about the rest of your
   day and night.

9. Write about your experience in your journal.

Psyche: The Sacred Well of Initiation

The archetypal well is a compelling metaphor and symbol that draws one into
an initiatory relationship with soul, the feminine mysteries, the Source, the
unconscious, and more. Sacred wells hold within them great power of revelation and healing-transformation. Wells have been both revered and feared
throughout history and folktale, as they are thought to be magical gateways
to the underworld as well as home to a wide range of spirits and mysterious
others. Within the depths of the well, the promise of enchantment, nourish-
ment, healing, and remembrance compels one to drink deeply—and to give
freely, for the well requires an offering, a sacrifice. The wishing-well requires
some change for some change. Knowing this, you offer a gift for a gift as you
walk the sacrificial path of initiation.

The process of initiation is an integral part of any immersive spiritual path
into the mysteries. To be an initiate is to be acknowledged as someone who is
knowing. Having made the appropriate sacrifice to drink from the well, the initiate has come to know something that the uninitiated does not. Every mystery
school, ancient and modern, guides the aspirant on a ritual path to the well(s)
of initiation(s). Each time the aspirant arrives at the well, something must be
left behind in order to drink. Sacred reciprocity must be upheld.

The initiatory path—as exemplified by working through the grades of
a magical order, or by the therapy process, or by life itself—is not a one-

and-done ordeal. Like a snake, you must slough off old skin many times over during the meandering course of your life. With each initiation, a sacrifice must be made. In a wyrd, spiral-like fashion, the transmutation of soul proceeds from ordeal to ordeal, from life to death to life to death to life to death again—ever expanding, ever deepening, ever becoming on the way.

This well—this deep void where on the edge the wanderer considers whether or not to drink or dive or turn away—is psyche. Shapeshifting mercurial quicksilver trickster, psyche, is at the epicenter of every initiation. Psyche is the mystery through which being, consciousness, and soul become and flow. Wyrd works directly on and through psyche. Integration and healing-transformation happen here. Your relationship with psyche is in many ways the most important relationship you have. You experience everything through the medium of your psyche. Psyche is with you always, from birth to death and beyond; it lives through you, and you live through it.

Another word for *psyche*—other than *soul*—is *self*. The *self* is both a psychological and a spiritual term, but generally speaking, one's self is equivalent to the wholeness of one's being. Self is a diamond-onion; like a diamond, it has many facets, and like an onion, it has many layers. The outer layers and facets are easier to see than the inner ones, but the more you explore, the more your wholeness can be known. This whole is called the Self. Both self and Self are in the Well, as is so much more.

Jung defined the *Self* as the "totality of the psyche."[34] The process of unveiling this totality he referred to as individuation. Though I am grossly oversimplifying, according to Jungian theory, individuation is the process of integrating the persona (the masks we wear in the world), the ego (your entire conscious self), the personal and collective unconscious, the shadow, and the soul (anima, animus, and the archetypes) into the Self.

If the term *individuation* sounds solipsistic to you, know that it is not. True individuation does not occur at the expense of the community, but rather for the benefit and empowerment of the community. Individuation—and integration, for that matter—is Self-centered. In other words, one who is fully self-empowered sees and experiences Self, the Self that all share, the Self that is within all, connects all, and is All. The individuated, initiated,

---

34. Josepf Henderson, "Ancient Myths and Modern Man" in *Man and His Symbols*, ed. C. G. Jung (London: Dell, 1978), 120.

Self-empowered person has re-membered (i.e., healed) the fragments of psyche into its weblike unity and awakened to the natural law of interdependence, interconnection, and interrelationship within the whole.

Individuation, too, is contagious; the individuated person encourages the individuation of others, which leads to an individuated collective. The individuated, initiated person and collective see who they truly are, as well as who they are in relationship to everything and everyone else—human, divine, natural. In other words, the Self they have found deep within themselves is the very same Self found deep within everyone and all things. From this place, we are empowered by empowering others. From this place, we are in cooperation rather than competition. From this place, we heal, transform, and become together. There is powerful magic here.

The Magic of Psychetherapy

You may have wondered why you are reading so much about therapy in a book that's supposed to be about magic. The reason is simple: *therapy is magic.* How so, you ask? Though we will delve into magic more deeply in chapters 11 and 12, let's start by taking a quick look at the nature of magic now. Generally speaking, magical practice makes use of sacred space, altered states, ritual objects, special techniques, and communion with other-than-human forces to cause changes to one's consciousness, being, and world. Therapy does the same. Therapy is at the very least a weekly ritual that takes place within a sacred space. Therapy also utilizes altered states and specialized techniques to communicate with one's Higher Self with the intent to cause change to one's consciousness and world in accordance with one's will. Like magic, the waves that emanate from one's psychetherapeutic ritual transformations ripple into the world and change it. Psychetherapy is psychological magic, and it is some of the most real-time, practical magic one can do.

Suffering is usually the result of a lack of consciousness. Psychetherapy strives to alleviate suffering by making the unconscious conscious and cultivating the emergence of wholeness—i.e., soulfulness. It is healing to see and experience wholeness—supposed flaws and supposed perfections and all. This whole-seeing happens every time one drinks from, and or dives into, the sacred well of psyche.

Through mindful, guided psychetherapeutic process, psychetherapy reveals wounds, which if left unaddressed, would continue to block or hinder the free flow of healing, magical life-energy within the individual, family, and larger human and other-than-human community. Psychetherapy works to bring soul-magic into the world; thus, psychetherapy is itself soul-magic. This type of soul-magic is naturally healing. The healing-magic of psychetherapy is so powerful that it can transmute insanity into sanity; it can transform hubris, narcissism, and other antisocial behaviors into humanity, humility, and divinity; it can heal ecosystems. Within each of our individual and collective wounds and blocks, the unbridled fullness of soul, divinity, and magic waits to emerge. Holistic, soul-centered, magic-centered psychetherapy is an amazing tool—the perfect alchemical crucible—for inviting healing-magic and natural magic into the flow of life.

Psychetherapy is an initiatory process, albeit often a slow one. Every week, the client, patient, or analysand sacrifices their time, energy, and money, as well as their tightly held delusions, so that they might drink from the well and become ever more so one who is knowing. Therapy is certainly not always easy, but it is a highly potent ritual container for transformative magic. I can say this from personal experience as both a client and as a therapist. Every session is another opportunity to drink from the well of psyche and see.

Like ecotherapy and magic, psychetherapy is built for exploring the mystery of wyrd's many facets—fate, destiny, nature, soul, the web, and becoming. It is an experiential, experimental, and holistic process of revelation, healing-transformation, and becoming. There are many ways to approach psychetherapy by both traditional and nontraditional means. I encourage you to explore multiple paths. Go with the flow, follow your heart, follow your wounds and gifts, follow the Fates' call. Take your time with each method you practice, and know that there is a deeper process at play within them all. Sink into each process and let the process sink into you. Drink deeply from the Well. Some examples of psychetherapy include the following:

- Any psychotherapeutic approach (CBT, narrative, somatic, psychodynamic, etc.)
- Any meditation or contemplation practice (self-inquiry, vipassanā, guided imagery, etc.)

- Yoga, ecstatic dance, mindful movement
- Mindful use of psychedelics
- Creative arts (painting, drawing, writing, music, etc.)
- Bodywork (massage, acupuncture, Reiki)
- Divination (tarot, runes, *I Ching*)
- Soul-systems (the Enneagram, Human Design, Archetypal Astrology, etc.)
- And more…

Wyrding Ways
Parts-Work with a Block or Wound

This experiment, which reveals the intersection between psychotherapy and magic, offers a way to psychetherapeutically work with internal blocks and wounds. This is another gestalt therapy intervention I learned during my practicum at the Integral Counseling Center at Church Street in San Francisco. I regularly do this experiment with my clients. It is called an experiment because nothing specific is *supposed* to happen. Who knows what will arise as you do it? Even though I recommend doing this experiment—sometimes called parts-work or the empty chair—with a licensed therapist, you can also try it alone or with a friend. I will present it here as a solo exercise. Read through it first and use your best judgment as to whether it might be best to have a professional guide you through this process.

You will need:
- At least thirty minutes of undisturbed time-space
- A comfortable place to sit (a meditation cushion, pillow, or chair)
- An empty meditation cushion, pillow, or chair you can place in front of you or near you

1. Take a seat and adopt a meditative posture—still, relaxed, and alert with your spine straight. Close your eyes, go within, and take a few slow, deep belly-breaths in through your nose and out through your mouth. Take a couple of minutes to bring awareness to your natural breathing pattern and your body as you settle into the moment.

2. Call to mind a specific situation that has been bothering you: a fight with your partner or friend, an unsettling experience at work, a big decision that has been vexing you, a recent accident. If you can't think of anything specific, sense into whatever may be present in your felt sense in the here-and-now and see what comes to the foreground.

3. Notice how your memory of this experience, emotion, or sensation is affecting you on a somatic level. Perhaps you feel a heaviness in your shoulders, or a tightness or agitation in your neck, chest, belly, or head. Whatever feeling comes to the foreground in your felt sense, stay with it; lightly hold your awareness on it. Remember to breathe.

4. Ask yourself, "Is it okay to feel this right now, and is it okay to go deeper into this feeling right now?" If you get a no, acknowledge the uncomfortable feeling, take a few breaths in and out of it, and say, "I see you, I acknowledge you, and I will catch up with you more later, but I am going for now." Take a few more breaths and end your meditation.

5. If you get a yes, stay with the feelings and sensations and keep your awareness on them and in them. As uncomfortable as the sensation may be, try to stay with it. Don't try to change it; allow it to have a life of its own. Let it *be*. As you do this, notice any emergent qualities within the sensation (tingling, heat, movement, vibration, etc.). See if you can sense where the outer boundaries of the sensation are. See if you can locate its center. Breathe.

6. As you sit with and allow the sensation to be, open the gate of your imagination and see if any colors, textures, or images emerge from it. Try not to force anything. Let that which emerges to do so organically. Be with the image for a couple of minutes. Again, let it *be*. If no image emerges, that is okay; just be with what is.

7. Now, imagine that this sensation takes the form of a being. It may take any form at all; let psyche decide. It may become a person, an alien, a goblin, or even an object (an orb of light or shadow, an animate blob, or an oozing ball of hair, for example). Again, don't force it. Let the image arise organically. Perhaps no image will arise; that is okay, too.

8. When you get a clear-enough image of this symbolic representation, imaginally lift it out of your body and place it on the empty cushion or chair in front of you or next to you. (You may not want it to be close, so feel free to put the cushion anywhere.) Look at this being with your mind's eye as it sits there. What does he, she, they, it, look like? What is it doing as it sits on the cushion?

9. Now is the time for a dialogue and to ask questions and tell this being—this part of you—what you think and feel. It is also a time for this part of you to tell you what he, she, they, or it thinks and feels. Don't think about the responses too much; let your stream of consciousness flow. Whenever it is time for the part to speak, get up and move to its cushion or seat, embody it, and answer in the first person, as if you *are* that being. When you are done, return to your seat and see if there is a response. Go back and forth in this manner as many times as you'd like—as long as the conversation keeps going. This standing up, going back and forth, and speaking for the part may seem odd, but give it a try. If it's too distracting or difficult, you can have the dialogue from where you sit, internally. Just so long as you extract the so-called being from your body and put it on the cushion outside of you and have a dialogue with it there. Here are some icebreakers:

   – Who are you?
   – What are you doing here?
   – What do you want?
   – What do you need?
   – Where did you come from?

   The conversation may be short or long. Often times, these dialogues go places you wouldn't expect, into deeper layers of your psyche and your emotional experience. This is one reason it is best to have a therapist help guide and contain the process for you. You may reach a deeper insight, have a reparative moment, or have an emotional catharsis—you may not. Try not to have an agenda. This is simply an experiment. At the most basic level, the goal is simply to increase awareness of the parts of your psyche.

10. When the conversation feels like it is over, you can do a few different things: you can thank this part of you for being there and talking with you, pick it up, and put it back in your being; you

can say goodbye to it and imagine it dissolving or blowing away in the wind; or you can imagine throwing it out the window, putting it on a compost pile, or even forcefully banishing it with inner light, burning sage, or laughter. Again, do what feels right in the moment.

11. After you have done this, take a few slow, deep belly-breaths, stand up, and give your feet, hands, limbs, head, and body a shake. Imagine the stuff you don't want or need sloughing off you and blowing away in the wind, falling on the same compost pile, or running off you like water. Write about your experience in your journal.

On Working with a Therapist

In the great ritual of life, there is a good chance that unprocessed psychological material will arise that would behest you to enlist a trained professional to help you process it—i.e., come to know it, deeply feel it, and learn to reweave it. There is a lot in the deep well of the psyche just itching to spill out. Though there are many ways to practice psychetherapy without a therapist or guide, I highly encourage you to experiment with a psychetherapeutic guide for a bit if possible. Psychetherapy is a form of ritual spellwork of the revealing and healing kind, and as any ritualist knows, powerful spellwork requires solid containment—and benefits from it! Psychetherapists are trained to do just that: contain. They are trained to do many other things as well. As soul-rangers, psychetherapists maintain the wild and active boundaries of the inner and outer wilderness of psyche. They are bushwhackers, trackers, hunters, wildcrafters, and guides dedicated to the revelation, healing-transformation, and becoming of soul.

For those concerned about the cost of therapy, consider the cost a form of sacrifice—a gift for a gift, if you will. Also, know that there are sliding-scale therapists out there. You can find them easily online. You could begin your search on the Psychology Today website (listed in the resources section at the end of this book). If you are looking for a therapist who might better align with your animist, pantheist, and magical worldview, I recommend including terms such as *holistic, integral, archetypal, imaginal, depth-oriented,* or *transpersonal* in your search. You can also search for a Jungian analyst or practitioner of gestalt therapy, psychosynthesis, or internal family systems. Each of these approaches understands the animated, polyfaceted, and kaleidoscopic nature of being. Note: A search for the term *psychetherapist* may not yield many results as it is not an official term for a licensed profession. Rather, it is a term used by a number of soul-oriented psychotherapists and psychoanalysts seeking to reclaim the concept of soul within the greater field of psychotherapy and psychology. I am one of them.

Though you can certainly do a lot of healing solo or with friends, family, and even consenting strangers, a psychetherapist can be of immense help when it comes to the heavy lifting required to do deep shadow work. Shadow work is difficult to do completely solo. A therapist can help you contain your process and all that arises within it. This containment will help you integrate and heal more efficiently and holistically. Believe it or not, this can help you become a more effective spellcaster as well, as it clears psychological blocks and heals wounds that may be tying up or misdirecting the natural flow of magical energy through your system. Contrary to popular belief, a therapist will not "fix" you; they will help you "fix" yourself. They will help you take your destiny into your own hands and reweave your personal, relational, and systemic wyrd in empowering, healing, and transformative ways.

Exploring Wyrd in Therapy

I get the opportunity to witness and explore my clients' wyrd with them every day. With every session, my clients' fate, destiny, nature, soul, and process of becoming come more and more into view—as does the Web of Wyrd. Together, we explore the fibers, strings, and weave of their life-thread and life-weave. I need not even mention the concept of wyrd to my clients. In fact, many of them couldn't care less about wyrd. That is fine. Whether they are aware of it or not, we are still exploring their wyrd and how wyrd manifests within the domains of their life. We are still doing wyrdcraft, whether it's called cognitive behavioral therapy, psychodynamic psychoanalysis, somatic trauma processing, solutions-focused therapy, or something else.

You are a web woven into a larger Web, a braid woven into a larger Braid, a gestalt within a larger Gestalt. There are myriads of threads that come together to create your wyrd. There are myriad mind-body-relationship-environment-soul-spirit threads to explore within your life. Some of these threads are torn, tattered, knotted, and need to be tended, healed, and rewoven.

I help facilitate this process. Whether it's called psychetherapy, wyrdcraft, spiritual counseling, psychotherapy, coaching, or counseling—it is all revelation, healing-transformation, and becoming. It's all the integration and remembering of the Web.

Wyrd shows up in therapy in novel ways. When a client of mine unconsciously says something was *weird* or *felt weird*, a deeper curiosity within me says, "Maybe there's something there." "Follow that deeper." "What does that experience have to say about my client's fate, destiny, or process of becoming?" Time and time again, I have found that the word *weird* is often a doorway that opens into the vast realm of wyrd. In this realm, the seemingly trivial experiences that are referred to as weird, if explored therapeutically, can reveal a great depth out of which meaning, purpose, healing, and spiritual process emerge.

As I have experienced within my own life and witnessed in the lives of my clients, as you practice psychetherapy, you can see your fate and destiny emerge before your eyes as you bring awareness to your inner and outer workings—your habits, assumptions, conditioning, and environmental influences. You can find the threads that connect past, present, and future, see what challenges you, what blocks your fullest becoming, what nourishes you, what empowers you, what ties you to others, and how and why you think and do the things you think and do.

What I have seen working with my clients is that we are all contagious. Our suffering and healing are contagious. As we are all woven into the larger Web, we are relational beings and empathic beings. Because of this, when one suffers and doesn't process that suffering, this will likely lead to another's suffering, which will lead to another's suffering, and to another's, and to another's, on and on, spreading through the web of life. The same can be said for healing, joy, pleasure, love, and awareness—these things are contagious as well. As you heal, you promote healing in others around you. Not by preaching and proselytizing, but by simply being your true, whole self.

How is your suffering and healing connected to the world around you? Psychetherapy will reveal both. Within the great Web, your life and actions are connected to the lives and actions of all. Your fate is tied to the fate of all people, and your destiny will impact the destiny of all. As you cultivate wyrd consciousness, you will see that we are all channels, catalysts, crossroads, and sources for the sharing of experience and existence with others. For better or for worse, whether we admit to it or not, we are all connected.

A symptom does not have to be a negative thing. That definition is old and cold. A warmer, more holistic definition might define a symptom as an outward expression of an inner experience—itself connected to a long chain of both inner and outer experiences. A symptom of joy, for example, might be a smile. A symptom of love might be a laugh. A symptom of anger might be abuse. A symptom of anxiety might be a shortness of breath or a jittery limb. Our symptoms, whatever they may be (and they are unique to everyone), can tell us a lot about our wyrd. Psychetherapy is a process for inquiring into these symptoms.

There is a stigma against therapy. "Only crazy people go to therapy," is the refrain. Because therapy has been equated primarily with psychopathology and mental illness for so long, most people don't go to therapy until they have a problem on their hands that they can't deal with using their ordinary go-to methods. And if they do finally go, they do so guiltily, ashamedly, and begrudgingly.

The symptoms that usually bring people to therapy are not the so-called positive ones, but rather the so-called negative ones. These symptoms are usually experienced as problematic, as they have a way of knocking our life out of balance. They usually arise when an issue cannot be resolved and is left to linger and fester unaddressed. As symptoms remain unaddressed, the underlying issues fester, often leading to worse symptoms or more symptoms, or both, which then lead to imbalance, which leads to more symptoms, which lead to further imbalance, which leads to further symptoms, ad infinitum. Thus spirals the self-perpetuating symptom cycle. Eventually, this cycle will become too much to handle, and the person will finally go to see a therapist.

We forget that our positive symptoms work like this, too. If we bring our awareness to and process our positive symptoms, we cultivate and generate that which is at their root; we feed our inner flame, encourage the emergence of our light, and create a feedback loop for more positive symptomology to come. Why don't we do this more? What if therapy was seen as preventative medicine? What if therapy did not have the stigma and shame attached to it? Our world would look much different.

We do ourselves a disservice when we neglect to acknowledge, address, and process any of our symptoms—positive or negative. We keep our wholeness, and our full potential, at bay. What are your symptoms in your life right now? Start with the ones that are the most present, in your face, in the foreground. Start on the surface and go deeper. Follow your symptoms as if they were threads. Follow each symptom-thread. Is it anxiety, depression, addiction, insomnia, ecstasy, joy, peace? Where does the symptom-thread go if you follow it inward and outward? Follow it as it meanders through multiple domains. If you follow the threads of your symptoms, where do you end up? You can follow your symptom thread with the help of your therapist, and you can also follow it by yourself. As you do, do your best to take a nonpathologizing approach. Each symptom is a window, doorway, and pathway to healing. Your symptoms reveal to you valuable information about you and your life. They reveal to you your wyrd. They are an integral part of your wyrd, your constitution, your makeup, and the direction you are headed—for better or for worse.

An essential tenet of wyrdcraft is this: *You must see the strings of fate before you can pull the strings of fate.* Likewise, *you must see the wound and feel the wound if you wish to heal the wound.* The unaddressed and unhealed wound will act as a block or veil that keeps you from seeing your wholeness, which could hinder your magic. By looking into the symptoms that bring you to therapy, you can begin to follow the thread of each symptom until you reach an understanding of its superficial and deep-rooted causes. Often, following the symptom-thread takes one to places they don't expect or want to go to— a trademark sign of the path to health, well-being, and Self-discovery.

Each symptom is a thread that connects past, present, and future. These threads can be explored, healed, transformed, and rewoven. In addition, each symptom-thread also connects all the domains. Mind-body symptoms affect relationship-environment-soul-spirit health and well-being, relational symptoms affect mind-body-environment-soul-spirit health and well-being, and soul-spirit symptoms affect mind-body-relationship-environment health and well-being. By bringing awareness to each thread, you can eventually see what you need to do to mend the thread and reweave it into a healthier braid of being. You can heal the past, present, and future; you can heal all domains.

You can craft your wyrd toward more favorable outcomes. Psychetherapy is a holistic process and practice. The more you practice—whatever you practice—the better you will get, and because all is connected, the better you get, the better we all get. Psychetherapy is win-win-win for all.

Wyrding Ways
Exploring Your Symptom-Threads

There are several ways to explore your symptom-threads. Here is just one example that brings together the psychological and spiritual through a process of meditation, guided imagery, and devotion.

You will need:
- Tarot cards, oracle cards, or a set of runes
- A quiet and comfortable place to meditate
- A special incense and offering for the Well

1. Sit down. Set the cards or runes in front of you. Ready your incense for burning, but do not light. Take a meditative posture with spine straight. Close your eyes. Take a few slow, deep belly-breaths in through your nose and out through your mouth. Return to your normal breathing pattern.

2. Imagine a thread reaching down from the Sun, into the crown of your head, down your spine, into your core. Draw and receive warm, loving solar energy through this thread. Do this for a minute as you fill your core with the Sun's light, love, and warmth. Now, imagine a thread reaching up from the core of the Earth, into and through your spine, up into your core. Draw and receive grounding, loving growth energy up from the Earth, through the thread. Do this for a minute as you fill your core with the Earth's stability, solidity, generativity, and love. Feel the energy flowing through the whole thread for a minute or so.

3. Imagine that you sit at the Well of Wyrd. Take a moment to let it materialize before you. Using your mind's eye, gaze softly upon the water's surface, then gaze into its depths. Feel how deep it is—immeasurable. Relax your core; feel the ambient energy or aura of the Well. Light the incense and present your offering

to the Well. Say something to the effect of, "Well of Wyrd, Well of Soul, what do I need to see? Fates Three, what do I need to know? What wounds and blocks keep me from growing and knowing Self? What symptom-threads must I follow? I make these offerings to you so that I might receive your wisdom. I open my mind-body-heart-soul to receive." Make your offering.

4. Ready the tarot or oracle deck or runes. As you shuffle, embody the energies of flow, depth, rest, stillness, and silence. Before you draw the card or rune, take a few minutes to bring your awareness to your breath and body. Breathe. Then draw the card(s) or rune(s). The first few times you do this exercise, pull one to three cards or runes. The more you do it, the more you can pull. I rarely pull more than nine at any given time. Keep in mind that the more cards you pull, the more threads you will have to explore, which will take more time, energy, skill, and will.

5. Softly gaze at the card or rune, soaking in its image in a spirit of receptivity and self-inquiry. Be mindful of every somatic sensation, thought, memory, or vision that comes with it. Ask yourself how it might apply to the domains of your life and the fragmentation occurring within. The more time you spend exploring the card or rune, the more time you spend coming to know this thread of your wyrd. Each thread has many different facets. For example, the Fool card has innumerable meanings and interpretations. Use the card or rune as a mirror. It is the light of the Sun and Moon reflecting material from within your unconscious. Allow the material within the unconscious to move from the invisible background to the visible foreground, into conscious awareness. You may also pick up a book and read about the card or rune at this point. Reflect upon what you read.

6. When you are done, light your incense, give your offering, and say, "I give thanks to you, deep Well of Psyche, for this message. Thank you for revealing my symptom-threads. Thank you for showing me my healing-path to Self. Thank you for your guidance and blessings. I will continue to follow this thread as I live my day-to-day life. I will return again." Take a few slow, deep belly-breaths, open your eyes, slowly move your body, stand up, take a deep bow of gratitude, and bring this awareness with you throughout your day.

The Archetypal

Another way to explore wyrd psychetherapeutically is to explore the archetypal. An archetype is an ordering principle, pattern, or natural law that manifests within the greater fabric of reality, through the transpersonal field of psyche. Archetypes exist as bridges between the so-called spiritual and mundane worlds. One way to think of an archetype is as a transpersonal being or living symbol that serves as an intermediary between our ordinary consciousness and the mysterious realm of the collective unconscious—the archetypal realm of soul. Each archetype is a gestalt, a constellation of energies, natural processes, behaviors, and symbolic correspondences that operates according to its own wyrd; each has its own way of being, in that it occupies its own niche within the greater ecosystem of the psycheverse.

Archetypes show up cross-culturally as commonly occurring themes or motifs throughout world mythology, art, and literature and within religious, social, and psychological spheres. From culture to culture, each archetype will manifest within the cultural fabric in culturally specific ways, yet cross-culturally they will share many traits in common. Some of the most common archetypes as delineated by Jungian and archetypal psychologists are the King or Queen, Warrior, Magician, Wanderer, and Lover. There are many others.

What we consider archetypes, and even symbols for that matter, can be thought of as energetic currents or rivers that influence mind and matter according to natural patterns. The archetypes are very much wyrd. We find ourselves falling into archetypal patterns of thinking, behaving, and being without even knowing it. They push us and pull us this way and that in surprisingly predictable ways—at least once we become aware of them. Without awareness, the archetypes will run our lives from behind the scenes; we will call this fate. With awareness, we can align with them and channel their energies toward fruition in healthy, life-affirming ways; this we will call destiny.

No matter your gender, age, ability, or cultural, spiritual, or philosophical orientation, you have the potential to commune with (i.e., enter into the gift-cycle with) any number of these archetypal patterns and processes. The more you do this, the more whole you will become. Which ones you commune with will depend upon your wyrd.

Just like nature, humanity, and divinity, each archetype has positive and negative, creative and destructive, healthy and unhealthy poles. The Mother—

loving, providing, and protective—can be smothering and controlling, for example. The Father can be protective and authoritarian; the Lover, supportive and possessive; the Magician, inspiring and manipulative.[35] Part of the psychetherapy process consists of developing awareness of the nature and powers of the wholeness of the archetypes and how they come into play within our lives in both positive and negative ways. As you come to know the archetypal, you will be given glimpses into your many parts, gifts, challenges, habits, and potentials—into the wholeness of Self.

Archetypal communion requires a high degree of care and awareness, for whenever one intentionally relates to the powerful primordial energies of the multiverse, one risks the potential of being overwhelmed and possessed by the archetype. The psychological word for this is *inflation*. During inflation, one's naturally imperfect human ego-self gets overwhelmed and replaced by the embodied experience of the archetypal. This is a powerful, ecstatic feeling in which all the perceived limits that come with being human appear to be meaningless. Archetypal possession can lead to a level of grandiosity that, if left unchecked by the conscious ego, can be so overwhelming it could lead to psychosis or some other form of hubristic self-destruction. Inflation is largely an unconscious process and can occur subtly and slowly over time, which is why it is so important to have trained, experienced professionals—elders, therapists, mentors—as well as time-tested myths, initiatory processes, and ritual containment to guide the process and warn the seeker of this possibility in real time. The hubris that occurs as a result of archetypal inflation—the "I am a God" delusion—often leads one to overstep the boundaries Fate has set for them. As evidenced in myth, as well as in the news, hubris often ends in tragedy. As you commune with divinity, go with guidance, go mindfully, go slowly, and go prepared.

---

35. Robert Moore and Douglas Gillette, *King, Warrior, Magician, Lover: Rediscovering the Archetypes of the Mature Masculine* (New York: Harper Collins, 1991).

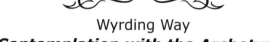

Wyrding Way
Contemplation with the Archetypal

Some of the most common archetypes found within pagan and heathen circles are the Seeker or Wanderer, the Witch, the Sage or Seeress, the Hunter or Huntress, the Warrior, the Lover, the Trickster, the Maiden, Mother, Crone, and so on. There are many more. Do any of these archetypes, or any others, resonate with you? In this exercise, I invite you to take a deeper look into the archetypal as it manifests within your life. As you do this, you will be coming to know your wholeness and wyrd.

You will need:
- Twenty to thirty minutes
- Your journal

1. Choose one (or more) of the archetypes listed above, or another of your choosing, for your contemplation and journaling.

2. Which goddesses, gods, or other characters from the myth or lore represent this archetype for you? For example, the Witch might be represented by Freyja, Cerridwen, or Hecate; the Wanderer may be represented by Odin, Pan, or Hermes; the Mother, by a number of different goddesses.

3. Based on the lore, and based on your personal experience, what are some of the positive qualities of this archetypal representation? How do these qualities show up in your own life—in your mind-body-relationship-environment-soul-spirit? Write them down in your journal.

4. What are some of the negative qualities of this archetypal representation? What are some of the shadow aspects of this god(dess) or being? How do these shadow qualities show up within the domains of your life and way of being? Write them down in your journal. Process with your therapist if you have one.

Shadow Work, the Underworld, and the Trickster

Because every archetype has a shadow and every archetype can be found within us, personal archetypal exploration gives each of us a great opportunity to do our personal shadow work. The shadow is the unconscious—that which is not-conscious. Mythologically and archetypally speaking, the unconscious is called the underworld. Shadow work, therefore, can refer to the exploration of the underworld and the processing of the material that is unearthed over its course.

The underworld is accessible everywhere, here, and now. It is deep within each of us. The quickest way to get there is by going within. Be careful, though. It is important to do shadow work slowly and mindfully. This can be done in phases: educating oneself about the concept and nature of the shadow, exploring the archetypal underworld, its myths, motifs, and denizens, engaging in deep ritualistic self-inquiry, and processing one's inquiry with a licensed therapist or skilled guide. If this sounds complicated or difficult, that's because it is, but try not to let this dishearten you. Though shadow work is not an easy or quick fix, it certainly is deeply meaningful, purposeful, and enlivening. The goal of shadow work is the same as the goal of psychetherapy, ecotherapy, and magic—not perfection, but wholeness: the awakening to perfection within imperfection.

Our world mythologies offer us a multitude of beautifully crafted archetypal maps of the human psyche and cosmic psyche. These maps serve as guides on our trip into the wilderness of the underworld, otherworld, and upperworld. They guide us when we are lost and confused, warn us when we are flying too close to the sun, and help us reorient when we forget what we are doing and where we are. In the end, however, these maps are just maps, and as we all know, the map is not the same as the landscape. Maps are helpful, but you don't live *in* the map. The maps will *help* you live, but you must do the actual living. You must face the wild, weird unknown with your own mortal and immortal mind-body. You must take each grueling step up the mountain in the snowstorm and endure the dark of the soul.

On your underworld journey, as you do your shadow work, it can be particularly helpful to commune directly with a psychopomp—a guide of souls. A psychopomp can take the form of a ritual guide, mentor, elder, therapist, and/or any number of other nonhuman entities or deities. Hermes, Charon,

Persephone, Odin, and Isis are just some examples of our world's archetypal psychopomps. The psychopomp is an expert when it comes to the shapeshifting transmutation and transportation of being-consciousness-soul. The psychopomp knows the way in, the way out, and the way in-between the underworld, otherworld, and upperworld. These realms are vast and, just like any ocean, forest, jungle, or neighborhood, can be tricky to navigate. Therein lies the expertise of the psychopomp.

A psychopomp is a guide, magician, trickster, and shapeshifter. The psychopomp is most at home within liminality and can be of great service as you ritually explore the liminal terrain of the psycheverse. The psychopomp's skill set allows them travel between different worlds and dimensions like no other. They are quick, adaptable, creative, and brilliant. They are our indispensable guides as they shift and guide from one form to another and one realm to another. Psychopomps, especially in their trickster capacity, are powerful awakeners. Sometimes these awakenings come gently on a soft breeze; other times they come quite harshly, slapping you out of a deep sleep. The trickster loves to reveal things, regardless of if you are ready to see them or not. Loki, Hermes, Coyote, Raven, and Rabbit are just some of the world's tricksters.

The trickster will keep you on your toes. Like any other deity or archetype, the trickster has both positive and negative poles. From the vantage point of the positive pole, the trickster is the magical, fertile void, the creator, initiator, inventor, and inspirer. From the vantage point of the negative pole, the trickster does all these things, but in unpleasant, painful, shocking, and/or traumatic ways. It is the way of the trickster to turn everything inside-out and shine a light on things. In my opinion, this is usually a good thing—even if it is incredibly embarrassing from time to time. The trickster serves many functions—psychopomp, clown, fool, magician. In each of these functions, the trickster helps us come to know and navigate the amorphous boundary between unconsciousness and consciousness—the place where destruction and creation blend, where foolishness and enlightenment share a dance. The trickster is the archetypal clown and fool. If you ever play the fool—as everyone does sometimes—if you ever put your own foot in our mouth, or cause undue suffering to yourself and others, this is the trickster at play. It is the trickster that helps us become aware of when and why we do this. The clowning fool keeps us entertained, awakens us, and pulls one over on all at once.

They laugh at us and with us. There is a fool within us all. They remind us of the cosmic joke and giggle.

Tricksters seem to love weirding people out, making us question things, do a double take. They are much more than just magicians doing sleight of hand. They do reality-magic. They shapeshift Nature in the least expected ways. This surprise can be shocking, inspiring, entertaining, and educational. Being but a fractal of a greater natural law, the tricksters live their wryd and do what they do. They help reveal, heal, and transform in their own weird ways, and they teach us to do the same—in our own weird ways. How and why they do what they do can be discovered by communing with them. If you want to see the work of the trickster in real time, practice magic; experiment with consciousness, expansion, and alteration; study the clowns, comedians, politicians, artists, and magicians. Take a deep look into your mind and into your life, ask yourself the following: What accidents have occurred in my life lately? How have I surprised myself and others lately? What I have been creating—for better or for worse? How do I get in the way of my own love, joy, health, and well-being? Are there limits I impose upon myself that no longer serve me? Am I living my life fully and wisely on purpose? Is it possible I might be entertaining a bit of hubris? These are all questions you can contemplate as you commune with the trickster in your life.

From a psycho-magical point of view, you can both do your psychological shadow work and come to know the psychopomp and trickster by inquiring into the concepts of suppression, repression, denial, and projection. These psychological mechanisms are some of the most common ways we invite the trickster into our lives.

At the risk of oversimplifying, suppression is the conscious avoidance and denial of all that makes us uncomfortable, repression is the unconscious avoidance and denial of all that makes us uncomfortable, and projection is when we unconsciously project our own unaddressed shadow material onto others. Rather than acknowledge and process our own deep guilt, shame, anger, anxiety, or sadness, we project it outward, point our fingers at others, and blame or judge them for what we fear to take ownership of within ourselves. The fact that this happens unconsciously points to the existence of the trickster. If you have an unprocessed emotion or trauma, you are going to project it outward and see it in others, and it will become a trigger for you.

It is a lot easier to suppress, repress, and project than it is to investigate our own psyches and take self-responsibility for the healing and transmutation of our own shadow material.

Wyrding Ways
Self-Inquiry and Shadow-Integration Journaling

The goal of this wyrding is to explore and feel into your personal habits around suppression, repression, and projection. This will help you become more aware of your shadow and how the trickster shows up in your life.

You will need:

- Fifteen to thirty minutes of uninterrupted time-space for contemplation
- Your journal
- Optional: A therapist to help you process

1. *Suppression:* What kinds of things do I suppress? What emotions, feelings and ideas do I push to the side? What emotions are overwhelming to me? Are there problems or conflicts in my life that I am currently avoiding?

2. *Repression:* What kind of things have I repressed? This question is harder to answer as repression happens unconsciously. Take an honest inventory. Are there any emotional states or lived experiences that are weirdly absent from your life? Sadness, anger, anxiety, joy, ecstasy? Sex, argument, play, laughter, adventure? Have I ever had any repressed memories return? If so, what were they?

3. *Projection:* When I lose inner balance, how do I act and react toward others, to the world, to myself? Pay particular attention to moments when you blame, judge, or criticize someone or yourself. What emotions make me feel uncomfortable when other people express them? What are my triggers? Are there any groups of people I blame for the world's ills? Pay close attention to how your emotions on any given day influence the way you relate to others and the world.

Again, this is a difficult exercise, as these processes often happen unconsciously. They are more apt to be answered if you work with a therapist or a
psychologically aware guide or friend. Record your insights in your journal
and, if you have one, process them with your therapist.

The Light within the Shadow

When I was doing my internship to become a Marriage and Family Therapist (MFT), my clinical supervisor—imaginal, phenomenological, depth psychotherapist Anthony Guarnieri—shared with me a great definition of the
shadow. He said, "The shadow is all that is unlived." The shadow is not inherently bad or evil. It is not a black-and-white, either-or kind of thing. As well as
being a hiding place for guilt, shame, anger, and despair, the shadow is paradoxically a hiding place of great untapped power, potential, magic, creativity,
and healing-transformation.

The shadow is very much a trickster. As we suppress and repress our shadow
material, we keep at bay much more than our dislikes, discomfort, empathy,
and soul. We also inadvertently push away our very potential for growth,
change, healing, and Self-realization. We block ourselves from magic, and we
block ourselves from our personal magic. We don't really want to do this, but
this is often what happens. This is the trickster at work.

So long as we avoid the material within our unconscious, we deprive ourselves of the challenges and resources we need to become who and what we
are meant to become. We block our "fullest blossoming for the greatest good,"
as another teacher of mine, psychologist, shamanic healer, and ritual elder
Tom Pinkson, says. When we deny ourselves the experiences of confusion,
shame, guilt, lust, messiness, or whatever else, we deny ourselves the opportunity to find our courage, power, empathy, and compassion.

Luckily, the story doesn't end there. Because our magic, potential, and
growth are hidden within our shadow and shadow material, we have the great
opportunity to unleash these things as we feel into and explore the wyrd of
each of the domains and do our shadow work. As we explore and process the
disavowed and unseen contents of our shadow and drink deeply from the well
of psyche, we have the potential to integrate, heal, transform, and become.
We have the potential to become wyrd conscious, to realize the archetypal at
play within ourselves and our world. Wyrd conscious, we have the potential to

work in union with the trickster to awaken the revealing, healing, and transformative powers of the magical, brilliant, shapeshifting psychopomp, and
welcome the magical potential of our inner wyrd-wielder and, in so doing,
bring clarity to our gifts and purpose in this life.

Wyrding Ways
A Light in the Shadow

In this exercise, you will be engaging in shadow work through meditation, divination with the tarot or runes, and contemplation. Let
your psychopomp, whatever and whomever they may be (and you
needn't necessarily be clear on this), speak through the cards to tell
you something of that which lies hidden within your shadow—specifically in relationship to your hidden gifts, emerging potentials, and
soul-purpose. Listen deeply for the messenger's message.

You will need:

- A deck of tarot or oracle cards or a set of runes
- A candle set somewhere at eye level or lower
- A quiet and comfortable place to meditate (preferably in a dark
  room)
- A special incense or offering to the Well and your psychopomp
- Your journal

1. Sit down. Set the cards or runes in front of you. Ready your
   incense for burning, but do not light. Take a meditative posture
   with spine straight. Close your eyes. Take a few slow, deep belly-
   breaths in through your nose and out through your mouth.
   Return to your normal breathing pattern.

2. Imagine a thread reaching down from the Sun, into the crown
   of your head, down your spine, into your core. Draw and receive
   warm, loving solar energy through this thread. Do this for a minute as you fill your core with the Sun's light, love, and warmth.
   Now imagine a thread reaching up from the core of the Earth,
   into and through your spine, up into your core. Draw and receive
   grounding, loving growth energy up from the Earth, through the
   thread. Do this for a minute as you fill your heart-space with the

Earth's stability, solidness, love, and teachings. Feel the energy flow through the whole thread for a minute or so.

3. Imagine you sit at the Well of Wyrd. Take a moment to let it materialize before you. Using your mind's eye, gaze softly upon the water's surface, then gaze into its depths. Feel how deep it is, how immeasurable. Relax your core; feel the ambient energy or aura of the Well. Light the incense and present your offering to the Well. Imagine that within its dark depths, you begin to see a faint light emerge. The longer you gaze at this light, the bigger and brighter it gets. It moves closer, bigger, brighter. Feel the warmth of this light within your being.

4. Open your eyes and light the candle in front of you. You have brought the light into the world. Soften your gaze and focus on the flame. Try to maintain your focus and concentration on the flame for as long as you can. Each time you inadvertently look away, gently return your gaze to the flame. Notice the subtleties in the flame—the range of colors; the shape, size, movements; the light refracting from it and reaching into the surrounding dark.

5. Say something like, "Well of Wyrd and Light within, what would you like me to see? What would you like me to know? How can I glow and grow, ever more and more? What are my gifts, and what light am I meant to bring into and share with the world? What am I meant to express? How am I meant to be? Please accept my offerings as I open my mind-body-heart-soul to receive your wisdom."

6. Draw the card(s) or rune(s)—anywhere from one to three. As you gaze at each card, let its symbology soak into your mind-body. Acknowledge, "This is from my unconscious. These are my gifts that I must come to know more and more. This is what I am meant to bring into the world. This is my wyrd magic." Take time with each card until you somaticize each message. Feel it in your body. Cultivate the energy. Breathe in and out of it. Keep in mind that you may receive a message telling you what might be blocking your light.

7. At this point, you can do any number of things. You can sit with the card or rune longer and gaze at it, being mindful of every association, thought, memory, or vision that comes with it, or you can pick up a book and read about it. No matter what you do, do it in the spirit of receptivity and self-inquiry. You may also

ask yourself *how* you can bring these qualities or this way of being into the world. The more time you spend contemplating the card or rune, the clearer your wyrd will become. Use the card as a mirror, a reminder, and a motivator. This is your destiny!

8. When you are done, make your offerings and say, "I give thanks to you, deep Well of Psyche. Thank you for your guidance and blessings. I give thanks to the psychopomp, to my soul-guide. Thank you for bringing me this soul-wisdom" As you blow out the candle, take its light within you, feel the flame ignite within your heart or solar plexus. Take a few slow, deep breaths into this light. You are done. Carry this light and awareness into the world with you.

9. Write about your experience in your journal.

10. Optional: Process your experiences with your therapist.

Psychetherapy in Summary

Holistic healing is the hardest, but also the most rewarding healing you can do. To do it, you must explore the depths and expanses of every domain: mind-body-relationship-environment-soul-spirit. Psychetherapy is a tool that can help you attune to and explore the depths and expanses of the natural laws and mysteries of psyche. Psychetherapy is an integral facet of the process of crafting wyrd. The therapy for the soul that psychetherapy enables can take many forms, from traditional psychotherapy to archetypal therapy, to body-work, to divinatory practices, to mindfully taking psychedelic medicines. Whichever form it may take in your life, prepare yourself for an experiential process of revelation, healing-transformation, and becoming—and prepare for things to get weird.

As you practice your wyrdcraft, prepare yourself to look into and feel both the individual and the collective shadow. The shadow is one of our most powerful allies in our process of integration. There are unlimited amounts of creativity, power, and presence that lie latent and hidden within, waiting to be engaged, processed, and unleashed. It is imperative that we turn toward our shadow and do our shadow work—each one of us. That is, if we wish to heal and move toward a more just, peaceful, and meaningful existence together. Shadow work is difficult and dangerous, but with the right maps, awareness, education, courage, and compassion, as well as the guidance of trusted and skilled mentors, therapists, elders, and other ritual guides, it can be done. We can heal and transform—we can affect change to our destiny. I have seen it so many times. In many ways, our individual and collective fate and destiny waits to be revealed within the deep well that is psyche. Prepare yourself, bring offerings, and drink deeply from the Well. Do it as if your life depends on it.

Wyrding Ways
Healing the Web I

I would like to close this chapter with a healing exercise. You will be using meditation, guided imagery, and wyrd consciousness to send healing-energy through the Web to multiple beings in need of healing. By extension, you will also send healing-energy to the Web itself and to you yourself.

You will need:
- A place to meditate (a chair, seat, or meditation cushion)
- Incense (specifically chosen with the intention to send healing-love)

1. Take a seat and settle into a meditative posture—spine straight, relaxed yet alert. Close your eyes and take a few slow, deep belly-breaths in through your nose and out through your mouth. With each out-breath relax just a little bit more. Return to breathing naturally in and out through your nose.

2. Call to mind someone in need of healing. Hold their image in your mind's eye and heart for a few minutes. As you do, speak to them, speak to the image. Tell them you love them. As you say it, see if you can feel it. If you don't feel it right away, that's okay. Thank them for what they bring to your life: "Thank you for _____ (fill in the blank with multiple things)."

3. Imagine there is a thread that connects your heart to their heart. Feel into this thread and the flow of energy that moves in both directions through it. Send your love and healing-energy to this person from heart to heart through the thread. Imagine love and healing-energy coming back to you from them. Imagine the thread itself, healthy, glowing, flowing.

4. Repeat steps 2 and 3 with two or more people. The more the merrier. As you add people, add strings. Simultaneously hold all these strings in your awareness and send love and healing-energy through each of them. Feel the love and healing-energy return.

5. Now, imagine—one at a time—that there are threads reaching out from the heart of these people to other people (some you may know, others you may not). Imagine all the threads connecting everyone to each other. The more people you add, the more threads you will add, and the bigger the web will become. Imagine the grandeur and beauty of this web. Feel the life-energy, love, and healing-energy flowing through this web. Send love into it, offer your love to the flow, let it go. Feel it return.

6. Finally, light your incense and make your offering to the Web. As the smoke rises, send prayers with it. Send love and send blessings to every being within it, all connected by the threads of wyrd. Say, "May you be happy. May you be healthy. May you be safe. May you trust this process of becoming. May you be filled with the light, love, and awareness of Self, Soul, and Wyrd. May all Being be filled with the light, love, and awareness of Self, Soul, and Wyrd."

7. When you are done, take a few slow, deep belly-breaths and open your eyes. Try to carry this openhearted love and healing-energy with you throughout your day or evening. Carry it into every encounter.

Chapter 10
The Mysteries of the Tree:
Ecotherapy and Nature Worship

There are many cultures around the world, past and present, whose cosmologies describe the body of the multiverse to be that of a sacred tree. According to heathenry, this World-Tree, thought to be an oak, yew, or ash, is called Yggdrasil. Yggdrasil was, and remains, the cosmological fulcrum around which the heathen worldview revolves. Yggdrasil is the central soul-image and transpersonal being upon which, within which, and around which all beings live. It is the totality of existence—nine-worlds in one—immeasurably grand, deeply rooted, and expansive beyond comprehension. The word *Yggdrasil* translates to "Odin's stead or gallows." It is the tree that Odin rides as he traverses the multiverse, and the tree upon which he hangs in shamanic death-rebirth. Other names for Yggdrasil include Hoddmímis holt, Mímameiðr, and Læraðr.

According to Norse myth, there are several beings that live in and near the great Tree. Apart from the Norns, whom you will come to know more intimately in the next chapter, there's the chattering, screaming squirrel, Ratatöskr, who runs up and down Yggdrasil's trunk, delivering messages and insults back and forth between the all-seeing eagle who sits perched at the Tree's apex and the dragon, Níðhöggr, who lives under the ground, gnawing on the Tree's roots. There are also four stags who feed on the leaves of the Tree.

So sacred was this Tree that the Norns themselves took on the duties of caring for it. They soothe its bark with sacred mud and quench its thirst with sacred waters from the Well, all the while giving thanks for its being and blessings of wisdom and guidance. They offer their blood, sweat, and tears to the Tree, and the Tree gives shelter, sustenance, inspiration, and purpose in return. As a gift demands a gift, both were always giving.

At the base of the World-Tree, the Norns sit, sing, dance, and work entranced, day and night—listening, learning, carving, weaving, and protecting. There they commune with the Tree and learn its secret teachings of natural wisdom and natural magic. It is through this very communion that the Norns learned their magical arts. They were taught how to be by the Tree—and so, too, can we. This is a place of powerful magic, a place of deep healing and being. Even the gods know this, for it is there where they gather in times of strife to sit in communion and council with the Well, the Tree, and the Three.

Wyrding Ways
Communing with the Wyrd Tree

In this exercise, you will commune with the World-Tree—the body of the multiverse—through meditation, grounding, and guided imagery. This is an exercise you could include in your daily spiritual practice. If possible, practice in a forest in the presence of a special, sacred tree.

You will need:
- Fifteen to sixty minutes (or more) of undisturbed time-space
- A meditation cushion or chair
- Incense and an offering specifically chosen for the Tree
- Your journal

1. Stand or sit in a meditative posture with spine upright, chest, solar plexus, and belly open and relaxed—like the trunk of a tree. Close your eyes; take three slow, deep belly-breaths in through the nose and out through the mouth. Bring your awareness to your body as whole. Feel into the presence of your being in the present moment as you return to breathing naturally, in and out through your nose.

2. Focus your awareness within your center (your heart-space or solar plexus). Breathe into this space. As you do, feel the energy present there. Imagine you are breathing even more energy into this space. Do this for at least a few minutes.

3. Imagine there is a spinning spindle of energetic raw material in your core. From this spindle of prima materia, draw a thread up your spine and out the crown of your head. Pull it all the way up to the Sun and weave it into its core. Feel the energy of the Sun flow down the thread into your core. Then, from the spindle at your core, pull a thread of prima materia down your spine into the Earth, down, down, down until it reaches the Earth's core. Weave it into the Earth's core; feel the energy from the core flow through the thread up into your core. Now imagine the thread in its entirety, reaching all the way from the core of the Earth, through the core of you, to the core of the Sun. Feel the energy circulating up and down this thread.

4. Now, imagine this thread transforms into a pillar—a great, cosmic pillar. This is Irmunsil—the Anglo-Saxon World-Axis. Become the pillar. Meditate in this state—as World-Axis—for five minutes (or longer, if you'd like).

5. Now imagine the pillar grows roots at its bottom and branches at its top. They are many, strong and far-reaching. Imagine the roots reaching deeply into the mystery, pulling life-energy, magical energy, and soul into the trunk, strengthening it. Imagine the branches of the great Tree, reaching far into the expansive mystery of space, soaking in life-energy, magical energy, pulling light into your being, down your trunk, into your roots. Now imagine the Tree in its totality. This is the World-Tree, Yggdrasil. Be the Tree. Feel the energy circulating through you. Sit in this state of relaxed, rooted, strong, flexible, expansive presence for anywhere from ten to thirty minutes (or more). Just Being, giving and receiving all at once. Allow whatever images, thoughts, emotions, or body sensations to pass through you like clouds in the sky.

6. Before you finish, light the incense and make your offering to the Tree. Say, "Thank you, Great Tree, for this opportunity to sit with you. Thank you for your being. Thank you for your breath, your shelter, your wisdom, and your magic—thank you for all your gifts. I will return another time. Until then, blessed be." When

you are done, take a few deep breaths, open your eyes, wiggle your toes and fingers, stand up, shake your body, and carry the energy you accumulated during your communion with the Tree as you go about the rest of your day and night.

7. Write about your experience in your journal.

Ecotherapy or Nature Worship?

As a pagan and a licensed psychotherapist, I have a foot in two different worlds—the world of soul and the world of science, the world of magic and the world of psychology. Each of these worlds is vast, and each has its own associated paradigm and vocabulary. There are pagan terms and ways of understanding psyche, and there are psychological terms and ways of understanding psyche. I have done my best to bridge this gap between these worlds, but sometimes this is not easy.

If you happen to be a pagan, a heathen, a native, or an indigenous person, you might find the practice of ecotherapy I describe here sounds familiar. I acknowledge that it may be strange, to say the least, to hear your way of life compared to an evidence-based healing modality. When I use the term *ecotherapy*, my intention is not to erase or dishonor the indigenous and pagan roots, trunk, and branches through which the field of ecopsychology eventually came to fruition. My intention is not to replace the old ways with the new. If anything, it is to honor both.

Ecotherapy is just another vehicle for helping people remember the timeless yet largely forgotten reality that everything is One, that separation is an illusion, and that unconscious adherence to this illusion is the primary cause of most, if not all, of the unnecessary suffering we experience in the world. The underlying and overarching goal of ecotherapy, therefore, is one of transpersonal, relational healing through remembering and re-membering, of bringing one back into the sacred knowing of our interconnection and interdependence with each other, nature, and the divine. This holistic healing happens naturally as one engages in the wyrding ways of ecotherapy.

In short, ecotherapy is nature worship. Both ecotherapy and nature worship lead the practitioner back into contact with nature, and thus, back into relationship with Nature—with natural laws, natural truths, natural wisdom, and natural healing. Ecotherapy is therapy that takes place in the forest, in the desert, in the garden, by the water, under the sun, stars, and moon, in direct connection with the elements and the soul of the Earth. It can be practiced solo, one-on-one, or in small to large groups with or without a trained therapist or guide. Though I do recommend an elder, guide, or licensed therapist when it comes to doing any soul-oriented psychospiritual depth-work.

Ecotherapy, or nature worship, can take many forms:

- *Wilderness rites of passage:* These rites differ from culture to culture and landscape to landscape. They all contain some sort of ordeal that must be endured or overcome, such as fasting, sleep deprivation, or other physical and psychological obstacles. A rite of passage usually marks a transition from one stage of life to the next.

- *Forest bathing:* Forest bathing (shinrin-yoku) is a practice that originated in Japan. Forest bathing entails a systematic and organic opening of the senses and cultivation of mindfulness while sitting, standing, lying, or walking very slowly through the forest. Scientific studies suggest forest bathing benefits one psychologically, physically, and spiritually.

- *Mindful exercise:* Hiking, trail running, swimming, walking, yoga, martial arts, or any other outdoor-based exercise all help reintegrate the human body-mind, Earth body-mind connection. Nature-centered exercise is a tried-and-true way to facilitate physical-mental-spiritual balance and well-being.

- *Herbalism:* The practice of learning the medicinal and psychotropic qualities and capabilities of plants and utilizing their essence for the means of healing-transformation. Herbalists are perhaps the world's oldest doctors.

- *Protecting and tending the land:* This is perhaps the most important and most forgotten form of ecotherapeutic healing—direct action. This type of ecotherapy leads to both short- and long-term healing. We are the earth, so as you protect and tend the earth, you protect and tend yourself and all others. To tend and protect is to make sacrifices of time, money, blood, sweat, and tears and uphold the sacred reciprocity of the gift-cycle. Whatever you tend and protect will share its being, wisdom, and gifts with you.

- *Learning ancestral skills:* The ability to start a fire, build a shelter, make clothing, and procure food and water using only the tools and materials of the natural world. The process of learning how to survive in the wilderness with the assistance of nature alone is one of the quickest and most engaging ways you can reconnect with the soul of the Earth.

- *Grief-work:* The Earth and everything on it, around it, and in it is suffering. Its people, flora, fauna, and ecosystems are slowly being poisoned; the web is fragmenting. Much of this destruction is natural and inescapable, yet much of it is also transmutable. Grief-work promotes transmutation. It honors the suffering, the damage done, the unconsciousness and ignorance of it all, and the fear and pain that touch all—some much more violently and traumatically than others. As one grieves, one drops deeper and deeper into soul, which enables the emergence of empathy, compassion, love, healing, and action.

- *Ritual:* Ritual can take a myriad of ecotherapeutic forms: gardening, taking plant medicines ceremonially, working with the elements and deities of nature, seasonal rituals, and so on. These are just a few ways to ritualize along with nature and commune with her/his/their/its soul.

- Other ecotherapeutic activities include making natural art; studying the flora, fauna, and geology of place; learning from indigenous elders; gardening; tending a houseplant; and so on.

Ecotherapy—nature worship—is inherently healing on many levels. Scientific studies have shown that ecotherapy lowers stress, boosts immune system functioning, and improves mental performance, mood, and creativity. In addition, it has been shown time and time again to offer solace, insight, and even life-changing, peak spiritual experiences.[36] Ecotherapy also generates a love for nature, called biophilia, which motivates people to become stewards and activists for nature.[37] None of this should be surprising. In fact, the fact

36. Marco Mencagli and Marco Nieri, *The Secret Therapy of Trees: Harness the Healing Energy of Forest Bathing and Natural Landscapes* (Emmaus, PA: Rodale Books, 2019).
37. Richard Louv, *Last Child in the Woods: Saving Our Children from Nature-Deficit Disorder* (Chapel Hill, NC: Algonquin Books, 2009), 149–158.

that human beings have come to the point where we need scientific studies to prove that nature is healing, and needs healing, highlights just how separated from the natural world we in the so-called modernized world have become.

On the other hand, it also makes sense why we need these studies and use these terms considering how many, and how long, humans have distanced themselves from the natural world. How many people across the globe are growing up glued to screens? How many people have forgotten that they themselves are one in the same as nature, and that their health and well-being rest in balance with the health and well-being of the natural world? Far too many. Simply put, spending quality time in nature is healing, as it is taking time to remember our deeply inherent connection and unity with the natural world and the Nature of cosmos.

Wyrding Ways
The Ancient Practice of Tree-Hugging

Here is an example of ecotherapy. In this exercise, you will be practicing one of the oldest and simplest forms of ecotherapeutic nature worship: tree-hugging. Before you roll your eyes, know that there is a lot more to tree-hugging than meets the eye. This exercise can be done outside in any kind of weather. Be mindful. Though it is very rare, people have been injured or killed by falling branches and trees. Choose your spot wisely, be aware, relax, and trust in the process.

You will need:

- Anywhere from ten to thirty or more minutes of uninterrupted time-space for meditation

1. Find a tree. Try to choose a special tree for this exercise—one you are especially drawn to. Maybe it is an exceptionally large or majestic tree; maybe it is small and beautiful. It could be its presence that draws you in, or perhaps you have a personal history and connection. As always, when venturing into the wild, watch out for ticks and poison oak or ivy. If inside, imagine!

2. As you walk toward the tree, take in its size, color, texture, and general presence. Look at the landscape around it. Approach the tree slowly and intentionally. Keep an eye out for any insects

or animals. Be mindful not to damage them or their habitat. As always, do your best to do least harm. Embrace the tree. Give the tree a good, solid hug, and get comfortable; you will be hugging the tree for anywhere from ten to thirty minutes or more. Give the tree a full-body hug. Feel the contact on your cheek, chest, arms, belly, and legs. As you settle into the hug, pay particular attention to the contact between your heart-space and the trunk of the tree. There is an invisible thread that connects you—heart-to-heart.

3. For a couple of minutes, invoke love into your mind-body heart-space. Call to mind people you love—living or deceased. Call to mind things you love and loving experiences you've had. After you can feel the love growing and accumulating in your heart-space, start sending it into the tree through the heart-thread that connects you. Feel the love flow from your heart into the trunk, roots, branches, and leaves of the tree.

4. Say something to the effect of, "I love you! Thank you for your being. Thank you for everything you and your relatives give and have given me throughout my life! Thank you for your breath, for the oxygen I breathe right now, that which you offer so freely. Thank you for your body, for your protection, shade, and shelter. It is obvious you love me! Thank you for your love. Thank you for the objects and tools made from your body—from your lumber—that improve my well-being. Thank you for the warmth of your sacrificial body—for your firewood. Thank you for your many fruits, seeds, and medicines that keep so many healthy and alive. Thank you for teaching me about giving and receiving—for helping me remember sacred reciprocity. And thank you for teaching me how to stay grounded, steadfast, flexible, expansive, equanimous, trusting, and loving. Thank you for your imperfect perfection, thank you for your teachings, your offerings, and your abiding love. For all of this, I love you. I love you. I love you! Thank you!"

5. Imagine you hug the World-Tree itself. Send love and gratitude and wonder into this great mystery of a Tree. Merge with the Tree. Stay in communion like this, feeling the circular flow of loving, healing-energy for as long as possible. Sending and receiving. Feel free to shift around the tree as necessary. Feel the tree move in the wind. Listen to the creaks, whooshes, and bumps. Listen to the landscape around the tree. Let the tree teach you

about its being—still, equanimous, trusting—and the forest in which it is but a thread. Let it reveal to you its natural magic.

6. When you feel as if your communion is coming to an end, see if you can stay a little longer. Send a little bit more love and gratitude from your heart to the tree's heart. Give the tree a final squeeze and a kiss. Kiss it like you would kiss anything or anyone you deeply love, and who deeply loves you in return. End the hug, step back from the tree, and give it a heartfelt, deep bow of thanks, saying, "Until next time, so long, and be well, friend."

7. Bring this awareness and energy you have cultivated into the world as you go. See if you can retain the embodied teachings of the tree throughout your day.

Natural Healing

Nature is humanity's first and last teacher. We have learned everything from her many faces and facets (gender nature as you will: her, him, them, it). One thing nature teaches that often gets overlooked is that nature is self-healing. The is the way and wyrd of nature. Nature doesn't need to be taught how to heal; he/she/they/it just heals. As you attune to and commune with Nature, you will learn how to heal like Nature.

Healing comes naturally to life. When the skin sustains a cut, or when a bone is broken, the body heals itself. You don't need to teach the body how to heal; though there are ways to facilitate or speed up the process, healing just happens naturally. If you break your ankle and don't give yourself ample time-space-attention to heal, but rather continue to walk on it, it will take longer to heal and could even heal incorrectly. In the medical field, this is called a malunion or a nonunion (when a break never heals). In either case, improper healing could lead to a ripple effect of symptoms that could eventually move through the entire system. Due to prolonged or inadequate compensation for the injury, you could develop other problems; a slight but persistent change in your gait could lead to knee problems, hip problems, and back problems, as well as emotional and psychological problems as a result of dealing with chronic pain and lifestyle changes. Eventually, these psychological symptoms, which originated from a broken ankle, could end up impacting your relationships as well as your surroundings. The world could lose its sunny luster, and you could be more prone to mistreating it. The ripples will continue outward and onward from there.

It's not only our bodies that sustain injuries and need healing, but also our minds. If you experience a psychological or emotional wound or break, you need to give yourself unhindered time-space-attention to heal. If you don't, if you try to rush your healing process, your psyche will likely experience a malunion, or nonunion. Just like a bodily injury, if the injury isn't properly addressed and healed, other symptoms will manifest. Psychologically speaking, an unprocessed or unhealed trauma could lead to other symptoms: PTSD, anxiety, depression, addiction, and so on. If unaddressed, these symptoms will ripple out into the other domains.

Our systems move fast and require us to move fast. Unfortunately, because of this, we are not given the necessary time-space-resources to heal—physically, mentally, psychologically, relationally, ecologically, or spiritually. This is bad for everybody and for all domains as it perpetuates harm through the entirety of the Web. If we can't, don't, or aren't allowed to slow down—psychologically or physically—we won't be able to get to the roots of our wounds, and we will never fully heal. We will go on perpetuating injury without being aware we are doing so. We need to *take* the time to heal. We need to set boundaries, reclaim our agency to heal, and take back our health and healing from all the entities that hinder it. We need to slow down until we are still and silent enough that we can feel our way into healing.

Anything that makes this process more difficult than it needs to be needs to be acknowledged and transformed. Healing life-energy and natural magic needs to flow. Whether it is our own identities and ideologies, or our unskillful ways of relating to each other, or the unskillful ways our governments govern, if it blocks the spread of life-energy, love, and healing, it needs to be transformed. No longer can we afford to enable the self-destructive paradigms, worldviews, and actions that privilege existential competition and wounding over existential cooperation and healing.

Wyrding Ways
Opening the Doors of Perception to Natural Healing

Ecotherapy helps one learn how to slow down and attune to the healing powers inherent in the natural world. This wyrding way is similar to chapter 4's Mindfulness of the Senses exercise; however, this time you be doing it within the natural world. Additionally, you will be intentionally attuning to and accessing nature's inherent healing powers. Before you go into the wild, go prepared. Educate yourself about ticks, mosquitos, local fauna and flora, poison oak or ivy; bring water and a healthy snack; be mindful of the weather; and try not to get lost or damage anything in your path. The aim is to go into nature, be with nature, and do least harm. The farther you can get from distractions and the deeper into the wilderness you can go, the better. If you cannot go into nature, bring nature to you. You can do this wyrding with a houseplant, or even within your mythic imagination.

You will need:

- Thirty minutes to three hours of time-space
- Access to a natural space (a park, garden, nature preserve, wilderness) or a plant or tree
- A blanket, meditation cushion, or camping chair (if you don't have any of these things, you can sit on a rock, a stump, or the ground)
- An offering to give to Nature (water, an apple, some nuts and berries, natural decomposable art, etc.)

1. Find a spot to sit, stand, or lie down. If you are in the wild, watch out for ticks and poison oak or ivy. Take some moments to settle in. Turn off your phone and put it out of sight.

2. As you sit, bring your awareness to your natural breathing. Notice the felt sense of breathing—in and out, in and out. Take some minutes to do this. Give thanks to your breath and the air you breathe. Then bring your awareness to the felt sense of your body. Notice any aches or pains. Get as comfortable as you can. If you need to get up and stretch a little before you continue, go for it. Give thanks to your body. Relax your body.

3. Open your senses to the natural world. Spend about three to five minutes (or longer) on each sense.

   – **Sound:** Close your eyes and listen to nature. Pay attention to all the noises around you, near and far. Be mindful of the coming and going of each noise and the unique qualities of each sound—the volume, duration, timbre, melody, tempo. Take in the stillness between the sounds. Each audial experience is a thread. Together, all the sounds weave to create a tapestry of sound. Imagine the thread of each sound as well as the tapestry as a whole. Give thanks to your ears and to all you hear. If you can't hear, be in the stillness and silence, open.

   – **Sight:** Open your eyes to nature. Pay attention to everything you see. Notice as many details as you can. The different shapes, sizes, and colors; the different movements; the different parts, the larger whole, the shadows, and the lights. Notice all the different flora, fauna, and insects. If you can't see, imagine what you might see—"see" with your other senses. Each thing you see is a thread. All together, they create the greater weave of the tapestry of life. Give thanks to your eyes, to sight, and to that which you see. If you can't see, give thanks to your *in*-sight.

   – **Touch:** Reach out to nature and touch something near— a tree, a plant, the ground, a stone. Feel the shape, texture, temperature, weight, thickness, and fragility of each thing. If it is big, test your weight against it, push it, pull it, hug it. If it is small, gently hold it in your hand. Caress it and squeeze it between your fingers—be careful not to damage it or yourself. Touch your body. Feel the elements on your skin—the wind, the rain, the warmth of the sun. Soak in the feel of everything you touch, everything that touches you. Experiment with your eyes open and closed. Each felt perception is a thread woven together into the greater tapestry. Give thanks to your sense of touch. Give thanks to all you touch. If you are unable to move, feel what you can. Feel the presence of your body-mind. Feel the light, the moisture in the air.

   – **Smell:** With eyes open and with eyes closed, take in the bouquet of smells in this natural environment. What do you smell? Grass, dirt, mud, detritus, the warmth of the sun?

Open your eyes; take a closer smell. Smell the tree, plant, flower, grass, scat, dead animal. Explore the smell of many different things around you. Try not to avoid any smells. Each smell is a thread woven into a larger tapestry that is the entirety of smell. Give thanks to your sense of smell; give thanks to that which arises as you smell, as well as to that which you smell. If you can't smell, meditate on the absence of smell.

- *Taste:* Taste your environment. Be careful of what you taste and what you ingest. Some things in nature are poisonous to humans. Try things you know to be safe—a wild raspberry, a dry leaf on the ground, some grains of sand, a blade of grass. You need not swallow. Simply touch the thing to your tongue. Savor the flavors of nature. Bring out the snack you brought with you. Eat very, very slowly and mindfully. Play with the snack in your mouth. Pay attention to the complexity of the taste. Taste with the tip of your tongue, the sides, the back. What flavors and textures do you notice? Each taste perception is a thread that makes up a larger weave of the tapestry of tasting. Give thanks to the experience of tasting and to all you taste.

- Now, open all your senses together at once. For as long as you can. Just Be. Give thanks for Being.

4. Close your eyes. It is time to passively receive and actively draw in the healing power of the natural world. With each in-breath—slow, calm, and deep—draw in the color, sound, touch, smell, taste of nature. Draw in nature's aliveness—feel it within you. With each out-breath, send the aliveness of life-energy back into the world around you. Feel the life-energy circulating between you and your surroundings. Feel it circulating within your body-mind, flowing through all your cells. Feel it circulating within nature's body-mind—through the Web. Guide the energy to any areas of your body-mind that may be injured or sick. Breathe into these areas and imagine the life-force, creativity, warmth, health, and well-being permeating these areas. Soak the energy in. Let life-energy vibrate within you. Let it move how and where it wants to move. Send healing life-energy out into the Web where you sense it is needed, to the places that need healing. Let nature's intelligent, healing life-energy flow how and where it wants to flow.

5. When you feel you are done, take a few slow, deep belly-breaths in through your nose and out through your mouth. Send gratitude to your body-mind and to the body-mind of nature. Thank nature for the healing-energy and for the experience you just had. Make your offerings to the Web. When you are ready, stand up, and carry this relaxed and powerful energy and feeling state with you as you go about your day and evening.

Natural Magic and Ecological Awareness

In the last chapter, I described the process of psychetherapy as a form of magic—a process through which the revelation and healing-transformation of the blocks and wounds within psyche facilitate the emergence of soul-magic into the world. Ecotherapy, too, facilitates the same process. Ecotherapy, too, is soul-magic.

Largely disconnected from nature, many human beings have largely, though not completely, hindered their potential to access the healing powers of soul and natural magic that permeate nature—and thus, permeate us. We have lost touch with our roots and, as a result, lost our ecological consciousness. Ecological consciousness is—along with Web consciousness, soul consciousness and magical consciousness—a facet of wyrd consciousness. Far too many physical and psychological walls have been erected both around and within humanity that have kept nature, soul, and magic out for far too long. Ecotherapy or nature worship aims to correct this by opening locked doors, closed windows, and blocked arches in these walls so that nature can come on in and we can go out more freely, returning the organic cyclical flow of life-energy to the larger system that is the Web.

Through the ecotherapeutic activation of ecological consciousness—and the wyrdcraftian activation of wyrd consciousness—you can illuminate the Web, its natural laws and natural flow. Within the Web, threads connect the Sun, the Moon, the Earth, the elements, all ecosystems, you, and the divine together. Through these threads flow life-energy, soul, and consciousness, and along with it, healing-energy and magical energy. Ecotherapy works to reveal and heal these threads, thus encouraging the healthy flow of life-energy and healing-magic throughout all domains of the Web. This is not merely an intellectual exercise, but a lived, felt experience. Ultimately, this illumination will lead to what the Anglo-Saxons referred to as *hæl*, what the ancient Norse referred to as *heill,* and what the ancient Greek referred to as *eudaimonia*—holistic health and well-being.[38]

Ecotherapy—and nature worship in general—helps one cultivate eco-logical/Web/wyrd consciousness by teaching one how to attune, how to be aware, feel deeply, and uphold sacred reciprocity with Nature. The more you do these things in tandem, the more you will open channels through which healing-magic can return to its natural organic flow within the transpersonal Web. Watch and *be* as the false separations between inside and outside, self and other, above and below are exposed for what they are—illusions that only serve to get in the way of hæl, frith, and eudaimonia. The more you can let nature in, and the more you can go into nature, the more you will feel into the presence of natural magic that already permeates all. This awareness will return like a memory, long repressed and forgotten. With each returning memory, you will feel more whole, at home, in presence, and on purpose; hæl, frith, and eudaimonia will flow into your life. Let us remember together and let us heal together.

Wyrding Ways
Being in Stillness and Silence in Nature

All the wyrding ways in this book will help you cultivate ecological/Web/wyrd consciousness, hæl, frith, and eudaimonia, though perhaps one of the most effective ways of them all is this one I will describe now. In this exercise, you will learn how to be still and silent—through meditation, guided imagery, and movement—which will enable you to become a clearer channel through which healing, magical life-energy may flow more freely.

You will need:
- Anywhere from thirty minutes to several hours of uninterrupted time in nature
- A natural compostable offering (seeds, nuts, raisins, apple)
- Optional: A cushion, camping chair, or blanket

---

38. Cat Heath, *Elves, Witches & Gods: Spinning Old Heathen Magic in the Modern Day* (Woodbury, MN: Llewellyn Publications, 2021), 90–91.

- Optional: Water and snacks
- Note: As with other exercises that involve going into nature, edu-cate yourself about ticks and other wildlife, as well as any poison oak, ivy, or sumac in your area. Prepare for the time of day and the weather, wear clothes fit for the season, put on some sun-block, and bring a map, flashlight, lighter, water, and snack if you plan on going far.

1. Find a secluded natural spot where you will be undisturbed. (Though it is true that the wilder and more secluded the spot the better, you can also do this exercise in a park, with a houseplant, or in the inner wilderness of your personal psyche.)

2. When you find your spot, stand still, take a few deep breaths, and turn around slowly in place as you take in the environment that will be your home for the next thirty minutes to several hours. Then either remain standing or take a seat (on your cush-ion or blanket, or on a stump, a stone, or the ground). Take a moment to get comfortable and adopt a meditative posture—spine upright, straight, relaxed, alert. Close your eyes and take a few slow, deep belly-breaths in through your nose and out through your mouth. With each out-breath, relax just a little bit more. Return to your natural breathing pattern.

3. Imagine there is a spinning spindle of energetic raw material in your core. From this spindle of prima materia, draw a thread up your spine and out the crown of your head. Pull it all the way up to the Sun and weave it into its core. Feel the energy of the Sun flow down the thread into your core. Then, from the spindle at your core, pull a thread of prima materia down your spine into the Earth. Weave it into the Earth's core. Feel the energy from the Earth's core flow through the thread up into your core. Now imagine the thread in its entirety, reaching all the way from the core of the Earth, through the core of you, to the core of the Sun. Feel the energy circulating up and down this thread.

4. Allow your awareness to settle into your presence as a whole, living being. Keep your senses open, your body relaxed yet alert. You will notice the emergence of many thoughts, memories, and fantasies as you do this. Every time you become aware of a thought or realize you are lost in thought, return to being in presence. Open your senses, take a slow, deep breath, and be

still and silent. Relax your body, especially your face muscles, chest, diaphragm, and belly. Just be.

5. This experiment is an exercise in sensation, intuition, trust, patience, and boredom. Nothing is *supposed* to happen. Just do your best to stay still, silent, and open for as long as possible. Even if the world is very un-still and un-silent around you, be very mindful of what comes through the stillness and silence that permeates everything. At any point if you wish to move, do so very slowly, silently, and mindfully. The goal is to create as few ripples in space-time-consciousness as possible. In your presence, you may feel a flow. This flow may draw you into movement—go with it. Let nature's flowing flow through you and move you—move like the wind, water, fire, and earth. You will create less ripples if you flow *with* nature. Don't worry about how it looks—your worry will cause ripples. As weird as it may look to some, be a natural channel. This is a good thing, and it matters not what others think. After your movement is finished, return to stillness and silence.

6. When you feel your open meditation in stillness and silence has come to an end, take a few slow, deep breaths in through your nose and out through your mouth. Slowly stand up and look around at all that surrounds you. Soak it in, breathe it in. Give thanks to the experience, to Nature, saying something like, "Thank you, Nature, for this opportunity to experience Being. Thank you for everything you give me—all the food, water, inspiration, healing-magic, and soul. Thank you for life, awareness, and being."

7. Make your offering to Nature. Stand, slowly and deeply bow, and mindfully walk away. Go about the rest of your day doing your best to remain alert, open, and attentive to the stillness and silence permeating everything.

This simple—yet not always very easy—practice will help you cultivate ecological awareness, which will in turn help you invite soul, magic, and healing into your mind-body-relationship-environment-soul-spirit. The more awareness you can bring to the braid that connects you with nature, the more you open the channel between your psyche and the psyche of nature, through which—like a live wire—life-energy, soul, and healing-magic will flow. Go with the flow.

Elemental Healing

The elements of air, fire, water, and earth are powerful allies on our individual and collective path to revelation, healing-transformation, and becoming. Spending extended amounts of time in the natural world in direct relationship with the elements is powerful because it puts one in touch with the healing powers and divinity inherent within the natural world, which are also inherent within all of us, as we are one and the same as the natural world. Though it is easy to forget, *you are nature*. This is something you will remember more and more as you attune to Nature, as you commune with the elements of air, fire, water, and earth. The elements are like threads that connect inner and outer, self and other, self and nature. Like the archetypes, they are bridges between the worlds.

One of the best ways to remember this is to get as still and as silent as you can for as long as you can in the wilderness. This is the way of deep attunement. The more you practice this, the more you will tap into the elemental healing powers of Nature. The elements will teach you as you attune and commune. Air, for example, can breathe new life into stagnant places and bring new ideas, new ways, and newfound hope into being. Fire can bring warmth, light, and transformation when and where you need it, and courage and faith to let go of that which no longer serves you. Water can remind you to relax, to go deep, and teach you how to go with the flow as you navigate the depths of soul. Earth can remind you of the necessity for grounding, stillness, solidity, and connect you with the wisdom of ancestors and other guides. Altogether, the elements give you access to powerful generative and healing magic.

Wyrding Ways
Elemental Healing Meditation

Here is an example of a more active form of ecotherapy and healing-magic that works directly with the elements. The aim of this exercise is to go into nature, be with nature, and open to nature's healing-teachings and energies through the elements. The farther you can get from distractions and the deeper into the wild you can go, the better—but again, you can also do this exercise by venturing deeply into the wilderness of your psyche, wherever you are. Before you begin your meditation, internally acknowledge that each element is a mystery and has the power to create and destroy. Remind yourself to remain mindful of the importance of maintaining healthy boundaries with the elements. In other words, don't let the wind, fire, water, or earth hurt you or kill you. And remember to uphold sacred reciprocity and the gift-cycle.

You will need:
- Thirty to ninety minutes of undisturbed time-space
- Access to a natural space (a park, garden, nature preserve, wilderness) or a plant or tree
- A blanket, meditation cushion, or camping chair (if you don't have any of these things, you can sit on a rock, a stump, or the ground)
- An offering to give to Nature (water, an apple, some nuts and berries, a decomposable artistic creation, etc.)
- Note: Go prepared. Educate yourself about ticks, mosquitos, local fauna and flora, poison oak or ivy; bring water and a healthy snack; be mindful of the weather; and try not to get lost or damage anything in your path.

1. Take some moments to settle in, turn off your phone, and put it out of sight. Bring your awareness to your breath as you breathe naturally. Notice the felt sense of breathing—in and out, in and out. Take a minute or two to do this.

2. Bring your awareness to the felt sense of your body. Notice any aches or pains. Get as comfortable as you can. If you need to stretch a little before you continue, take a few minutes to do this. Return to a sitting or standing meditative posture (alert and relaxed), put a hand on your heart and a hand on your belly, and breathe deeply. Give thanks to your body.

3. As you sit or stand, imagine a thread that reaches from the core of the Sun downward through the crown of your head, down through your spine, into the core of the Earth. Feel the energy moving downward from the Sun into your body, filling you with energy, light, love, and warmth. Breathe it in. Imagine it soaking into and permeating all your cells. Take your time. Do the same with the energy moving upward through the thread from the core of the Earth. Breathe it in. Imagine it soaking into and

permeating all your cells. Take your time. Feel the flow through the thread in its entirety. Then move on to the elements: air, fire, water, and earth.

- *Air:* Breathe mindfully. Notice the qualities of the air as you breathe it. How cool or warm it is, how dry or wet it is. This air you breathe is life. Without this substance, you would not be alive. Give thanks as you breathe slowly and deeply through your nose into your belly. Breathe out through your nose or mouth; try both. Imagine life-energy, or chi, permeating the air. Feel its living vibration all around you. Breathe this vibrancy in. Imagine it soaking into and permeating every cell within your body. With each breath, you draw in life-energy, healing-energy; you draw in loving, calm rejuvenation—hæl, heill, eudaimonia, frith. If you have an injury, draw the light, cleansing vibrancy of air into the wound. Picture the cells healing and healthy. Imagine you transform into the wind. Let your soul move like the wind—dance, play, fly. Give thanks.

- *Fire:* The element of fire can be most easily accessed while communing with the Sun, a candle, or a campfire. As you sit under the Sun or before a fire, feel its light and warmth on your skin. Imagine the fierce power within fire's core. There would be no Earth and no light or life without the Sun. Give thanks to the Sun for your life, for all life. As you sit in the warmth and light of the Sun, allow the vibrancy of light-energy and life-energy to soak into and permeate your body. This energy is revealing, warming, enlightening, and reassuring. If you have an injury or mental block—physically or psychologically—draw the solar fire-energy into it. This fire destroys and creates simultaneously. Imagine the fire devouring all that is not serving your health and well-being and fueling everything that is. Imagine the fire healing your cells—filling each cell with hæl, eudaimonia, and frith. Spend some minutes collecting fire-energy in your solar plexus for later use. Imagine you transform into flame. Dance, play, burn, devour. Give thanks!

- *Water:* If you can find a place to sit next to or in a natural water source, great; if not, you can connect with water wherever you are. There is water in your body, in the air, and in the plants, animals, and soils around you. Water permeates life. Water is life. Give thanks. As you sit, bring your awareness to the water in your body and around you. Feel water's waves and flows. As you breathe in, imagine a wave coming in. As you breathe out, imagine a wave going out. Take a drink of water from your water bottle. Soak it in, feel the cool clear water quench your thirst, feel its powerful life-giving energy soak into your being, replenishing your cells. If you have an injury, send clear, cool, healing water-energy there. Feel the ripples, waves, and currents of life-energy flowing through your wounds, cleansing them of psychic bacteria. With each in-breath and out-breath, imagine water washing away what no longer serves you. Imagine it feeding everything that does serve you, quenching the seeds you want to grow. Feel the watery waves cleansing your mind-body-soul, bringing you hæl, eudaimonia, and frith. Imagine you transform into water. Let your soul move like water—dance—flow, whirl, undulate. Give thanks!

- *Earth:* Jump up and down, stomp, touch the Earth, touch the trees around you, push your weight against them. Sit down, make yourself comfortable, alert, and still. Breathe naturally. Bring awareness to your body and to the space your body occupies. Feel the force of gravity keeping you earthbound. Bring your attention to the points of contact between you and the Earth—your feet, butt, legs. Feel the elemental earth-energy all around you—in the soil, in the stones, in the plants, in matter, in every cell in your body. Generative earth-energy is alive, feeding, nourishing, growing. Imagine you are a plant, flower, tree, moss, or mountain. Become the rotting log. Let the decaying parts of you decay; let them add to the nutrient-dense soil, become this fecundity of the fertile void known as soil. Draw elemental earth upward into your growing, healing being. Feel the growth energy rise from the core of the earth, through your grounding thread and through the threads all around you. If you have an injury, send this life-energy there. Imagine the healthy growth and renewal of your cells—imbibe in hæl, eudaimonia, and frith. Become the green, healthy plant and blooming flower. Become the mountain. Sit. Eternally solid. Give thanks!

4. After spending time communing with each element, take a few slow, deep belly-breaths, make your offering to Nature, give thanks, and bow slowly and deeply in the spirit of gratitude. Carry this energy into the world with you as you go about your day. Offer hæl, eudaimonia, and frith to all you encounter.

The elements are teachers. The more you commune with them, the more they will teach you their mysteries. Each is a wellspring for natural wisdom, natural magic, and natural healing. Practice this exercise as often as you can. You can commune with the elements in the wilderness as well as in the city or at home. Get creative; there are many ways to access the elements. They weave through all domains.

Nature as Teacher: Spider Medicine

If you spend enough time in natural spaces, you will find nature is home to many teachers. The forests, oceans, and deserts are teeming with teachers and teachings. The magic of Raven, the dream of Dragonfly, the gentle presence of Deer, the stillness and equanimity of Mountain, the flowing purposefulness of River—these are just some of the lessons of nature's many teachers. These teachers—which take the form of archetypes, land-spirits, deities, and more— are both threads and doorways into the greater Web of Being. Each has their own teachings, or medicine, that leads the fragmented back to wholeness.

I use the term *medicine* as Native Americans and other indigenous peoples around the world have used it: as an honoring of nature's wisdom and healing powers; as a recognition that nature is a conduit for the healing-teachings of Higher Self, God, Goddess, Great Spirit, and so on; and as a form of guidance and medicine that can be applied to our inner and outer lives in any moment.

Though we have explored several of nature's teachings throughout this book—the elements, the Sun, the Tree, and several deities, just to name some—I would like to focus now on the medicine teachings of Spider. Spider is a powerful teacher of wyrd and ally for spiritual healing and emergence. We already learned something about Spider medicine in chapter 3 as we explored some of the world's animist cosmologies and myths—those of Thought Woman, Anansi, and Arachne, for example—but what about the spiritual medicine of actual living spiders? If we get quiet, still, and curious, what medicine will come through this eight-legged, many-eyed magician?

Creativity

One of the first things I notice about spiders is that they are prolific creators. Spiders spin their web from their own body and construct beautiful, intricate, ephemeral creations that mesmerize—especially when seen at dawn or dusk or when covered by dew. The spider's silk is multipurpose. Spiders use their silk to build webs, swath prey, fly, build shelters, and create egg sacs.[39] Those who identify or work with Spider are usually adept at some form(s) of creative art; great with their hands and bodies, they may be builders, crafters, writers, or dancers. Their creations, just like the spider's web, often draw others closer with their mesmerizing beauty, otherworldliness, and magnetism. Spider's creations often inspire others to create. Spider is a symbol of new technologies and inventions that have both creative and destructive capacities. Like any other archetype, spiders have a shadow side—spiders are venomous, after all. They stun, paralyze, and immobilize. They are highly evolved, masterful hunters and efficient killers. Spiders can be coldly calculative in their ways as they use their creations to ensnare and devour their enemy. Without awareness or empathy, shadow-spider can lead human beings down a very destructive path.

Persistence, Skill, and Efficiency

Spider also teaches us about persistence, dexterity, and hard work. Spider's webs, though remarkably strong for their size, are constantly being destroyed. Because of this, Spider must rebuild time and time again. Spiders work hard for their meals. Though some spiders leave damaged webs behind to build anew, others make repairs and even eat their damaged web so they can recycle it into a new one. The dexterity, balance, and skill they exhibit as they do the work of constructing and repairing their webs remind us to be mindful, to never give up, to not take ourselves or our creations too seriously, and to always strive to do our best.

If you've ever watched a spider build a web, you know that it takes time, skill, and a certain amount of luck to create and place a bountiful web. If the web isn't in a good spot, not many insects will get caught. If it is, Spider will

---

39. Larry Weber, *Spiders of the North Woods: A Handy Field Reference to Our Most Common Northern Spiders* (Duluth, MN: Kollath-Stensaas Publishing, 2003), 118–119.

never go hungry. Spider teaches us to be mindful of the timing and placement of our metaphorical webs. Context matters.

Spider is a role model of efficiency. Spiders work hard, but they also know how to rest and wait. They are masters of patience. Even after a spider finishes building their web, they spend a lot more time in stillness. As such, they are wonderful exemplars of self-care. Spiders don't sleep; rather, they slow their metabolic rate to rest and recuperate. They are smart and efficient with their energy expenditure. At the same time, spiders are decisive and incredibly quick to act when it is time. Even after going months without eating, spiders can dart into motion at the drop of a dime to catch their prey.

Consciousness Expansion, Empathy, and Psychic Abilities

Spiders have anywhere between zero to twelve eyes, some of which are on the side, top, or back of their heads. While some spiders can't see at all and primarily rely on touch and sensing vibrations, some spiders have nearly 360-degree vision. With so many eyes, Spider medicine teaches us about kaleidoscopic vision—how to see the bigger picture from many different angles at once.

Spider medicine teaches us about the expansion of consciousness. Scientists have found that spiders' awareness reaches outside of their body and into their web.[40] They are intimately attuned to their web and the world around them. Through the web, spiders can sense the vibrations of the world. The web is an extension of the spider's mind. Those with close Spider allyship find it all too easy to expand their consciousness beyond their physical body. As such, they are highly empathic, intuitive, and psychic beings, hypersensitive to the energetic vibrations of other minds, of other beings, and of the Web itself. Through this heightened empathic awareness of vibration, Spider is highly attuned to the underlying weblike structure of nature, consciousness, being, and existence.

---

40. Hilton F. Japyassú, Kevin N. Laland, "Extended Spider Cognition," *Animal Cognition* 20 (February 7, 2017): 375–395, https://doi.org/10.1007/s10071-017-1069-7.

Sacrifice, Ceremony, and Right Living

As spiders sit at the center of their web in wait, they remind us to stay centered, aware, and ready—within ourselves, within the world, and within the greater cosmic web. From this center, we can focus, meditate, and tune in to the Web, as well as to the spiral-process of creation-destruction-transformation. Like Snake, Spider is a medicine of transformation and sacrifice. Spider reminds us that we must molt our outer shell if we wish to continue growing. Spider shows us what we need to let die to become that which we are meant to become. An expert at the balancing act of give-and-take, Spider teaches—through their persistent web-building—that we must make sacrifices and go all in to receive that which we want and need. Spider keeps us on the balanced path by teaching us the ways of right living, contemplation, ceremony, and healing.

The ritualistic aspect of web-building is very much like the slow, contemplative walking of a fifteen-circuit labyrinth. If you ever find yourself at a walking labyrinth, use it as an opportunity to commune with Spider. Evoke and invoke Spider as you walk. Ask for Spider's guidance as you weave your contemplative web.

If you ever feel stuck, paralyzed by fear, stunned by circumstance, or immobilized by the sticky webs of your own trickster machinations, take some advice from Spider—get creative, keep learning, never give up, be patient, be efficient, meditate, rest, feel deeply, trust your intuition, look at it from a different angle, deepen and expand your consciousness, remember sacred reciprocity. Let Spider be your guide.

Wyrding Ways
Dancing Spider

In this exercise, you will have the opportunity to honor, celebrate, and embody the teachings of Spider through dance. This dance will be done without music, but feel free to try it with music as well. A prerequisite of this exercise is taking time to study Spider. Spend some time observing spiders in your home and outdoors in their natural habitats. Take some time to learn about your favorite or least favorite spiders online or in books. If you are unable to dance or move, dance in the theater of your mind.

Chapter 10

You will need:
- Around twenty or more minutes of undisturbed time to dance
- Space enough to move around (preferably outside or in front of your altar)
- Incense or another offering

1. This is an improvised dance that will begin sitting down. Begin by taking a meditative posture: spine straight, alert and relaxed. Take a few slow, deep, belly-breaths in through your nose and out through your mouth. With each out-breath, relax just a little bit more. Breathe naturally as you bring awareness to your body. Do a quick body scan starting with your feet and ending with the crown of your head. Take notice of any tension, aches, or pains, if you have any. Be mindful of these areas that ache as you dance.

2. Begin to conjure images of spiders and spider movements within your mind. Let all you have learned and observed loosely guide you, but try not to overthink it or force it. Feel into the mystery that is the being of Spider. Give up control and let Spider pull the strings, so to speak. Let Spider's medicine, energy, and being move your body, and see what comes through. Call in Spider's creativity, balance, patience, efficiency. How does Spider move through you? How does Spider dance, fly, weave? You can interpret Spider as you wish. Weave a web as you dance. Get creative. Improvise. Go with the flow. There is no right or wrong way to dance Spider. Have fun! Allow yourself to be weird.

Ecotherapy in Summary: Into the Wilderness

From a dualistic point of view, the wilderness within you and the wilderness outside and around you are two different things. From a nondualistic point of view, however, both inner and outer wilderness blend together into one vast, unknown, and weird web of wilderness—some of it is known, but most of it is unknown. You could call this wilderness psyche or soul. If this wilderness remains unexplored, you leave your wholeness hidden, your wounds unhealed, and your potentials blocked and unlived. The unconscious, fragmentative ripple effects from this will spread throughout every domain. There is reason for hopefulness, though. The more you go into the wilderness—the more you bring intentional, mindful time-space-awareness into the psyche as it can be found both within and without—the more you can reveal, heal, transform, and become whole. You can re-animate and re-enchant the Web. You can course-correct in alignment with your soul's natural becoming.

What we call the wilderness or psyche is a deep and expansive mysterious realm permeated by magic, medicine, and natural wisdom. The more you explore, the more you will reveal. There are some wild, weird, and timeless truths hidden in the threads that connect *in here* and *out there*. By practicing psychetherapy and ecotherapy—by practicing good old-fashioned nature worship—by getting as still and silent as you can for as long as you can, staying aware, taking care, and feeling deeply, you can reveal, heal, transform, and become the Web. What a process! What a gift! With the connections of the Web reforged and energized—with personal psyche realigned with the psyche of nature—you gain access to a very deep and ancient part of you, a fecund and enchanting wilderness in which a wellspring of natural magic and healing-magic will flow unhindered.

Let us wander onward now from our communion with the Tree to our communion with the Three. Let us venture into the realm of magic.

Chapter 11
The Mysteries of the Fates: Magic

Under the Tree of Wyrd, near the Well of Wyrd, sit the Wyrd Three—the Norns. Shrouded in mystery, each within their looks-within place, deeply entranced in communion with Wyrd, they wield the magic that allows them to lay down the fate of all beings and all worlds. So shrouded in mystery and liminality they are that not much is known about these primordial three—Urðr, Verðandi, and Skuld. Urðr is *fate*; she is the oldest. It is from her name that the Well of Wyrd, Urðrbrunnr, gets its name. Verðandi is the second; she is *becoming*—the power of emergence, great grandmother growth of the North. The third, Skuld, is the reckoner, *debt*. It is she who decides what sacrifices are owed by each being, and when and how each debt must be paid. Together, they are Fate.

Woven out of the enchanted fabric of mystery themselves, it is they, the Three who are One, who taught magic to those who taught those who taught those who taught *you*. As they exist somewhere beyond the gods and goddesses, the details of these fate-weaving beings are not mentioned with any clarity of vision, only their purpose—to care for the Tree, to decide the fates of all, and to guide the underlying mechanics and process of the multiverse. The fact that so little is known about them only speaks to their otherworldly weirdness. A weirdness you will only know if you heed the Fates' call—as you attune and commune with the Three.

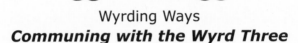

Wyrding Ways
Communing with the Wyrd Three

This is an introductory exercise for attuning and communing with the Wyrd Three—the Norns, the Fates—through meditation, centering, grounding, and guided imagery. Go slowly; the power of these primordial giantesses is beyond comprehension. The purpose of this communion is simply to offer loving devotion. They may talk with you; they may not. Go with an open mind-heart, see what you see, feel what you feel, know what you know.

You will need:

- Fifteen to sixty minutes (or more) of undisturbed time-space
- A meditation cushion or chair
- Incense specifically chosen to offer to the Three
- Your journal

1. Stand or sit in a meditative posture with spine upright, chest open, belly relaxed. Take three slow, deep belly-breaths in through your nose and out through your mouth. Relax just a little bit more with every out-breath. Return to your natural breathing pattern. Bring your awareness to your body as whole. Feel into the presence of your being in the present moment as you breathe.

2. Focus your awareness within your center, your core, your heart-space or solar plexus. Breathe into this space. As you do, feel the energy present there. Imagine that you are breathing energy into this space and filling it with light and energy. Do this for at least a few minutes.

3. Imagine there is a spinning spindle of energetic raw material in your core. From this spindle of prima materia, draw a thread up your spine, out the crown of your head. Pull it all the way up to the Sun and weave it into its core. Feel the energy of the Sun flow down the thread into your core. Then, again from the spindle, pull a thread of prima materia down your spine into the Earth. Weave it into the Earth's core. Feel the energy from the Earth's core flow through the thread up into your core. Now imagine the thread in its entirety, reaching all the way from the

core of the Earth, through the core of you, to the core of the Sun. Feel the energy circulating up and down through this thread.

4. As you sit or stand, feeling this energy circulating up and down through you, imagine you take the form of a massive tree—a World-Tree. Feel your roots and branches reach into the mystery below and mystery above, uniting the two into one mystery, one void. Become the Tree, be the Tree—breathing in and out, giving and receiving. As the Tree, you begin to sense a powerful presence somewhere near your base. This presence is deep, full of magic and mystery. It is the Well of Souls. For a minute or so, picture it there; feel it there, gently pulsating with energy and magical wisdom. Before too long, you begin to sense another presence, also near your base. This presence also feels intensely magical and mysterious and powerfully expansive. It dances, it flows, it weaves and knows; it is also still and silent and titan. The more you feel it, the clearer this presence becomes. It is one, but it is also three. Cloaked, sitting very still and silent, sit the Norns. Exuding magic, weavers of light and matter and love, they meditate, each within their looks-within place. Ask them no questions. Just sit before them; sit with them. Offer them your time-space-awareness. Offer them your gratitude, wonder, and deepest respect.

5. Light the incense you have chosen specially for them. Say, "I offer this incense to you, Wyrd Three. Please accept my enduring love and respect, please accept my wonder, my being. It is an honor to sit before you. Thank you for your magic, for your wisdom, for your healing-teachings. You teach me the ways of wyrd—the ways of magic. You teach me how to live my life in attunement with Wyrd. I ask nothing of you today except to sit in your presence and offer my devotion."

6. Sit, meditate, receive, soak in the energy and teachings they exude just by being. Remember to breathe, relax, and offer your love to the Wyrd Three. Stay receptive. They may have a message for you, they may not.

7. When you are done, say, "Thank you for allowing me to sit with you today. I will return another time, bearing gifts, and perhaps questions. Until then, blessed be, and thank you for your wisdom teachings!" Hold the gestalt of the image of the Three, the Tree, and the Well in your consciousness and being. It emanates

powerful, wild, cosmic energy and mystery through the threads that connect you and all—through the Web. Feel this energy and mystery in your core as you let the image drift away. When you are ready, open your eyes, stand up. With your hands in prayer mudra at your heart, slowly bow to the experience, to the moment. Take the residual energy into the world with you as you go about the rest of your day and night. Offer hæl, eudaimonia, and frith to everyone and everything you encounter.

8. Write about your experience in your journal.

Strange Magical Mysticism

Magic is the third string in the braid of the wyrdcraftian-triad. The essence of magic cannot be encapsulated in a sentence, a paragraph, a chapter, a book, or even in a collection of books. Magic is a bottomless ocean, an endless sky. Magic is mystery, and like all mysteries, it eludes definitive explanation and understanding. I don't see this as a problem in the least. In fact, I think it's a great thing, for it is the mystery of magic that draws one deeper into its currents and workings, pushing and pulling one toward magical becoming.

Magic is simultaneously a noun, adjective and verb, a thing, quality, and process, as well as a presence, feeling, and happening that—even though it may not always be seen, felt, or understood—is nevertheless always present within, through, and beyond both spiritual and mundane existence. Basically, magic permeates everything; magic is everywhere, just like psyche, soul, and wyrd are everywhere.

Wyrdcraft, like any other magical path, teaches the practitioner to "locate" magic. To locate something is to sense it, see it, feel it, attune to it, come to know its ways and names. I dare say that locating magic is both easier and harder than it seems, as magic, like anything else that is deeply meaningful and purposeful, is deeply paradoxical.

I like to think of magic as a divine being far stranger and more incomprehensible in its totality than can be imagined. Sure, we can come to know this *being* or *thing* or *force* called magic in many ways through many guises—as Cerridwen, Oya, Itzam-Ye, and others—however, its deepest and most expansive essence cannot be fully *known* until we *become* it. In other words, magic cannot be fully known until we experience ourselves *as it* and until *it* experiences itself through us and as us. This is magical mysticism.

Take a moment to ponder the Sufi mystic Rumi's famous words: "What you seek is seeking you." One could argue that Rumi was not referring to magic, but rather, to the Beloved, nameless, divine essence. I would argue that they are one in the same—the Beloved *is* Magic. The Magic you seek is also seeking you. This means that as you practice magic—i.e., as you live and cultivate magical consciousness—you are not only coming to know yourself and the nature of reality, but also coming to know Magic, and at the same time, Magic is coming to know not only you, but it is coming to know itself and the world *through you* and *as you*. In other words, Magic is wyrding its way into Self-realization through form, through you, and you are wyrding your way into Self-realization through Magic, simultaneously. What could be weirder than that?

How many times have you heard someone say that their patron god or goddess called out to them first? How many have said, "It was Hecate (or Jesus, or Kali) who found me." Sometimes it is a deity who says, "You're mine now!" or even, "I know you thought you were mine, but you're not; you actually belong to Freyja." Often, when someone finally does connect with their patron deity in this way, they experience a sort of retroactive awakening in which they can look back at their life and see all the trademark signs of their deity's handiwork that have guided them there. "It was Freyja all along!" they exclaim. That which you are seeking is also seeking you. What could be weirder—yet also more natural—than the ordinary becoming extraordinary in this way?

Anytime you practice magic, you commune with the being that is Magic. Whether it be through spellcasting, divination, manifesting, sigil-casting, spellsong, spelldance, or any ritual of any sort, you invoke Magic into your being and evoke Magic into the world. When you court Magic, you court weirdness. There is no way around this weirdness; there is only through it. The weird thing—and this I find very encouraging—is that the destiny, nature, and purpose of Magic might just very well be the same as our own: to re-member, to become whole. We help each other do these things. The co-awakening of you and Magic is the result of the evolution of wyrd and the flowering of wyrd consciousness. This process has been occurring since time immemorial. Magic has reached out through deep time, deep space, and deep consciousness and wyrded its way into conscious awareness through you. Even now, Magic is experimenting and learning and evolving through you, and you are doing the same through Magic until one day, together, you will experience union and return as One, into Infinity—the state of pure magic.

The practice of magic has a highly experimental and experiential nature. This experiential drive and experimental tendency leads people to the *strange to them* and *strange in them* and encourages them to explore, attune, commune, celebrate, and express in the ways most suited to one's wyrd. When I think about the magicians, witches, and mystics I've known over the course of my life, I see a diverse, sensitive, curious, adventurous, and strange lot. I see deep feelers and perceivers of subtle and cosmic energies, of nonhuman entities and psychic phenomena. When the status quo sees these people, they see "weird" people who draw bizarre symbols, gather in wild places, sing odd songs, dance in unusual ways, and make questionable offerings to unfamiliar gods. I see people deeply in relationship with the mysteries of the cosmos and psyche.

The deep, transformative nature of magic is nothing if not queer. This I celebrate, for there is deep magic that emerges through the firsthand exploration of queerness. Queerness reminds us that—beyond that which is currently known and considered "normal"—there is powerful magic waiting to come into being. Fear-based normativity tends to fear this shapeshifting queerness; it has the tendency to close windows, shut doors, and fill in cracks so that the light of queerness, magic, and soul can't emerge from the shadow, so that deep experiential transformation—which is ultimately inevitable—might be held at bay for just a little longer. This is futile, for wyrd-soul-magic wants to flow freely, fully, naturally, infinitely.

To practice magic is to be engaged in an intimate relationship with Nature's transformation. The more you attune to this magical transformation, the more magical transformation will flow through your life. The more it flows through your life, the more you see, feel, and understand it. The more you see, feel, and understand it, the more you see *how* it flows and *how* it is blocked from flowing. The more you see this, the more you can unblock the blocks and enable, increase, and channel its flow (or, in other words, get out of Magic's way). The more you get out of Magic's way, the more it can flow into all the domains of the Web. The more it can flow into the Web, the more it can heal and transform the Web. It only flows on from there.

Nature only reveals its mysteries to those who are ready, or ready-enough, to enter into sacred reciprocity with it. The same applies with magic. Magic is one of these mysteries; so, too, is love, truth, soul, and wyrd. No matter the mystery with which you commune, be prepared to step outside your comfort zone and dance, and be prepared to act, to will, to open and surrender. Be prepared to make offerings to truths much stranger than you can imagine. Be prepared to let go into the flow, as layer after layer of your being heals, transforms, and becomes—en route to your ultimate fate and destiny.

The Liminal

If you wish to experience, work with, and be worked by magic, all you need to do is step outside of the ordinary into the non-ordinary, into the weirdness known as the *liminal*. The liminal is the time-space-consciousness where magicians, witches, and mystics hang out when they work their magic. It is also where psychetherapists, social workers, bodyworkers, and other healers commune with their clients and the healing energies inherent in the domains. The liminal is the in-between zone: the boundary, gateway, and threshold. It is the crack where the magic comes through. It is within and through the liminal where the power of healing-soul-magic can be felt most fully, so if you wish to practice magic, seek the liminal—liminal time, liminal space, and liminal consciousness.

Liminal times:

- Dawn
- Dusk
- Noon, midnight, the witching hour, 3:33, etc.
- Solstices and equinoxes
- Eclipses, transits
- The phases of the moon
- The moment of death, as well as the many little deaths one transits through one's life

Liminal spaces:

- Altars
- Graveyards

- Crossroads, pathways
- Doorways, gateways, windows, mirrors
- Bridges
- Ritual circles
- Sacred groves, caves, cliffsides, mountains, swamps, shorelines
- Temples, sanctuaries
- Healing offices (psychetherapy, bodywork, etc.)
- Elevators, trains, buses, trains, and bus stations

Liminal consciousness:

- Meditation
- Contemplation
- Trance, exhaustion, ecstasy
- Sleep, dream, hypnogogia
- Psychedelic experiences, psychosis
- Love
- Death, grief

Liminal activities:

- Ritual
- Drumming
- Singing, humming, chanting
- Fasting
- Divination
- Dancing
- Sleep deprivation
- Psychedelic (soul-revealing) and entheogenic (god-invoking) substances, plant medicines
- Sexual stimulation
- Overexertion, exhaustion
- Creative arts
- Dying

Liminal time-space-consciousness is somewhere between wakefulness and sleep, here and there, past-present-future, this world and otherworld, conscious and unconscious. In the liminal you enter into a current that brings you further into liminality, until you arrive at a place where near and far don't matter, self and other become one, gender becomes fluid, above and below become one, things become malleable, ensouled, charged with potential, and readied. You get one step, or many steps, closer to re-uniting with essence.

The liminal is where one may find cracks within the veils of time, space, and consciousness. It is within these cracks and through these cracks where wyrd-soul-magic can be experienced and wielded most viscerally and effectively. As you get farther along into your magical practice, you will spend more and more of your time-space-consciousness in these liminal times, places, and states of being. Explore, experiment, and see what comes through. Welcome Weird!

Wyrding Ways
Centering, Grounding, and Balancing in the Liminal

The weirdness of liminality has a way of bending, blending, distorting, and dispersing boundaries, so it's good to know how to ground and center oneself before, while, and after exploring liminality. Magical weirdness can be quite disorienting, to say the least. Here is a quick centering, grounding, and balancing exercise. Remember this technique as you court the liminal.

You will need:
- Five to twenty minutes
- A place where you will be undisturbed
- A meditation cushion, chair, or blanket (if you wish to sit)

1. Take a seat and sit with spine upright and lengthened, alert yet relaxed. Close your eyes if it helps you go within. Take a few slow, deep belly-breaths in through your nose and out through your mouth. With each out-breath, relax just a little bit more. Return to your natural breathing pattern.

2. Bring your awareness to your body. Feel into the internal space that your body is occupying within the space around it. Hold both spaces in your awareness. Feel gravity as it keeps you earthed, so to speak. Center your awareness to your heart-space or solar plexus. Breathe into it—in, out, in, out. As you do this, imagine a glowing ball of energy growing there. Don't force it; allow it. This is your center.

3. Use an imaginary spindle to spin some of that energy into a thread that travels upward through your spine, out the crown of your head, all the way into the Sun where you weave it into its core. Feel the warmth, light, and love within the Sun flowing down the thread, into your crown, down your spine, and into your center. Breathe deeply. Make a home in your core for it.

4. From your center, use your magic spindle to spin energy into thread, downward through your spine, out your sacrum, through the layers of the Earth; weave it into the Earth's core. Feel the warmth, solidity, and love within this core. As you breathe in, draw that energy upward through the thread, through the root of your spine, into your heart. Breathe deeply. Make a home in your core for it.

5. Simultaneously—feel into your center and your centeredness. Feel into your rootedness and groundedness and feel the solidity and balance of the pillar that reaches from the core of the Earth, through the core of you, to the core of the Sun. This pillar is the sacred World-Axis. You are centered, grounded, and balanced. Be in this state for another five to ten minutes or longer. Soak in the experience. You can even reinforce the pillar by sending more threads up and down it, weaving them into and out of the core threads already there. Feel the solidity and stability strengthen as you do this.

6. Keep a part of your awareness on this centeredness, groundedness, and balance as you continue with whatever ritual you would like to perform, or just sit in this experience for another five to fifteen minutes or longer. Soak it in.

7. When your meditation is coming to an end, take a few slow, deep belly-breaths, open your eyes, slowly stand, stretch, and take a slow bow in a spirit of gratitude. Carry this feeling into the world as you go.

It is within the liminal where one may locate magic, attune to magic, learn to speak its language, and then guide it and be guided by it within and through the Web and beyond. It is here where the witch, mystic, druid, and wyrd-worker hang out and engage in their crafts. Liminal time-space-consciousness is a fertile void through which any number of phenomena can come—creative, preserving, and destructive energies, benevolent and malevolent entities, and archetypal encounters and communications of all sorts. What comes through will depend upon your wyrd, and how you encounter these phenomena will depend on your craft. Different traditions create and cultivate liminality and commune with energies and entities in their own ways. No matter which tradition you practice, each has its own best practices for attuning to and wielding magic. Learn these ways, read books, consult with elders and peers, practice ritual alone and with others, meditate, exercise, stay curious, and stay aware. The old ways await rediscovery as you walk your own path of magical and spiritual gnosis.

The non-ordinary and liminal are not always safe, but they are often safe-enough. Go slowly with as high degree of awareness and discernment as you can. You are using your mind-body-relationship-environment-soul-spirit as a vessel for the embodiment and evolution of a being, consciousness, and power beyond imagining. Remember that the mysteries of magic are far deeper and far more expansive than any book, person, or spellcrafting can tell you. Experiment and experience the transformation of magical living and magical dying on the growing-edge of being and becoming mindfully and prepare yourself for an experience that may just be far weirder, and far more ordinary, than you can ever imagine.

Close Encounters of the Weird Kind

It is inevitable that as you explore the inner and outer landscapes, you will find yourself at one crossroads after another, interacting with someone else or something else from time to time. Therefore, before you do any deep liminal magical work, after learning how to balance, center and ground, it is good to know how to create and maintain magical boundaries. We live a relational existence within this great Web, and at every intersection where thread meets thread, we have the opportunity for another encounter wherein we may learn something new or be reminded of something old, long forgotten.

Practicing the magical arts and crafts will lead to many close encounters of the weird kind. As a soul-ranger exploring the boundaries of consciousness, being, and reality, you traverse many dimensions populated by many beings. Have you ever been face-to-face with a land-spirit? How about your own inner demons? How about a mouse, snake, fox, or mountain lion? Have you ever had the opportunity to share minds with a giantess, a wraith, or even your beloved dead? Are you prepared to hold your ground and stay in your integrity when eye-to-eye with the sacred "other?"

Magic is nothing if not relational. Be forewarned here and now that if you practice magic—especially healing-magic—you will likely come face-to-face with many beings—gods, land-spirits, elementals, ghosts, and possibly psychic parasites. Some will be in you, while others will be around you, and they will be curious about you. Some will want to come close. Are you ready for this? Are you ready to face the poisons of regret, fear, and trauma that your ancestors have experienced and passed down? Are you ready to face the confusion of the wandering lost ghost, or the wild exuberance of nature's divinity? Are you ready-enough to face your own fears, traumas, and wounds?

You have to see the wound and feel the wound if you wish to heal the wound. Healing-magic is not always the safest, most fun, or easiest magic one can practice. Like any other healing work, it requires training, skill, courage, and empathy to do it well. It also requires the ability to stand strong in one's being and project clear boundaries when needed—in trance, in ritual, in community, and in life.

Wyrding Ways
Creating Boundaries

In this exercise, you will practice a technique for creating and maintaining energetic and magical boundaries.

You will need:
- About thirty minutes of undisturbed time-space
- A place to stand

1. Stand in a meditative posture—feet shoulder-width apart, knees slightly bent, spine straight, alert yet relaxed, shoulders broadened, chin slightly tucked. Take three slow, deep belly-breaths in through your nose. With each one, feel your breath expand in your lower belly first and slowly move upward into your chest and end at your nose. Feel your diaphragm expand. Breathe out starting at your mouth or nose. As you do, feel your chest, diaphragm, and belly pull toward your spine. End your breath out at your belly button. Return to your regular breathing pattern.

2. Bring your awareness to the entirety of your body at once. Feel your feet firmly planted in the Earth. Then, bring your awareness to your heart-space or solar plexus—your core. Breathe into and out of it—in, out, in, out. As you do this, image a ball of glowing energy growing there. What color is it? What does it look like in your mind's eye? This is your center. Stay here in your center, breathing in and out of it, for a few minutes.

3. From the ball of energy that is your center, draw a thread upward through your spine, out the crown of your head, until it reaches the Sun. Weave it into the Sun's core and draw the thread back down into your center. Do not stop there, but continue to draw the thread down your spine, out of your sacrum, until it reaches the core of the Earth. Weave it into the core. Again, do not stop there. Draw that same thread upward into your core, then onward to the core of the Sun, then back down. Creating a lemniscate—an infinity symbol—with your core at the center. Feel the energy flowing through this figure eight—from your core upward to the Sun's core, then back down to your core, onward to the Earth's core, then back up to your core, back up to the Sun's core, onward. Breathe deeply and feel this flow. If you'd like, you can breathe in alignment with this flow. From this flow, you can draw the energy you will use to create your magical boundary.

4. Lift your dominant arm and point with your finger (or with a feather, wand, or knife) to the horizon. Slowly turn in place 360 degrees until you've drawn a complete circle around you. You can make the circle any size, but start with no more than two meters in diameter. You can make the circle any color—silver, indigo, gold, white. You have just created an energetic boundary. Know that nothing can enter it or leave it unless you allow it to do so.

5. Feel the energetics of the boundary around you—feel its vibration and movement. Feel the vibrations of energy in your core. Now, project your core-energy outward until it completely fills this space in the form of a solid sphere of energy. Practice expanding it and contracting it at will. Feel the energy vibrating within this space. Affirm to yourself, "This is my space. I decide who and what may enter it and who and what must stay outside."

6. If you need more energy, pull energy from the lemniscate you have created.

Practice this exercise until you get a good feel for it. Boundary-setting and maintenance is a prerequisite before doing any kind of deep liminal magic or trance-work. You will inevitably meet other beings on your wanderings; therefore, it is good to be able to meet these beings ready, empowered, aware, and sensitive. Carry this sphere with you through your day. Create it on a whim. The more you regularly practice setting your energetic boundaries, the better. There are beings—human and other-than-human—you don't want attached to you, draining you of your life-energy.

It is equally as important to work on your emotional, psychological, and physical boundaries just as much as it is to work on your magical energetic boundaries. They all interact in a dance with each other. Embodying a solid sense of self—being in your soulful wholeness—you exude a personal presence that will create a natural boundary. This is another reason I consider psychetherapy to be magic, as a big part of therapy is learning about one's boundaries and how to express them in healthy ways—when to say yes and when to say no. Explore your relational dynamics with the people in your life—your family, loved ones, strangers—with your therapist. Psychological processing of your past experiences and present expression of your boundaries can be of great assistance when it comes to learning how to banish unwanted energies from your life. It's one thing to hold someone in your heart, and it's another thing to invite them into your home.

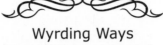

Wyrding Ways
Banishing Growl

Regularly working on your magical, psychological, and relational boundaries is necessary, but sometimes even they cannot prevent unwanted things, energies, and entities from entering your bubble. Sometimes life gets uncomfortably close. In these cases, what can you do? There are many ways to banish unwanted energies, people, beings from your immediate sphere. Laughter—especially maniacal laughter—glaring, standing your ground, voicing a command to back off, shouting, expanding, and projecting your energy outward, for example, all can be amazing tools for setting magical boundaries and banishing unwanted energies. I would like to share one more with you—growling. Growling is a very effective tool that Mother Nature teaches for expressing boundaries. Think about it; you don't have to ask twice what a dog or cat is trying to say when they are growling. The message is clear: "Back off now!"

You will need:

- Five or more minutes of time-space where you will be undisturbed by others

1. Stand in a meditative, alert posture—feet shoulder-width apart, knees slightly bent, spine upright, alert, and relaxed, shoulders broad, chin slightly tucked.

2. Take three slow, deep belly-breaths in through your nose. Feel your breath expand in your lower belly first and slowly move upward into your chest. Breathe out through your mouth. Bring your awareness to the entirety of your body at once. Feel your feet firmly planted in the Earth.

3. Create another lemniscate as you did in the previous exercise. This will be the source of your banishment energy. After you have created the lemniscate and tapped into its flow, focus your awareness on your center. Imagine and feel energy accumulating there. Breathe in and out of it. Concentrate the energy and prepare to direct it toward that which you wish to banish.

4. Take a deep breath in. As you breathe out, begin a slow, quiet, calm growl. Engage your diaphragm. Feel the low rumble deep

in your throat and chest. Imagine the energy moving outward from your solar plexus. Start quietly and slowly raise the volume until it is loud, sustained, and powerful. Practice as many times as you'd like. Experiment with your body. Where do you feel the growl the strongest? From where does the growl originate? Try growling from your upper throat, middle throat, lower throat, and chest. Try it with your mouth open, closed, teeth bared. See how many ways you can growl. Try different volumes. Imagine you are a wolf, a coyote, a cat. Growl louder until it comes out as a shout. Project the energy outward. Project it in different directions. You can use the vibrations in your growl to break up, dissolve, and disperse unwanted energies near and far.

5. Practice doing this quickly, in the form of a blast of energy. Shout "No!" Yell. Bark. Roar. Use your diaphragm. Like a gunslinger in a duel, see how quickly you can ground yourself, drop into presence, center, tap into the energy of the lemniscate, and fire a round directly at what you wish to banish. Decimate it.

Growling can be a highly effective boundary-setting tool for practicing natural magic out in the wilderness, especially at night when you can't necessarily see what's around you. Animals understand the growl and the energy behind it. Some animals you might not mind being close to you, but others you might want to keep away. Before you venture into the wilderness, learn who else might be out there, and what to do if you encounter someone—a bear, mountain lion, snake, and so on. As always, be mindful where you go and do least harm. And remember, when you are in nature, you are in their house, on their mating ground and hunting ground. Be a good guest, and they will be a good host.

Learning to banish toxic and parasitic energies and entities is incredibly important when it comes to working magic, maintaining good magical hygiene, and living a life of abundant frith, hæl, and eudaimonia. No matter what kind of relationship it is, it is good to enter it with a solid sense of self and boundaries. Your powerful inner light is a vital force that can help you safely navigate any realm. Wherever you are, it will be there when all other lights go out. It will remind you to stay strong, centered, rooted, and expansive—all at once. It will remind you that you are a powerful being when you are engaged in the process of becoming more and more wholly *yourself*. Trust in your emerging light and let it shine. It will guide you and protect you.

The Magical Altar

One way to engage with liminality, centeredness, groundedness, balance, and boundaries is through the creation of an altar. An altar is a sacred cross-roads—just one juncture in the great Web of Wyrd—where you can attune and commune directly with magic and its many manifestations. An altar is a shapeshifting being in and of itself, constantly in flux, as it witnesses the coming and going of many energies and entities. At this crossroads that is your altar, you have the option to practice your boundary-setting, invoke, evoke, and explore many different paths, deities, archetypes, correspondences, and so on. You will also have the opportunity to learn from many different far-travelers who come your way, as your altar and your magical workings will serve as an antenna, attracting spirits, energies, and otherworldly beings toward you in accordance with your wyrd. In addition, your altar can act as a magical battery and resource for magical energy when it is needed for your trance-work, healing work, and spellwork. At the same time, your altar will also serve as a type of World-Axis, a grounding cord, a safe base to return to as you traverse the in-between-in-between place. At the center of the mandala, the magician can merge with his/her/their altar, steadfast and immovable within the mystery of liminality.

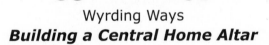

Wyrding Ways
Building a Central Home Altar

In this exercise, you will construct a home altar—a gateway that leads into the Web and into the many crossroads within it. Though you can build altars pretty much anywhere—in the bathroom, on the bookshelf, or on the kitchen counter, for example—I recommend you designate a special place that is not shared—a place that is its own, so to speak—for your primary home altar. Treat it like a spiritual fireplace or hearth. I have found that bedside tables or small coffee tables (optimally with shelves or storage space underneath) work perfectly when set up against a wall. If possible, try to leave enough room for sitting and moving in front of your altar.

To have an altar is to have a sacred place in which to cultivate liminal time-space-consciousness through a wide range of daily ritual activities, such as meditation, journeying, prayer, spellcraft, spellsong, spelldance, divination, and so on. When adorning the crossroads that is your altar, start simple, functional, and beautiful. A candle, an incense burner, a bowl or cup for offerings, a piece of art, and a sacred object such as a stone, statue, or magical tool (I will discuss magical tools in the next chapter) are a great place to begin, after which you can adorn your altar with any creation or found object you desire. Your altar is a place for you to attune and commune creatively, experiment, and have fun as you court liminality and attune to the flow of Magic through your life.

A Magical Musing on Raven, Faerie, and the Daimon

As much as I have emphasized threads and webs and spiders throughout this book, wyrdcraft can also be thought of as Raven magic and Raven medicine. This is a shapeshifting being-consciousness-existence form of magic and medicine. Raven is a revealer of the paradoxical blending of death and darkness and life and light. Raven, though black as night, bears as a result of this blending a magical light. This light you can see if you look closely at its obsidian plumage, through which hints of iridescence shimmer. Behold this light behind your very own closed eyes, or even while meditating wide-eyed in a darkened forest. Watch it shimmer through day and night.

Raven is a powerful teacher of Light. Raven teaches us that there is light in darkness, and darkness in light. This nondual Light is not opposed to or separate from darkness; rather, its magic permeates both darkness and light. This is the Light that illuminates wholeness and shines out when wholeness comes in being. Raven's Light brings the magic and medicine of death and darkness to life and light *within you* as Raven reveals the magical emergence of soulful wholeness. Behold a similar rainbow iridescence—and a similar medicine—in Dragonfly, Butterfly, Moth, and Salmon. Every being expresses Light in their own ways—Tree, Eagle, River, you, me—the Light comes through the fabric of wyrd in kaleidoscopic and mesmerizing ways.

The native peoples of the Pacific Northwest knew this. So goes the tale that tells of the first emergence of light. Long ago, Raven got so frustrated and bored with the primordial darkness that he used his magic to shapeshift himself into a baby to trick those who held the light captive into adopting him. They did just that and took him into their home, where he set himself to kicking and screaming until they could no longer bear it. "What do you need?!" they asked, exacerbated. He pointed to a sacred bentwood box in the corner of the room—the one he knew contained the light. After giving it to him, when they weren't looking, Raven transformed into his original form and flew with the box through the smoke hole in the roof, turning himself black in the process. Out he flew into the darkness, where he opened the box, releasing the Sun, Moon, and Stars into the world.[41] At last, there was light!

This is only one version of similar tales told by native peoples all over the world. Many of them reflect Raven's intelligence, trickster nature, and magical abilities. Many others also tell us that Raven was born white or even rainbow colored. Ravens, as well as many other birds and animals, have tetrachromatic vision, which allows them to see ultraviolet light.[42] Having this type of four-dimensional vision means that Ravens see each other as rainbow colored.

Raven is just another manifestation for that weird *being* called Magic. Raven is mind-psyche-soul transmutation magic, shapeshifting—ever changing, learning, integrating, and wisdom seeking, forevermore. "Quoth the raven, Nevermore."[43] What a weird night it was, when Poe's raven—the winged "prophet" from "Night's Plutonian-shore"—visited a grief-stricken man, wrestling with his reveries of his lost Lenore, only to remind him again and again of the eternal wisdom—Nevermore.[44] Raven, here, represents nostalgia—the deep wish and call to return to soul. This soulful depth is Raven's sky, through which ravens fly, reminding us all that all must die, and all with just one simple cry—Nevermore!

Wise, too, were Odin's ravens, Hugin and Munin—*Thought* and *Memory*—and wise was Odin as a result. For each day, as Hugin and Munin venture out into the nine-worlds, so, too, goes Odin's consciousness with them, soaring in shamanic soul-flight, searching the multiverse for answers, magic, purpose, and pattern. Each day Odin's ravens return with tales of distant lands, distant stories, distant people, and distant happenings—tales of waves and ripples that may lead to new ways to wander and wonder.

41. Lynn Hassler, *The Raven: Soaring Through History, Legend & Lore* (Tucson, AZ: Rio Nuevo Publishers, 2008), 98–99.
42. Andrew Bennett and Marc Théry, "Avian Color Vision and Coloration: Multidisciplinary Evolutionary Biology," *American Naturalist* 169, no. 1 (January, 2007): S1–S6. https://doi.org/10.1086/510163.
43. Edgar Allan Poe, *The Poetry of Edgar Allan Poe* (London: Arcturus Publishing, 2020), 98.
44. Poe, *The Poetry of Edgar Allan Poe*, 98.

To say that Odin's ravens are simply Thought and Memory and leave it at that does us a disservice, for what *is* thought, and what really *is* memory—if not more mysteries? We must remember that Odin and his ravens are part of a larger animist cosmology—one permeated by soul. Looking through the lens of soul, then, what is thought if not the soul/imagination? And what is memory if not the act of re-membering soul? And so Hugin and Munin fly as Odin's consciousness, not just as thought and memory, but as the soulful imagination and the desire and quest for soul-spirit re-membering. This interpretation makes this quote of Odin, taken from Jackson Crawford's translation of *Grimnismal*, much more arresting: "Thought and Memory, my ravens, fly every day the whole world over. Each day I fear that Thought might not return, but I fear more for Memory."[45] Does Odin fear the loss of his mind, his shamanic abilities? Does he fear the loss of his Self, the loss of his soul? The loss of his magic?

I can say with confidence that it was in large part Raven who opened the box out of which the Light of this book has come into the world; however, Raven also had helpers. It was also through the mysterious workings of the Fae—my wildwood and wildhearted friends of the inner and outer wilderness that wyrdcraft came into being. In my experience, Raven magic and Faerie magic are similar. Like Raven, the Fae are beings of Light that dwell in both darkness and light. Their medicine, too, is natural, playful, creative, experimental, shapeshifting magic. You could say that within each of us there is Light. This Light is not only your soul but your magic. Another name for this Light could be faelight; therefore, your Light could be seen—if you choose to see it this way—as something that you and the Fae share in common. Maybe your faelight is your very own Fae-nature.

And alas, there is the *daimon*, or *daemon*. The ancient Greek used the word *daimon* to describe a being occupying a space somewhere between humanity and divinity. The daimon is spirit-soul-essence in emergence. The daimon is the outward expansion and expression of one's inner light and flame, and, like Raven and Faerie, the daimon plays a magical game— transmuting and becoming, just the same. Much like the unbound elements of nature—the flood, lightning, wildfire, earthquake, and hurricane—the

---

45. Crawford, *The Poetic Edda*, 64.

daimon can manifest as a powerful, sometimes dangerous, force. If it is not engaged with in skillful ways, that is. Thankfully, we have the mystical and magical traditions to help us do this.

One's daimonic faelight expresses itself as one's magic, one's genius, inspiration, gifts, and power. The daimon desires to be, to grow, and to flow unhindered. Like animal instinct, like nature, like the elements, like the soul, if the daimon is repressed, suppressed, denied, or oppressed, it will fester within the depths of the shadow and turn sour, toxic, dangerous, and self-destructive. This is what happens to the trickster Loki in the Norse myths.

Magic's momentum toward becoming that which it is meant to become cannot be stopped. The magic of the daimon *must* come to fruition by any means necessary. As it does so, it naturally pushes against repressive and suppressive boundaries and hierarchies—physically, psychologically, systemically. The daimon's light is alchemical; it is a revealing, healing, transforming, and becoming kind of Light-magic. As magic changes everything and everyone it touches, the status quo—as created perpetuated by fundamentalism, fascism, and social and cultural normativity—fear Raven, the Fae, the daimon, Loki, and many of the magical others. From this place of fear, the status quo has turned wyrd into weird, made the raven a harbinger of doom, turned the wise woman into the witch, pushed the faelight into hiding, transformed the daimonic into the demonic, and turned Loki into the Devil.

Fear blocks the flow of Light—a.k.a magic, soul. If Light remains stuck and stagnant for too long, it will begin to self-immolate. Consciously communing with Raven, Faerie, Dragon, Phoenix, and others can help Light flow naturally and healthily. There are so many Light-magic loving guides woven throughout this wild, animated tapestry of psyche into which we are all woven who can help us channel, guide, and harness this flow. Communing with them is an integral facet of wyrdcraft. Communion can mean a lot of different things and take many different forms, but basically, it means to uphold the gift-cycle, to relate, to attune, to honor. Sacred flame: you give to it, and it gives to you—as such, you give to You, and You become that which You are meant to become.

You may ask what you can offer to the being known as Magic? First and foremost, you can give your awareness, time-space, and energy. These are the first and ongoing offerings and, I have found, the most important ones. After so many centuries of trauma and stigma, you must regain Magic's trust and make a good home for Magic in your being and in your life. You must do your best to heal the ancestral, transgenerational traumas and stigmas that have been passed on through the ages. There are many wounds that need to be addressed. Practically speaking, you can do this by studying the myths, qualities, correspondences, life-purposes, and lifestyles of your patrons. Come to know them through ritual. Commune with as many or as few as feels right. Worship them; offer them gifts and delight. Sing to them, paint them a symbol, write them a letter stamped with your seal. Dance with them, for them, in them; adore them. Invite them into your mind-body-relationship-environment-soul-spirit; embody them in the great ritual of your life and in your great spellwork. Learn from their ways, respect them, and they will teach, help, heal, and transform you. Embody their teachings as you move through your life and unveil your Light. No need to preach their ways—just *be* their ways, then all will change; all will become that which is meant to become.

As your relationships with your magical patrons develop, other offerings will become clear—creative altars, sacred items, food, drink, blood, sweat, and tears. Magical patrons love creative, imaginative offerings. Though it isn't a hard rule, in general, the greater the ask, the greater the offering. In the great ritual of life, if you wish to cast a great spell, you will need to offer a great sacrifice. Do you wish to heal the domains of your life, unleash your full magical potential, and become that which you are meant to become? Then you will be asked to sacrifice bad habits, self-destructive worldviews, oppressive thoughts, words, actions. You will have to seek them out, find them, eat them, and digest them like Raven. Raven loves to eat the carcasses of expired identities and transmute them into new life, soul, magic, and Light. The inner flame loves to be fed with the shed and discarded layers of the crusty old ego. Add some much-needed compost to the garden of your Being and watch it grow and glow.

Who are your Beloved-Ones? Who are your magical patrons? What feeds their fire, their warmth, and their Light? And what is it that you hope they might offer to you in return? What do you want? What do you need? Live these questions and welcome Light, healing-magic, and soul-magic into your life.

Wyrding Ways
Communing with Magic

In this exercise, you will be communing with the weird and mystical being that is Magic—through meditation, grounding, centering, and guided imagery. You will also be engaging in a dialogue with Magic. As you do this, you will be making your life and the Web—your mind-body-relationship-environment-soul-spirit—into a loving container for Magic to return to.

You will need:
- Fifteen to thirty minutes of undisturbed time-space
- A place to meditate
- Incense or another offering for Magic

1. Take a seat and sit with spine upright and lengthened, alert yet relaxed. Close your eyes; take a few slow, deep belly-breaths in through your nose and out through your mouth. With each out-breath, relax just a little bit more. Return to your natural breathing pattern.

2. Bring your awareness to your body. Feel into the space your body is occupying within the space around it. Feel gravity as it keeps you earthed, so to speak. Bring your awareness to your heart-space, or solar plexus. Breathe into it—in, out, in, out. As you do this, imagine a glowing ball of energy growing there. This is your center.

3. From the ball of energy that is your center, draw a thread upward through your spine, out the crown of your head, until it reaches the Sun. Weave it into the Sun's core and draw the thread back down into your center. Do not stop there, but continue to draw the thread down your spine, out of your sacrum, until it reaches the core of the Earth. Weave it into the core. Again, do not stop there. Draw that same thread upward back into your heart, creating a lemniscate—an infinity symbol—with your core at the center. Feel the energy flowing through this figure eight—from your core upward to the Sun's core, then back down to your core, onward to the Earth's core, then back up to your core, back up to the Sun's core, onward. Breathe deeply and feel this flow.

If you'd like, you can weave several more threads in the same manner.

4. All while staying aware of the flow through the lemniscate, focus on your center. Speak into the void within the center: "Magic, mystery of mysteries, I call to you. Magic of many names and many faces from many places, I call out to you from the center of my being. Magic you are! Come to me if you will it and as I will it. Join me now in the spirit of love, creation-destruction-transformation. I open my mind-body-relationship-environ-ment-soul-spirit to you. I open my heart." Remain attuned— ready, alert, and flexible. Relax your core and diaphragm. Open and receive. Don't force anything to happen. Magic will arrive within the space you offer it. What does it feel like as Magic arrives? How does Magic arrive? A flow, a tingling, a buzzing? Do any images or thoughts come? Breathe into this experience.

5. Commune with Magic:

   - Welcome Magic back. Talk to it; say, "Hi there! It's nice to feel you. Thank you for joining me and thank you for your life and my life. Thank you for your guidance and for your revelation and healing-transformation. Thank you for your soul."

   - Tell Magic what it is you would like. With what could you use Magic's assistance? If you have a question for Magic regarding a difficult decision you must make, ask. Relax your core and diaphragm while remaining upright in med-itation. Open yourself to receive the answer in a variety of ways, and know that the answer may come when and how you least expect it. Tell Magic what it is you want, need, or don't want or need.

   - Then, ask Magic, "What is it that *you* want?" Again, relax your core and diaphragm while remaining upright in med-itation. Open yourself to receive the answer in a variety of ways, and know that the answer may come when and how you least expect it.

   - Before you end, just *be* with Magic. Sit with it and soak it in. Let it move through your body. Let it move you. Allow it to permeate your experience in the moment. Be still and allow. Be.

6. When your communion is coming to an end, make your offering to Magic, then take three slow, deep breaths, stand up, and slowly bow, thanking Magic for being present within this experience and throughout your life. Take Magic into the world as you go about your day, and do your best to remain open to Magic's revelations as you go about your life.

Magic in Summary

Magic seems very much to want to come into this world, to know itself through you, and to flow freely, and ultimately, to become. Magic will shape you in wyrd ways as you shape magic in wyrd ways; Magic will remember Self through you, and you will remember Self through the practice of magic.

The magical mysteries of the Fates are not off-limits—they are just incredibly weird. They are waiting, ready, and available to anyone with a strong will, a flexible mind, an open heart, and a high tolerance for weirdness. You cannot conquer Magic; you can only make yourself a humble vessel through which Magic may flow ever more freely by clearing the blocks, addressing the wounds, and re-relating to soul in naturally wise, existentially collaborative ways. Everything about our current zeitgeist is asking us to change. Wyrdcraft—through psychetherapy and the mysteries of the Well, ecotherapy and mysteries of the Tree, and magic and the mysteries of the Fates—will help you, and us, do this.

I believe our best bet for a miracle cure for our ailing world and aching hearts is magic. Magic is miracle. Magical miracles are possible so long as magic is possible. And magic is possible so long as there are beings alive who maintain sacred reciprocity with it. There are many ways to practice magic and many angles from which to view the magical arts, crafts, and sciences. How you view them and how you practice them is up to you and your wyrd. I ask again, what is your wyrd? Explore it and find out. Give and receive, take action, surrender, and relax your body, for deep within the homeostatic balance of all polarities is a stillness and silence that is but a doorway into the liminal, into the Light. Within this liminality is that which you have been seeking, and that which has been seeking you. The Fates call. Ready yourself, wyrd-walker, and walk on through.

Wyrding Ways
Healing the Web II

I'll end this chapter with an exercise in healing-magic. The goal of this ritual is manifold: to access healing-magic and send it to someone, something, or some place in need of it; to bring awareness to the Web of Wyrd; and to send healing-magic to the Web itself.

You will need:

- Thirty minutes or more of undisturbed time-space
- A cushion, chair, or place to sit or stand
- Incense or other offering

1. Find a special place that feels right, a place where you won't be disturbed (possibly in front of your home altar or in a natural sacred space). Turn off your phone. Close your eyes and take a few slow, deep belly-breaths in through your nose and out through your mouth. Relax a little bit more with each out-breath, then return to your natural breathing pattern.

2. Bring your awareness to your core—your heart-center or solar plexus. Breathe into this center; feel energy accumulating within. Do this for a few minutes.

3. From the ball of energy that is your center, draw a thread upward through your spine, out the crown of your head, until it reaches the Sun. Weave it into the Sun's core and draw the thread back down into your center. Do not stop there, but continue to draw the thread downward through your spine, out of your sacrum, until it reaches the core of the Earth. Weave it into the Earth's core. Again, do not stop there. Continue to guide that same thread upward into your heart, creating a lemniscate—an infinity symbol—with your core at the center. Feel the energy flowing through this figure eight—from your core upward to the Sun's core, then back down to your core, downward to the Earth's core, then back up to your core, back up to the Sun's core—on and on, circling, weaving. Breathe deeply and feel this flow. If you'd like, you can weave several more of these threads in the same manner. As you weave, you generate energy; you can use this energy for your healing-magic.

4. Using your finger and outstretched arm or your imagination, create a circle or sphere around you in which you stand or sit at its center. Feel the force of this magical boundary. Nothing may enter or leave that you don't allow. Stay present in your center for a minute or two. Feel the energy accumulate at the boundary.

5. Expand the energy in your core to fill your ritual circle. Feel into this expanded center. Let the entire space vibrate with your presence, your love, and your intention to do healing-magic. This larger sphere of energy in which you are centered is your thread—the one that connects you to Source, to divinity, to the Web, to the Norns, to all. Feel and listen to the hum of all the threads within.

6. Now bring someone to mind—a friend, family member, stranger, nemesis—anyone to whom you would like to send healing. As you imagine this person (or place), hold their image in your core. Imagine how your core and their core are connected by this thread. No need to pull them toward you; merely open yourself to the soul-thread that connects you. The channel is ready to give-receive.

7. Begin sending loving healing-energy through the thread, from your center to their center. Send them love. Imagine who they might become as they heal. Imagine them laughing, smiling; imagine them content, at peace, strong, patient, and trusting. Send them your gratitude for all they have brought to your life and to the world. Send them messages of hopefulness and healing. If you feel a block, or a kink, or a tear in the thread, send healing-energy right into that space. That is where the healing is needed. The goal is to open and heal that channel as much as possible, to heal the soul-thread that connects you, to heal the Web that connects us all. Perhaps a guide will show up and help you. Don't force anything to happen. Let it happen naturally. If you'd like to send healing to other people or places, repeat the same process with them.

8. Before you finish, call into your mind-heart as many people (or places) as you'd like. Imagine the threads connecting you all, then imagine the Web as a whole. Send healing-energy into this Web—to all. Imagine the Web itself becoming healthier and healthier, energy flowing freely. Do this for at least a few minutes. When you are done, take a few slow, deep belly-breaths, light incense, make your offering, send gratitude to the moment and into the Web. Stand up, bow deeply, and carry this healing-energy into the world with you as you go about your day.

Chapter 12
The Northern Magic of Seiðr

Now that we've explored the nature of magic and the practice of magic in a general philosophical sense, I'd like to shift focus toward a particular form of ancient Scandinavian and modern heathen magic called seiðr (pronounced *sayder, sayth,* or *say-thr*). Seiðr-workers—historically called völva (seeress), seiðrkona (seiðr-woman), seiðrmaðr (seiðr-man), vitki (witch), or spákona (prophecy woman)—were sorceresses and sorcerers who engaged with Wyrd through divination, meditation, and trance-induced ecstatic magic. Seiðr-practitioners were said to have offered their services as they travelled the land from farmstead to farmstead. Though they are not considered to have been shamans, per se, they practiced many of the typical shamanic practices we are familiar with from other parts of the world, such as spellsinging, spelldance, shapeshifting, soul-journeying, divination, weather control, human puppetry, battle-magic, and so on. It is thought, at least historically speaking, that men who practiced seiðr were looked down upon within Norse society. They were referred to as ergi—meaning "taboo," "unmanly," or "sexually receptive." Is this because of the strong association between seiðr and spinning and weaving, which were seen as traditional, indoor, female-occupied roles? Is it that the trance states in which the seiðr-worker engaged in were seen as weak, vulnerable, too physically draining, or too strange for a gender-typed warrior man? Or was it considered a cowardly, unmanly act to use magic to begin with? These are just some of the theories. What is known is that there have been, and still are, seiðr-practitioners of all genders and sexual orientations past and present.

Seiðr is not only still being practiced today, but it has also been going through somewhat of a renaissance. This is interesting because there is still an ongoing debate about the true nature of the historical practice of seiðr and the actual identity and role of the seiðr-practitioner. The sources only reveal so much, which leaves us with some important unanswered questions: What criteria must be met before one can identify as a seiðr-practitioner? Are there any extant lineages of seiðr out there? If not, how can one learn the practice of seiðr without living elders to pass it on?

The seiðr that is being practiced today seems to be an amalgam of both past and present practices, in forms that vary slightly from practitioner to practitioner. Modern seiðr, like most modern magic that has ancient roots, takes what we know of the historical practice and fills in the blanks with UPG—unverified personal gnosis. For example, well-known author and heathen elder Diana L. Paxson reconstructed a form of oracular seiðr based on accounts gleaned from the lore as well as from her personal experiences working with Core Shamanism—an approach developed by Michael Harner, author of *The Way of the Shaman: A Guide to Power and Healing*. She offers this form of oracular seiðr to the community through her kindred, Hrafnar.[46]

Another example comes from author and founder of the Cult of the Spinning Goddess, Cat Heath. In her book *Elves, Witches & Gods: Spinning Old Heathen Magic in the Modern Day*, Heath offers a well-researched reconstruction of the historical nature of seiðr.[47] She is able—through her study of history, myth, lore, psychology, and her own UPG—to weave together a practical synthesis of the past and present practice of seiðr and fiber magic.

I have included a list of books about the past and present practice of seiðr in the Resources section at the end of this book.

Based on my own UPG, I define seiðr as Nature-magic. And when I use the word *Nature*, I don't just mean the natural world, I mean the Nature of everything in existence—mind, matter, human, alien, and otherwise—everything

46. Diana L. Paxson, "Hrafnar: Thirty Years of Re-Inventing Heathenry," Hrafnar, May 7, 2022, https://hrafnar.org/.
47. Heath, *Elves, Witches & Gods*.

known and unknown, near and far, deep and wide, weird, wild, and mild. As already mentioned, another word for *Nature* is *Wyrd* or *Tao*. The practice of seiðr, therefore, can be thought of as a practice of attuning to and communing with Nature, Wyrd, or Tao and coming to know its ways. This is a practice that naturally leads to the cultivation of wyrd consciousness—the consciousness of Nature and the Fates, also referred to as magical consciousness, ecological consciousness, spiritual consciousness, or Web consciousness. This consciousness is exemplified by Raven, Faerie, Freyja, Odin, and the many other magical patrons of the world.

The Deities of Seiðr

Though many polytheistic pagans and heathens are known to cross spiritual borders and commune with a wide range of peoples, communities, cultures, deities, and entities that are not of their cultures of origin, here are some of the deities associated with the culture from whence seiðr has come forth.

- *Freyja:* Meaning "Lady," Freyja is the primary goddess of the Vanir (the nature-deities of the Norse pantheon, associated with magic, sex, fertility, abundance, beauty, and the practice of seiðr). It is Freyja who taught seiðr to Odin, allowing him to be the first non-Vanir deity to know and practice the craft. Freyja is the prototypical Northern "witch" and the patron goddess of many wyrd-workers. Freyja has many mysteries associated with her that her devotees seek to comprehend—her association with gold, her wandering, her wandering husband (Odr or Odin?), her relationship with her twin brother (Freyr), her cloak of falcon feathers and her shapeshifting, her sow familiars, her chariot drawn by two cats, and her dwarf-made amber necklace, Brísingamen. She is also associated with the dead, as half of those slain in battle are delivered to her hall, Sessrúmnir, which sits at the end of the vast otherworldly battlefield known as Folkvangr.

- *Frigg:* Goddess, wife of Odin, and queen of Asgard, Frigg, which translates to "love," is seen as the highest exemplar of womanhood, motherhood, and family. Frigg is known for her spinning and prophetic insight, though she was not known to work as a prophetess. She is often depicted with a distaff, which she uses to weave wyrd.

Frigg embodies Mother Earth and the qualities of love, freedom, sex, generativity, and abundance. Frigg shares many similarities with Freyja, so many say that Frigg and Freyja are one and the same.

- *Gullveig:* An ancient Vanir goddess and völva, Gullveig's seiðr was so powerful, mysterious, and threatening to the Aesir that they abducted her, stabbed her with a spear, and burnt her to death three times in the attempt to ascertain her nature and abilities and to be rid of her. This act started the first war between the Vanir and the Aesir. It has been conjectured that Gullveig, meaning "golden draught," is another form of Freyja. Gullveig represents spiritual power, determination, and the transformational initiatory process of shamanic death-rebirth. After she was burned three times, she returned, transformed into Heiðr.

- *Heiðr:* Apart from being Gullveig-reborn, Heiðr, "the bright one," is thought to perhaps be the völva consulted by Odin in the saga of the Völuspá. She is a soothsayer—a caster of spells and charms. She is known for practicing magic whenever and wherever she could. Etymologically speaking, the name *Heiðr* has close connections to the word *heathen.*

- *The Norns:* The three giantesses who live under the World-Tree, Yggdrasil. They are Urðr (destiny or spiritual purpose), Verðandi (the process of becoming), and Skuld (our karmic debt that must be paid). They are closest to the mysteries of wyrd, thus they are shrouded in mystery themselves. Not much is known about them except that they carve the fates of all beings, including the gods and goddesses, and preserve the health and well-being of the World-Tree, thus preserving the multiverse at large. I like to think of them as the first practitioners of magic. To know them and to know their ways, one must travel through and beyond the realm of the gods, beyond all realms, and beyond life-death to commune with the fundamental and primordial forces of nature and existence.

- *Odin:* Often translated as "ecstatic one." Also known as Wodan or Wotan. More is known about Odin than any other Norse deity. The ecstatic wanderer, trickster, warrior, scoundrel and chieftain of the Aesir gods, Odin practiced seiðr even though he was ridiculed for it.

He is known for many things, but most of all for his endless thirst for knowledge and his unswerving dedication to truth and Self-realization, which led to him putting himself through initiatory shamanic ordeals of death-rebirth. He sacrificed one of his eyes to gain *in*-sight into the past, present, and future and into the nature of existence. He fell on his own spear and hanged himself, sacrificing himself to himself, on the World-Tree, an ordeal through which he was said by some to have discovered the mysteries of the runes. Odin is a shapeshifter. Hugin (Thought/Soul/Imagination) and Munin (Soul-Memory/Soul-re-membering), Odin's ravens, travel about the multiverse and return to him with messages as he sits on his high seat, entranced. His shamanic journeying is also aided by his two wolves, Geri and Freki, and his eight-legged horse, Sleipnir. Odin has a magical golden ring and a magical spear, loves wine, and speaks in poetry.

Apart from these deities, seiðr-practitioners may also work with Loki, Hel, Heimdallr, or any other deity of the Aesir or Vanir—or any other deity from any pantheon, for that matter. It may also be more likely that the bulk of the seiðr-practitioner's communion will involve ancestors, the dead, animal and plant allies, the elements, otherworldly beings, and land-spirits (landvættir)—and *not* the gods and goddesses. The Norse gods and goddesses are said to take a more hands-off approach when it comes to humans, whereas land-spirits and ancestors are much more involved with humans on a day-to-day basis.

Utiseta

One of the most well-known practices associated with seiðr is called utiseta. This practice is one of the primary keys that can be used to unlock the mysteries of seiðr and the magic of wyrdcraft. Whenever seiðr is mentioned, utiseta is usually not far behind, and like seiðr, not much is known about utiseta as well. Traditionally speaking, the practice of utiseta, which translates to "out-sitting," consists of sitting out from dusk to dawn—in the wilderness, at gravesites, burial mounds, hills, or crossroads—in order to attune and commune with Wyrd and a variety of otherworldly beings to gain guidance, healing, magical power, and gnosis.

Utiseta—and seiðr as a whole—offers an experiential study in liminality and natural magic. Though gravesites, burial mounds, wilderness, and crossroads may offer a more intense experience of liminality, the modern-day seiðrmaðr or vitki—similar to the mystic or tantric—communes with this magic and courts spiritual gnosis by seeking out and engaging liminality wherever and whenever possible—on the bus, at the beach, at home, on their lunch break. The liminal can be found wherever and whenever—in the here-and-now. What happens within this utisetic-liminality when the veils between self, other, nature, and divinity grow thin? This only the völva knows as they out-sit and in-sit hour upon hour, traversing the landscapes of psyche's wilderness and engaging in the crafts of meditation, wandering, dancing, and singing.

Meditation

The simplest way to practice utiseta is to find a sacred place and sit still for long periods of time. Sit for long enough, and you will eventually gravitate toward a meditative, entranced, and enchanted state. It is from this foundational practice of extended sitting that you can unveil the fundamental nature of seiðr and the ways of natural magic and the ways of Wyrd.

There are many ways to practice meditation, including mindfulness meditation, concentration meditation, active imagination, self-inquiry, and so on. Each in their own ways opens windows and doors that lead the sitter into wyrd. The out-sitter seeks to immerse oneself in direct experience, and through this, explore, experiment, and learn. This is an enchanted space and state. Within the entranced state of meditation, one engages in a process of learning how to attune to the underwill, to the pattern and flow of wyrd. Meditation opens you up to processes, energies, beings, and teachings that normally lie hidden beneath the surface of the sleepwalk unconsciousness of consensus reality where the subtler energies, quieter voices, and weirder encounters of the other-, under-, upperworlds occur.

Nature *is* magic. You will see. Sitting-out for extended periods in nature leads the out-sitter (and in-sitter) to natural magic, natural-wisdom, and natural healing. This magic-wisdom-healing can then be brought back and offered to community in support of the health and well-being of all. The out-sitter need not preach, they need only *be* in alignment with their wyrd.

Every time, the in- and out-sitter and the in- and out-seeker return from their meditations just a little bit more wyrd conscious, with just a little brighter Light.

Meditation—in whatever form it may take—is one of the most basic forms of magic. Having a solid meditation practice is not only a solid prerequisite for doing any kind of magical work, but also a necessary part of daily mind-body-relationship-environment-soul-spirit hygiene—along with centering, grounding, balancing, warding, and banishing. Meditation will help you commune with Magic and with the alchemical Light that reveals all and helps one transmute all. Meditation will help you see what you need to offer to Higher Self, what to feed to your inner flame—sometimes uncomfortable, but always worth it.

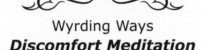

Wyrding Ways
Discomfort Meditation

This exercise consists of a simple meditation that one can practice to prepare for deeper magical work. The longer you can embody and tolerate physical discomfort, the larger and deeper your tolerance for ecstasy and the divine will become, and the more magical energy you will be able to contain, sustain, and channel within and through your being. If you are newer to meditation or magic, I recommend choosing a place that is not a graveyard, burial mound, or crossroads, at least not until you become adept at grounding, centering, balancing, boundary-setting, and banishing. One must prepare for this type of chthonic magic before venturing into the underworld in this manner. Note: This practice is not about self-flagellation or punishment or purification of your supposed impure soul. Rather, it is an evocation and celebration of your wholeness. Step in the river and see where it flows.

You will need:
- Ten to sixty minutes (or more) for meditation
- A comfortable place to sit, stand, or lie down (a cushion, chair, or blanket)

1. Sit down or stand in a meditative posture—spine straight, alert and relaxed. You can sit on a cushion, chair, boulder, or tree stump—anything that allows you to sit upright and remain relaxed, centered, and balanced.

2. Take three slow, deep belly-breaths in through your nose and out through your mouth. Bring your awareness to your body in the present moment. How do you feel? Do you notice any aches or pains? If you need to stretch for a moment, shake your legs, arms, or body for a moment before you continue.

3. Return to stillness, silence, and presence. Open your senses, relax your body, breathe, and remain as still and silent as you can—openly sensing, deeply feeling, being. Experiment with eyes closed and open. Every time you feel like moving, see if you can remain still for just a little bit longer. Steel yourself. You may notice an itch, an ache, an insect crawling on you. You may be hot or cold. You may be tired, anxious, or fidgety. You may even experience intense pain. Whatever your experience may be, surrender to its energy. Do your best to remain as still as possible for as long as possible. Breathe through it. Imagine that the energies of moment are flowing through you like a river. *This too shall pass.* Sit still, feel the flow, let it move you. Fear not, love lot. Watch as everything comes and goes—clouds in the sky. If you need support, if it becomes a lot, focus on your breath and relax your body. Stay with your breath, surrender to flow. Every time you are distracted, return to presence, return to energy, return to breath, return to stillness. Explore the paradox of relaxing your focus while remaining focused. Meditate on the *presence* of your body-mind, the ground of being. Allow yourself to feel the discomfort without instinctually adjusting it. You are exercising your ability to tolerate discomfort at the growing-edge of your being and becoming. It is here where your fate, destiny, nature, soul, magic will become clear. Breathe, feel, relax your body-mind, and try to remain as still as you can for as long as you can.

Other options for building one's tolerance for the ecstatic:
- Engage in extended exercise, like running, hiking up mountains, or other endurance activities. Push your limits. Explore your growing-edge.

- Test your limits of heat and cold. Go swimming in cold waters. Stand under cold waterfalls. Take hot baths, cold showers, cold baths, and hot showers.

Though utiseta can have one sitting through many hours of discomfort—through pain, extreme weather conditions, sleepiness, sleeplessness, darkness, insects, and more—the longer you sit and the stiller and quieter you can be, the more natural wisdom and wyrd consciousness may flow and grow. It is at your growing-edge where revelations into your wyrd will emerge. Exploring your boundaries in this way can hurt at times. It can even be dangerous, so take good care of yourself. Take care of your sweet, loving heart. Go with the flow of love. Be careful not to permanently damage your body or risk your life unless you are prepared to face the consequences with love in your heart. Always do your best to practice your wyrding in the spirit of love.

Wandering

Sometimes the flow of magical energy might get you moving. Utiseta is not all about sitting. It's also a lot about walking. Freya and Odin, two of the most well-known seiðr-practitioners, were notorious wanderers. If you are an out-sitter, then you are also a walker between worlds. Walking into the wilderness, down paths, up mountains, through valleys, you will find the crossroads, sacred places, and burial grounds waiting. There you will meet with your Beloved's revelations. You will also invariably meet those in need of healing—ghosts, lost or lonely travelers, excommunicated souls. A simple moment of kindness, connection, and intimacy can fill the tank of the far-traveling seeker. Out on the road, a shared story, laugh, and tear can nourish the wandering soul's sense of purpose. The web in which we are all but interconnected threads can be nurtured and strengthened everywhere and anywhere.

In many ways, the best soul-medicine may be moving—going with the flow. It may even be necessary to keep moving if you wish to keep living, and if you wish to thrive—physically and psychologically. If you are freezing, overheating, overexposed to the extremes of the elements, walking may very well keep you alive. If you have cut off circulation to your lower leg, it may be a good idea to move.

Wandering—along with sitting—just may be the oldest and most fruitful spiritual practice known to humanity. Wandering is simply walking, and it is so much more. It is *being* in motion, en route to no-where, to know-where, to now-here. The wanderer, rambler, drifter, and rover travel the pathless path of the mystic. As J. R. R. Tolkien writes in *The Fellowship of the Ring*, "Not all those who wander are lost."[48] The wanderer gives oneself over to the elemental ways of wyrd. The ongoing process of wandering is to relax the mind-body and go with the flow. Wandering is a somatic-soul-practice, a sweet surrender into devotion and foolishness. The wanderer goes with the flow, into the unknown, into the dark, into the light, into emptiness, into the wild, into the great wide-open and fertile void with a smile.

To wander is to attune to the sacred path of life. It is to welcome life's magic, natural wisdom, and wonder. To wander is to loosen the fetters of the grasping, compulsive, structure-obsessed mind and venture into the open roads and skies of the psyche, where wandering soul and spirit wait to be encountered. Soul and spirit are wanderers themselves, after all. Though they are certainly found within the stability and coziness of hearth and home, deeply rooted in the earth, souls and spirits drift across the land, they trace the coastline, traverse valleys and forests from village to town to city to haunt the status quo with their weird ways.

The wanderer walks a meandering and spiraling path of initiation. The path works on the wanderer as the alchemist works on the prima materia. When you wander—and come what may—you welcome fate, destiny, synchronicity, psychedelia, and magic; you welcome wyrd. The pathless path of the wanderer is certainly not an easy path, or necessarily a safe one, but it is a revealing, healing, transformative one. You will without a doubt encounter many an invaluable soul-memory on the trail. Something happens out on the road, on the winding path where soul- and spirit-encounters await. The call of the open road, water, and sky comes to us all at some point, or at many points, over the course of our lives. Some heed this call, some deny it. Some long for it, while others suppress it. Whether one heeds the call or not, it doesn't change the fact that there are distant lands, strange and kind people, revealing experiences, and untold wonders waiting out there, also seeking you, waiting to meet you at the crossroads.

---

48. J. R. R. Tolkien, *The Fellowship of the Ring* (Boston: Mariner Books, 2012), 167.

Wyrding Ways
Wyrd-Wandering

This fun experiment I call wyrd-wandering or following synchronicity. Though the name speaks for itself, this practice involves walking
around and surrendering to the momentary flow of wyrd as it moves
through life and through you. Consider this a practice for learning
how to follow synchronicity. Give it a try yourself; with time, you will
gain a better understanding of wyrd's magical flow. I recommend
practicing this in the city as well as in the wilderness. Remember,
wherever you go, go prepared, and do least harm.

You will need:
- Supplies for a long walk (water, snack, phone, map)
- An hour or three to wander "aimlessly"

1. After you gather your belongings and go to the place where your
   wyrd-wander will begin—whether out your front door or in a
   park, wilderness area, or city—sit down, close your eyes, and
   take a few deep, slow belly-breaths in through your nose and out
   through your mouth. With each out-breath relax just a little bit
   more. Return to your natural breathing pattern. Feel into your
   body, notice any aches or pains, and breathe into these places.
   Take a mental note of your emotional state. Are you well, fair-to-
   middling, not well? Take a mental note of your mental activity. Is
   your mind busy, calm, tired? Remind yourself of your intention:
   "For the next hour or three, I am going to go with the flow, open
   to what unfolds, and follow the signs and synchronicities."

2. Stand up, grab your belongings, and begin your wandering. At
   any point during your wandering, if you feel called in any direction by an intuition, a sound, a sign, a thought, or a feeling, go.
   If you feel called to pause, pause. If you feel called to stop, stop.
   If you feel called to go home, go home. Remember the following
   as you walk:

   - Be mindful of your breath, body-mind, and presence.
   - Open all your senses and allow for the blending of *inner* and
     outer.

- Be very aware and do your best to maintain a meditative openness—a walking trance.
- Let go of your expectations, hopes, doubts. Don't let your thoughts lead the way.
- Open to the communications of the universe, of your guides, of spirit and soul.
- Receive the flow and go with it.

3. If you come across a synchronicity, follow it. See what it has to say. Trust the process as soul and spirit emerge. Go down that street, hop on that bus, go into that store, talk to that person, take that path, bushwhack, stop, sit, meditate, stretch, open even more, go with the flow. Sometimes a synchronicity will lead you on a long circuitous journey, from one meaningful coincidence to the next; other times, the journey will offer up one moment of wyrd. There's no saying what will happen as you wander.

This is an intuitive, experiential meditation that takes practice. You may need to try it a few times before you get the knack for it—before the Light of Magic starts to come through.

Magical Movements and Sound

Magic is a somatic experience that can be felt in the body in several ways. It can elevate, tingle, buzz, snap, crackle, and pop in varying intensities. Many feel magic energetically or elementally, as one would feel electricity, water, wind, earth, or fire—as a flowing, blowing heaviness, warmth, or chill. Magic can feel erotic, sensual, ecstatic, and wild. Magic can also register emotionally through anxiety, excitement, a sense of elation or relaxation, or a clear, calm, and simple intuitive knowing. Again, it will depend on the individual, the moment, and the wyrding.

Apart from being felt in the body, magical energy can also move the body. Its flow can influence any part of your body. Yes, it can get you walking, but it can also get you spinning, shaking, jumping, dancing, flailing, and flying. A moment of magic can lead to spontaneous singing, humming, chanting, and glossolalia (speaking in tongues).

There are powerful energies at play throughout the multiverse. The völva attunes to and makes herself receptive to these energies and channels them into her magical workings. Just as tai chi offers one way to dance Tao, there are also ways to dance wyrd. One of these ways is seiðr. The name of the game is experimentation; become a vessel through which wyrd can flow. One way to do this is by embodying the movements, sounds, and behaviors of animal spirits and guides. You did this as you danced Spider in chapter 10. Dance with others. By dancing Raven, Deer, Faerie, or Dragonfly, for example, one can channel these primordial energies in safe-enough ways. The more you commune with wyrd—through utiseta, nature worship, and other trance-inducing practices—the more you will learn to embody and express these transcosmic movements and sounds, allow them to move you, and move them in return.

Because magic is so highly experiential and somatic, I recommend having a daily yoga and exercise practice, as well as a regular dance practice, to supplement your magical work. Exercise, yoga, and dance are all practices of attunement; they prepare the body to receive, channel, and express natural and cosmic energies in ways naturally aligned with your wyrd. The sorcerer uses voice, dance, sacred poses (mudras), and other magical movements—even ones as simple as bowing, swaying, shaking, and spinning—to attune to and channel the wild energies of the multiverse. The wilderness is just as much within you as around you. These energies may be collected, gathered, and stored within their body, within dance and song, within places, symbols, and magical items, which may later be used for spellwork, action, healing, or for any number of other purposes.

Wyrding Ways
The Song and Dance of the Cosmic Weaver

In this exercise, you will practice feeling magic and attuning to wyrd and the divine flow of archetypal energies as they move through here-and-now. No music is necessary for this dance as you will be listening internally to the cosmic sound and attuning to the cosmic dance of the multiverse. If your mobility is limited for any reason, you can dance using slow, small, careful movements of your arms, hands, head—or, your dance can occur on the internal dance floor in the theater of your mind. Your growing-edge is *your* growing-edge. Explore wherever and however you are.

You will need:

- Anywhere from twenty minutes to an hour or more to dance
- A space that will give you room to dance (you may wish to dance in the dark or by candlelight—if you do, be very mindful of the flame)
- An offering of incense or another offering

1. Begin by sitting or standing in a meditative posture—upright, still, alert, relaxed, and ready. Close your eyes; take a few slow, deep breaths in through your nose and out through your mouth. Relax just a little bit more with every out-breath. Return to your natural breathing pattern. Bring your awareness to your body. Feel the presence of your physical and energetic body as it takes up space in the present moment. Feel the outer boundaries of your being. Sense into the center of your being.

2. Using your finger and outstretched arm or your imagination, create a circle or sphere around you in which you stand or sit at its center. Feel the force of this magical boundary. Nothing may enter or leave that you don't allow. Stay present in your center for a minute or two. Feel the energy accumulate at the boundary.

3. Centered, grounded, and balanced in your magical circle, stand very still, be very silent, and remain receptive and open. Your eyes can be open or closed; whatever helps you stay centered. Go within. Imagine you hear through the stillness and silence the softest music wafting in on an almost imperceptible cosmic breeze. The faintest hum coming from the faintest light coming from the faintest stars, you hear the music of the spheres drifting toward you from very, very far away. As it comes closer, it gets louder. Louder. Louder. Closer. Until you begin to feel the song in your mind-body.

4. Slowly start to let the song move you. Improvise; let the music of the spheres guide your movements. Let the song move your limbs and hands—up and down, right and left, round and round. Be a conduit for the timeless melodies, rhythms, and sound. Dance like Shiva, Freyja, Dionysus. Sing if you feel called to— hum, whistle, moan, laugh, cry, intone. Let go, surrender to the flow. Allow yourself to be weird and dance your wyrd.

5. Light the incense and continue to dance. Let the incense transport you even more fully into the cosmic dance you now dance. Allow yourself to get weirder. Let go. As you do, emanate gratitude into

your movements and into the sound. Send thanks to the Weaver of the dance and the song and imagine they dance and sing along.

6. When you feel your dance coming to a natural end, imagine the music slowly drifting away from whence it came, far, far away (this may take many minutes). As it fades, slowly return to your still and silent center. Bring awareness to your body and the energy in your body. What do you feel?

7. Mindful of your breath, put your hands together in a prayer mudra and take a slow, low bow—to the experience you just had and still are having—and offer a sincere, heartfelt, and soulful thank-you.

8. Do your best to embody this feeling as you go about your day. We are all dancers in the world. Continue your wyrd dance as you encounter one wandering dancer after another—each dancing in their own way.

Magical Items

Well-known magical items associated with the modern practice of seiðr include the high seat, the staff, the cloak, jewelry, and tools for divination, such as the runes. These are not the only magical items used by seiðr-practitioners; however, they are the most common. Magical items like wands (sticks), feathers, gemstones, and cauldrons are tools one can use to learn about magic and wield magic. Remember, though, that you will not always have tools around when you need them. When this happens, you must become your own wand, your own cloak, and your own cauldron. You don't *need* these tools to become an effective spellcaster. Your body-mind is your most powerful tool for wielding magic. Just as you are the altar, you are also the wand, cup, staff, and cloak.

- *The ceremonial high seat:* The high seat—called a seiðrjallr—can be used during public, group, oracular seiðr, and/or for seiðr performed for an individual or for oneself. The high seat likely served multiple purposes. For one, the high seat made it easier for small or large audiences to see and hear the seer or seeress. Like a throne, the high seat was considered a sacred object reserved solely for the one giving prophecy and guidance as it helped them ritualize, deepen, and expand their seeing and being. So sacred was the role of the völva and the seat upon which she sat that she was often buried along-side it.[49] The high seat was also thought to be associated with Odin's throne, Hliðskjálf, on which he sat, also seeing far and deep.

- *The staff:* Along with the high seat, the staff was another common item found in the burial grounds of seiðr-practitioners. This leads many to believe that the staff—like the high seat and the cloak—was a social role signifier that identified one as a seiðr-practitioner to others. Some of these staffs were made of bronze or iron and were decorated with elaborate carvings, though most were likely made of wood. The exact use of these staffs during seiðr and utiseta is uncertain. However, if you spend any amount of time alone in the forest or in the graveyard doing utiseta at night, you will soon begin to see it has many uses. It can be used as a support and a balance when walking through rough terrain or standing for long periods of time. It can be used as an offensive and defensive weapon against human and nonhuman entities. It can also be used as a tool for spinning fiber, or even a dancing implement—especially when in a spinning flow-state. The staff can also be charged with magical energy, used to project magical energy, or used to create magical boundaries. The staff is also a meditation implement and journeying tool as a representation of the World-Tree, Yggdrasil, or the axis mundi, Irminsul.

- *The cloak:* For the wyrd-worker, wanderer, and out-sitter, the cloak is very useful and serves many purposes. It can certainly be used to protect oneself from the elements, but it can also be used to protect oneself from unwanted energies and entities that might come too close. It can serve quite literally as a cloaking device, keeping its wearer unseen or camouflaged. A cloak is a tool for liminality, as it can be especially useful for enabling deep trance, contemplation, meditation, and traveling between worlds. Raven wears a cloak all the time. The seiðr practice of "going under the cloak" consists of wholly covering oneself with one's cloak—while either sitting or lying down—so that no worldly light and distraction might come through and disturb one's

---

49. Neil Price, "The Archaeology of Seiðr: Circumpolar Traditions in Viking Pre-Christian Religion" *University of Uppsala Brathair* 4, no. 2 (2004): 109–126, https://ppg.revistas.uema.br/index.php/brathair/article/download/616/535/1730.

utiseta as one seeks the best inner and outer paths through a challenging situation or trance-induced journey on the way to the Light. Big decisions—such as whether to convert one's kingdom to Christianity, as seen in the story of Þorgeirr the Lawspeaker in the twelfth-century *Iselendingabók*—were done under the cloak.[50]

- **Jewelry:** Jewelry is often used as a talisman to attract, collect, and/ or repel energies, entities, and experiences. Moonstone jewelry, for example, can be used if you want to work with the magic of the Moon. Citrine jewelry can be used to work with the Sun. Labradorite can be worn to facilitate deep transformation and the acquisition of magical wisdom. Obsidian is known to absorb negative energies. Jewelry can be used for a variety of purposes—to awe, distract, repel, inspire, or honor. It can also be used as a form of currency that can be bartered, gifted, or offered. Two well-known magical items of jewelry found in the lore are Odin's ring, Draupnir—which can self-generate eight new versions of itself every nine days—and Freyja's gold and amber necklace, Brísingamen, imbued with magical powers of sexuality, fertility, beauty, and healing-magic.

Wyrding Ways
Wyrding Out with Others

In this exercise, you will have the opportunity to commune with the sacred other—in the form of a deity, ancestor, or land-spirit—in front of your home altar or nature altar. If you would like, you can decorate your altar with items that remind you of your love and dedication to this divine presence: statues, flowers, paintings, symbols, gems, and so on. You can don jewelry, paint symbols, and craft creations for your Other. Wear a favorite scent, sing a favorite song, dance a special dance.

---

50. Jenny Blain, *Nine Worlds of Seid-Magic: Ecstasy and Neo-Shamanism in Northern European Paganism* (London: Routledge, 2002), 60–63.

You will need:

- Ten to thirty minutes or more for meditation, devotion, and communion
- An altar
- A candle
- Incense and/or an offering of some kind
- Optional: A meditation cushion or chair

1. Put the candle on your altar and light it. If you are outside in a place where there are flammable objects, forgo the fire for now. The last thing you want is to start a forest fire. Light an internal candle in your heart-space. Take your seat or stand in front of your altar. Maintain a meditative posture, spine upright, ready yet relaxed. Close your eyes; take a few slow, deep belly-breaths, relaxed, alert, calm, awake. With each out-breath, relax just a little bit more. Return to your natural breathing pattern.

2. Focus your awareness on the flame (or your surroundings) for a couple of minutes. As you do this, simultaneously bring awareness to your felt sense within your core or belly. Feel your internal light as you gaze at the external light. Feel the thread that connects them. Breathe deeply.

3. Close your eyes and let this light permeate your mind-body. Feel it clear any extraneous thoughts and residual energies from your mind-body, then focus your awareness on, toward, and into the divine presence with which you wish to commune. Open your heart to receive.

4. Picture her, them, him, it in your mind. Imagine them in their glory and power. Feel into the qualities of their being. If it is Freyja, for example, feel the experience of beauty, love, attraction, abundance, magic, sexuality. If it is the Fae, feel their shapeshifting playfulness. If it is a land-spirit, embody their elemental qualities. If it is an ancestor, open to their essence. Feel these qualities in your body-mind. Let the images, thoughts, sensations, and emotions flow in meditation, in trance.

5. As you commune, say "Greetings _____! Blessed be YOU! Thank you for your being, for your wisdom, your magic, and your teachings! Thank you for _____! Our wyrd is interwoven. May we both be blessed with love and understanding. May our dance flow unimpeded. May it go where it wants to go and

flow how it wants to flow. May we re-member together!" Say whatever else you feel called to say.

6. As you stay in the flow, deeply feeling, consciousness attuned and semi-absorbed with this presence, open yourself to teaching, healing guidance—whatever it is you need in your life or in the moment. Open and trust that that which comes through is meant for you. Whatever it is, you are ready-enough to receive it.

7. When your communion feels like it is coming to a natural end, start sending gratitude through your mind-body felt sense into the presence. Light the incense, make your offering, and say, "Thank you _____ for being here today. Thank you for _____! Please accept this offering of _____. May I carry the memory of this experience and the wisdom you have shared with me as I move throughout my day."

8. Take a few slow, deep belly-breaths, rise, and bow slowly and deeply. Carry this energy into the world as you go about your day or evening.

Seiðr in Summary

As metaphysical naturalists and soul-rangers, seiðr-practitioners live to explore the edges of the inner and outer spiritual landscapes because they know it is at the furthest boundaries of consciousness, being, and existence where the unknown becomes known and where the revealing, healing, and transformative light of magic and soul may be found, accessed, and channeled most directly. Walkers between worlds, seiðr-practitioners are mystics who have wandered far, survived initiatory transformations, and returned to the community Web and Wyrd consciousness. With this consciousness, they support their communities as intermediaries between humanity and mystery, as psychopomps who deliver messages, and as counselors who maintain relationships—between humans, nature, ancestors, land-spirits, elves, giants, and gods. Adepts in the ways of wyrd, their *in*-sight into the interweaving of past, present, and future allows them to predict with a high degree of clarity what has occurred, what is occurring, and what will occur. Because of all this and more, they are indispensable members of the community.

As glamorous as all this might sound, I want to remind you that seiðr, and thus utiseta, is not for everyone. Seiðr is a chthonic, celestial, and middle-world path of ordeal and nonconformity. It's not easy. Because seiðr explores the growing-edges of consciousness, being, soul, and magic, the seiðr-practitioner may sometimes walk a fine line between life, death, sanity, and insanity. Seiðr-bearers are sometimes even treated with suspicion in the heathen community. Even for many open-minded, progressive nonconformists, they may be considered a little "too weird." If you choose to walk the magical, mystical path of seiðr—or, perhaps more accurately, if it chooses to walk you—thank you; goddess bless your wyrd, and god bless your fierce, sweet, loving heart! Whatever seiðr was, is, and will become, one thing is for sure: it will always be cloaked in mystery. Fare thee well through this mystery, and I look forward to meeting you at the crossroads—now-here, know-where, in the liminal no-where.

Chapter 13
Weaving It All Together

Every dimension of every facet of wyrd we have explored over the course of this book—fate, destiny, nature, magic, soul, and becoming—as grand and mysterious as they are, are nothing but the result of pattern—the pattern of Wyrd. Causes and effects play out in predictable ways. Subtleties can be inferred from other subtleties, so much so that uncertain leaps can be made with a measure of good faith, to great success. The Earth rotates, the stone weights, the apple falls and rots, the loss of love leads to sorrow, the echo returns, Magic finds its way. Waves, spirals, contractions, and expansions do what they do because of patterns. Civilizations rise and fall, systems collapse and rebalance, while prophecies and histories predict it all—all thanks to patterns.

All conform to the presence of the underlying metaphysics and geometry of the great pattern. This pattern is Wyrd, the fundamental pattern that contains all other patterns. Over the course of this book, we have explored only a few of the myriad ways this divine pattern manifests within the domains of human existence. We have explored mind-body-relationship-environment-soul-spirit and found within each and through all the pattern. We have seen the pattern connect past, present, and future, microcosm and macrocosm, inner and outer, self and other. We have seen the pattern manifest as infinity, archetype, mythological motif, thoughts, and emotion. We have seen the patterns within

fragmentation and integration, within revelation and healing-transformation, within the pattern's becoming.

I am beyond grateful, reader—fellow wyrd-walker—that your wyrd and
my wyrd led us here together, to this liminal crossroads, where fate, destiny,
nature, magic, and soul become something other, something more, something beyond other and more. I am happy to be in this pattern together. It is
deeply meaningful and purposeful to me that we are here-and-now, wherever
and whenever that here-and-now might be. There is so much promise here,
so much potential, so much love—and so much to do.

Tending the Fire

There is a sacred fire burning within you and me. The flame you tend within
your being is not completely yours and yours alone, just as mine is not mine
and mine alone. The flame is merely ours on temporary loan. Eventually we
must return our flame to the Source—the Source of the pattern. This flame,
this Light, which has been tended and passed down through the ages by our
ancestors, is a great gift. As you and I carry and tend this gift, it gets brighter
and warmer, until eventually others begin to see it and feel it and wonder if
it is the same gift they see and feel within themselves. It is! It is the gift of life,
light, warmth, love, and remembrance. It is the gift of soul and essence made
conscious, and it is a gift to be shared as wholly and freely as possible.

On this transformative return to Source, through and beyond the mysteries of wyrd, it is extremely helpful, if not necessary, to have guides along the
way to help us see, feel, and remember our gifts, as well as the way. It can be
hard sometimes to see one's inner light without a mirror. A guide is just that:
a mirror that reflects our inner flame and Light—our wholeness—back to us.
A guide is a flame that shines a light on our own flame and path. Just by being
who they are, guides show us who we are, as well as where we are and where
we are going. Our guides' and elders' flames are that bright.

Anything that carries the Light within it is a potential guide, and because
everything came from the Light and carries a piece of the Light within it,
everything and anything can be a guide that can help you see Light within
yourself and within others. It all depends on how open you are to see it and
what choices you make on your life path. What does it mean to choose Light?
What does it mean to look and live through the lens of Light?

If you are wondering how to find a guide, start by looking within, explore your wholeness, and then process it, embody it, and share it. As you do this, the right guide will certainly come at the right time. Who knows when and who knows where, but it will happen. Prepare yourself for your guides; ask yourself, "What do I love?" "What am I curious about?" "What fuels my passion?" "How can I feed my inner flame?" "Where are my gifts needed?" Answer these questions and follow the answers. Just as Theseus followed Ariadne's thread through the deadly maze of the minotaur, let the braided thread of your wyrd—your fate, destiny, nature, magic, and soul—lead you back to Light. Your Light, our Light, the Light.

The point of wyrdcraft is to see and feel and know the Light that permeates the wholeness of who you are and what you are—all your supposed imperfections and perfections and all—and not just you as an individual actor and agent in the world, but the transpersonal You that is not just you, but me and everyone and everything else. This ecopsychospiritual awakening doesn't happen sometime in the future, it happens in the present; it is happening right here and right now as I write this and as you read this. Blessed be the emergence of Light!

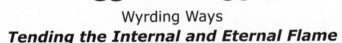

Wyrding Ways
Tending the Internal and Eternal Flame

In this exercise, you will be tending your inner flame through meditation and guided imagery. If you can, make this a daily practice. You will also be practicing a form of personal energetic composting in which you can transform mind-body-relationship-environment-soul-spirit.

You will need:
- A quiet place to meditate for thirty-three minutes
- A cushion or chair
- A candle
- Incense or another offering

1. Take a seat, get comfortable, maintain a meditative posture (relaxed and alert) with spine upright. Close your eyes, take a few slow, deep belly-breaths in through your nose and out

through your mouth. Relax a bit more with each out-breath. Return to your natural breathing pattern. Bring your awareness to your core. Breathe into it. As you do, imagine a ball of energy and light growing there.

2. From the ball of energy that is your center, draw a thread upward through your spine, out the crown of your head, until it reaches the Sun. Weave it into the Sun's core and draw the thread back down into your center. Do not stop there, but continue to draw the thread downward through your spine, out of your sacrum, until it reaches the core of the Earth. Weave it into the Earth's core. Again, do not stop there. Continue to guide that same thread upward back into your heart, creating a lemniscate—an infinity symbol—with your core at the center. Feel the energy flowing through this figure eight—from your core upward to the Sun's core, then back down to your core, downward to the Earth's core, then back up to your core, back up to the Sun's core—on and on, circling, weaving. Breathe deeply and feel this flow. If you'd like, you can continue to weave the thread in the same manner. As you weave, you generate energy. Focus on the center point of this great lemniscate in your core. Feel the energy collect and build here.

3. Light a candle in front of you. As you breathe, softly gaze into the light of the candle. Maintain your focus on the flame for the next ten to twenty minutes. As you do this, simultaneously feel the flame burning within your core—feel the light within. Gaze externally and internally into the same but different flame. Relax your diaphragm, breathe softly, and surrender to the glowing, growing fire within. This fire is your courage, your love, your grit, your creativity, and your passion. It is a healing flame. As it grows, imagine it consuming all your blocks and delusions. Let these things fuel the fire of your transpersonal becoming. Imagine the flame pulling everything toward it and transforming it into Light.

4. From your sun-light-flame, send courage, love, joy, creativity, and passion to all beings within the Web. Imagine these things feeding the inner flame of other beings. The light and warmth within them glows and grows. They are healing; the Web is healing. Imagine their inner flames devouring all that which does not serve their fullest becoming and greatest good. Feel the love

permeate the Web between all beings. Spend ten or more minutes engaging steps 3 and 4.

5. When you feel this wyrding coming to an end, take a few slow, deep breaths, stand up, bow, and carry this Light, warmth, and love into your world. Carry it with you for as long as you can into all you do. Carry it to the grocery store. Bring it into your art. Bring it to your family, to your friends, and to the strangers you see out and about. And if you forget for a while, so be it; you will soon remember to open your heart and glow again before too long. Be yourself.

The Will to Heal and Become

We have been living out of alignment with natural-soul-wisdom for far too long now. A wobbling top will eventually topple. An imbalanced and ill-constructed tower will eventually fall. Perhaps this fall is necessary for our collective awakening. Perhaps fragmentation and collective cataclysm are necessary for the fulfillment of our destiny. Perhaps we need suffering to remember. Perhaps. Regardless, no matter how far down this dangerous path we've gone, every day is a new day. Even if we do get to the point when everything does collapse, we can still turn toward each other and help each other out of the rubble. We can do this every day—today! It is never too late to start again from a place of love, empathy, and compassion. It is never too late to remember the magic of healing and the healing of magic. We can always choose to minimize harm and act from the truth of love and light, no matter how far down the road of Ragnarök and Revelations we have gone.

We have the opportunity—humans and gods alike—to meet in the rich and fecund relational space between us and within us. There is a lot of healing-magic to be found and done in this space, as we learn to manage the discomfort of communing face-to-face, side-by-side, and heart-to-heart without attacking or running away. This mysterious space where we meet each other is the liminal and alchemical crucible where revelation, healing-transformation, and becoming happen, and the evolution of being-consciousness becomes exponential. This is where magic meets matter and soul-emergence gets practical. This is where the will to love, the will to create, the will to heal, and the will to become can be found and strengthened as they are interwoven with each other. We can meet here-and-now, and/or we can meet here after we've hit rock bottom. Which one will it be? The choice seems pretty clear to me.

As ritual elder Tom Pinkson says and sings often, within each of us is the light, beauty, and power of a star, and we are here to shine, shine, shine—together. And as Aleister Crowley channeled and wrote in *The Book of the Law*, "Every man and every woman is a star."[51] Man, woman, neutral, or fluid, let's be stars together. Let us turn toward each other and open to each other mindfully, respectfully, and intentionally. Let the light of truth and the truth of Light shine healing remembrance upon us all.

Wyrd Love

As we near the end of this book, I look over my shoulder at the paths we've traversed along the way. These paths have manifested as many different themes—healing, transformation, magic, wholeness, soul, becoming—themes within themes, weaves within weaves, threads within threads, patterns within patterns, all interwoven in a wild and wonderful kaleidoscopic braid of wyrdness. As I ponder these themes and imagine them to be threads, I am re-minded of the concept of gestalt, and remember that there always seems to be a vaster, more inclusive braid that somehow encompasses all other braids within it. It's turtles, all the way down, as they say. This greater gestalt has been called by so many different names and symbolized through so many different forms over the millennia. I have called it by so many different things throughout this book—Mystery, Tao, God, Goddess, Wyrd. How about one more? How about love!

Like soul, magic, being, and nature, love is very much weird and wyrd is very much love. Love is a thing. Love is a process. Yes, it may be mysterious, but love is purposeful; it has a reason, a destiny, and a fate. Love is perhaps our most valuable and powerful guide. Though love may not always be visible, it is here for us, right here and right now. If you take the time to look, love can be found underneath, around, above, within, here, there, and everywhere, hiding in plain sight, guiding relationship, guiding becoming, guiding healing, guiding transformation, and guiding purpose.

Imagine a being called Love.

---

51. Aleister Crowley, *The Book of the Law: Liber Al Vel Legis* (Boston: Red Wheel/Weiser, 2004), 25.

Through the great ritual of existence, Love has all the while been wandering, growing, and evolving within each of us. Love, the highest witness, has been awakening us to the truth like no other. To receive the gifts Love offers, Love, too, requires offerings. Love works on the principle of sacred reciprocity as well. Love waits for you to meet it halfway on the dance floor, and Love loves to dance. The flame of Love feeds on the sacrifice of all that blocks it. Love asks us to relinquish unto it our fear, all our delusions, all those outdated, soul-less stories we tell ourselves, all the things we do that block the flow of Love. Love grows every time you face fear courageously. With every offering, every sacrifice of unnecessary suffering, Love flows and grows.

Look long enough, deep enough, and far enough, and you will see Love at the helm of all things. Every time you ask the question how (now)? you evoke and invoke Love. Love pushes and pulls us to a very special place—to a very special window, door, and path. It is Love behind all healing-transformation—from distrust to trust, hatred to compassion, mercilessness to forgiveness, prejudice to open-mindedness, deceit to truth, avoidance to responsibility, apathy to wonder, depression to aliveness, anxiety to action, unconsciousness to consciousness.

Love functions as a binding-agent and a change-agent. It is Love behind gravity, behind orbits. It is Love that brings people together and holds everything together. It is Love that illuminates the Web. Love is the great and mysterious organizing principle of the multiverse. It is also Love that helps us trust in the process of letting go when we need to. Love is there with us as we metabolize the alchemical transformations that occur at our growing-edge of being and becoming. Love integrates inner and outer, above and below, here and there, many and one. Love helps us embody and process the seemingly unbearable tensions of all the polarities and paradoxes of our dualistic world. It is with Love that we commune as we ritualize the great spell to heal all domains. To attune is to commune with Love. Love will help us as we turn and face each other and work through what we need to work through. Love will help us turn toward fear, meet fear, and transform fear into more love. A lighthouse in the distance on a stormy and dangerous sea, Love helps us endure through all manner of experiences, even sickness, misfortune, old age, and death. Love guides us through the door of death and beyond. In the end (or should I say beginning?) Love helps us surrender our individual light into the Light and flow, returning to Source.

One of the main goals of this book has been to help people love themselves. I want you to love your mind-body, your relationships, your environments, and your soul-spirit, because if you love these things, you will want to heal these things. And if you heal holistically, we all heal holistically. Healing is a labor of love and love is a manifestation of healing. Healing leads to love leads to healing leads to love leads to healing—forever—in an endless, evolving, spiraling positive feedback loop. This is the power and magic of Love. This is the power of remembering Love.

Our governments, institutions, and religions, as well as our justice, law, medical and economic systems, have somehow forgotten Love and *how* to love. They have pushed it away for far too long. Love is transformative, seemingly too transformative for the status quo called normalcy. True love is far too weird for many. True love has a way of exposing illusion, delusion, and lies. The light of love illuminates wholeness, everything. As a result, the light of love illuminates all we do that causes unnecessary harm to ourselves and others. Most of us don't want to see these things because we don't want to have to change our ways, and we don't want to take responsibility and feel the pain, guilt, and shame of our self-destructive and delusional ways. With greater love comes greater responsibility. Love will reveal the difficult yet rewarding path ahead.

Thankfully, love will give us the brilliance, guidance, strength, courage, and empathy to do what we need to do. We can suffer less, but we must decide to, again and again and again; we must remember to love every time we forget, and every time others forget. All of us must put love into action. Love will help us do this, too. Love will help us transform our self-destructive systems into Self-revelatory systems.

Thankfully, we have the potential to do all these things. We are smart, adaptive, and highly curious and conscious. We have evolved a lot over the millennia. Each of us are the heroines and heroes of this collective soul-story into which we have all been written and are continually writing ourselves. We are all loving warriors, teachers, and healers. We are shapeshifters all, magicians and witches, stars on Earth, spirit clothed, Light ensouled. Let us help each other remember this. Let us help each other tend our inner starfire and flame, as we learn to dance this cosmic dance with Love, and with Magic, together.

If you are wondering how to begin, how to continue, what to do in a practical, immediate sense, here are some options:

- Explore your wyrd within every domain.
- Ask the question *how (now)?* often.
- Dance, exercise, do yoga, meditate, and eat and sleep well.
- Spend more and more time at your growing-edge.
- Spend as much time as you can in the natural world practicing mindful awareness exercises, such as forest bathing or other ecotherapy practices.
- Explore psychotherapy and ecotherapy. You can start an initial search by typing *psychotherapist or ecotherapist near me* into the search bar, or do a more refined search by location, modality, fee, and so on through the Psychology Today website.
- Connect with an Earth-centered, soul-based spiritual wisdom tradition—including your own ancestral traditions. Learn about their worldviews and myths. Live by, and honor, the cycles of the seasons, planets, stars, Sun, and Moon.
- Maintain a daily magical, ritual, and meditation practice. Practice the wyrding ways, read, study, experiment.
- Reconnect with your friends and family. Speak your truth, share with them your Light, help them see their own. Again, don't preach—simply be, and your Light will come through.
- Connect with a magical community. The most well-known of these communities include the Troth, the Reclaiming community, ADF (Ár Ndraíocht Féin), OBOD (the Order of Ovates, Bards, and Druids), the Asatru Assembly, the Fellowship of Northern Traditions, and so on. (Webpages listed in the appendix under resources.) There are many more, large and small.
- Volunteer your time, energy, and money to those in need. Connect with an activist community—learn about and organize toward causes that promote and perpetuate healing-transformation within every domain. Speak truth to power! Never give up. Start again, and again, and again.

I will leave you with a few questions you can take into the great ritual of your life and fuel the great spell you are wyrding into existence.

- What does healing-transformation look like in my life? What needs to be healed in the domains of my life? What needs to be transformed?
- How can I be part of the collective healing process? What are my gifts that I can offer the world? Where are my gifts needed?
- What worldviews, lifestyles, behaviors, ideologies, and identities can I sacrifice that no longer serve the Web, my Higher Self, and the greater good?
- And finally, as often as you can remember, ask yourself the alchemical question: How (now)?

This book, once it's opened, will never close. Wyrdcraft, once begun, will never end. Not because I say so but because this is the way of wyrd—because the Fates say so, because Nature says so. Let the door remain open, let the path unfold, may the ups and downs of life wave, rave, and flow as they go.

The more you practice any kind of wyrdcraft, you will see life and death interwoven. You can't have one without the other. Death is woven through life and life is woven through death. You will see this as you wander through the domains. You can see clear as day as you walk through the forest, you will see death and life wedded in transformation. You will see life feeding death and death feeding life in a harmony of becoming.

Wyrdcraft is not just a guide to be used for living a healing life. It can also be used as a guide to prepare for dying a healing death. It is not often that people think about death as an experience of healing, but that is exactly what it can be. It just requires a shift in perception and understanding, one that may feel counterintuitive at first, but will eventually come more naturally with time, practice, and with the emergence of wyrd consciousness. Returning to Source, Self, Light is the ultimate healing, the ultimate re-membering.

No matter what happens, no matter what our fate and destiny may be together, no matter how things may come together or fall apart, it feels good to be part of this great soul-ritual with you. Our life-threads are woven together more tightly than ever. Thank you for that. Thank you for joining me on this path and in this process. There is so much love here. Thank you for dancing this beautiful, magical, weaving dance with me. Thank you for sharing your Light and the warmth of your flame with me and with everyone.

Now, go to the woods! Go into nature as much as you can for as long as you can and get very still and listen. Relax, root into the Earth, and reach your branches high. Soak in the sunlight, moonlight, and starlight conscious-ness of Nature. Soak in the darkness; swim in the rainfall. Feel the bitter cold and sweltering heat. Listen to the wind pass through your leaves. Meditate. Sit with the Tree, drink from the Well, marvel at Fate's weaving.

It is my hope that as you sit in the forest, as you lie in the center of the mandala in the sacred space you have found, looking up at the kaleidoscope of branches, leaves, and sky that fills your heart with such beauty and peace, such enchantment, such visions of infinity, you will forget all about wyrd-craft, all about process, suffering, work, shadow, and wholeness—and just be.

As you lie there on that soft bed of Earth, I pray she takes you in her womb and nourishes you. I hope the trees, branches, winds, and birds above and around you sing to you their being. I know the air will fill your lungs, your mind, your heart, soul, and spirit … and eventually, you will come to know your name and your Nature. The nameless name for the beingless being that has woven itself into existence through you. I pray that you will forget it, forget it all, and in that forgetting, remember everything.

Glossary of Heathen Terms

Aesir: The group of Norse gods and goddesses who live in the realm known as Asgard. This group includes Odin, Thor, Frigg, Tyr, and others. Associated with warfare, order, civilization.

Baldr: Norse Aesir god of beauty, light, and goodness. Son of Odin and Frigg. His death initiates the start of Ragnarök.

Brísingamen: Freyja's famous gold and amber necklace that was imbued with magical powers of fertility, beauty, and healing.

Disir: The spirits of dead female ancestors; described as weavers and decreers of fate.

Draupnir: Odin's magic ring, which self-replicates eight new versions of itself every nine days.

Ergi: Old Norse term used to describe those who engage in taboo behavior, such as men who practiced seiðr.

Fenrir: One of the trickster god Loki's children; the giant wolf who kills Odin at Ragnarök.

Fimbulwinter: The three-year winter that heralds the beginning of Ragnarök.

Folkvangr: The hall of the Vanir goddess, Freyja, where half of the battle-slain are taken upon their death.

Forn Siðr: "The old ways"; also a Danish religious organization.

Freyja: Meaning "Lady"; goddess of the Vanir, associated with fertility, beauty, wealth, magic, and the practice of seiðr. Twin sister to the Vanir god Freyr.

Freyr: Meaning "Lord"; god of the Vanir tribe, associated with kingship, harvest, fertility, virility, and peace. Twin brother to the Vanir goddess Freyja.

Frigg: Goddess of the Aesir tribe associated with the household, motherhood, fertility, love, marriage, and the domestic arts. Wife of Odin. Known for her prophetic skills of foreknowledge.

Frith: Old English, Anglo-Saxon term for peace, well-being, good health, security, and positive relations.

Garm: The wolf that guards Helheim, the Norse underworld.

Gift-cycle: Heathen concept of sacred reciprocity that states if you receive a gift, you are indebted to give one in return. Important for the upholding of homeostatic balance within divine relationships, social groups, tribes, families, and so on.

Going under the cloak: A seiðr practice that consisted of spending extended amounts of time completely covered by a cloak in meditative trance and ritual contemplation.

Grith: A temporary period of strictly enforced peace often instituted during large public gatherings known as Things.

Gullveig: Goddess from the Vanir tribe who was stabbed by spears and burned three times over by the Aesir gods (the act that started the very first war).

Hæl or **heill**: Old English and Old Norse terms, respectively, to describe health and well-being.

Heidr: Archetypal völva thought to have revealed the coming of Ragnarök to Odin.

Heimdallr: God of the Aesir tribe, all-seer, watcher of the nine-worlds and gatekeeper of the rainbow bridge, Bifrost. Father of all human beings.

Hel: One of the trickster god Loki's children. The half-dead, half-living goddess and ruler of the Norse underworld, also named Hel, located within Niflheim.

Hliðskjálf: The god Odin's throne upon which he sits in his hall Valhalla, where he watches over the nine-worlds.

Höd: Baldr's blind brother who was tricked by Loki into killing Baldr, thus initiating Ragnarök.

Hoenir: A god who survives Ragnarök and helps breathe life into humans.

Hugin: One of Odin's ravens; commonly translated as "Thought," though I prefer to define it as "Soul-imagination."

Hvergelmir: One of the three wells from which the roots of Yggdrasil draw sustenance; translates to "boiling spring." Located in the underworld, Niflheim.

Irminsul: Germanic, Saxon concept of the sacred pillar, axis mundi, or World-Axis of the multiverse.

Jormungandr: The giant, terrible serpent of Norse mythology, son of Loki, who kills Thor and is killed by Thor during the final battle of Ragnarök.

Landvaettir: Also referred to as land-spirits, nature-beings, the faerie folk of the Germanic religions.

Loki: Shapeshifting trickster giant-god of the Norse, blood brother of Odin, sometimes friend and sometimes foe of the Aesir. Father of Jormundgandr, Hel, and Fenrir.

Mimir: Wisest of the gods within Norse mythology. Odin kept his decapitated head alive by treating it with herbs and placed it in the bottom of Mímisbrunnr (the Well of Mimir).

Mímisbrunnr: The Well of Mimir. This well, located in Jötunheim, the realm of the giants, is the source of all wisdom-memory. Odin plucked out one of his own eyes and offered it to the omniscient giant Mimir in order to take a drink from this well so that he might apprehend the mysteries of existence.

Munin: One of Odin's ravens; commonly translated as "Memory," though I prefer to define it as "Soul-memory, or Desire to re-member soul."

Nerthus: Earth and fertility goddess worshipped by the Germanic peoples of the European subcontinent.

Nídhöggr: The dragon that incessantly gnaws on the roots of the World-Tree, Yggdrasil.

Niflheim: The primordial, icy, dark, cold Norse underworld; one of the nine-worlds.

Njord: Vanir god, father of Freyr and Freyja; associated with the sea, seafaring, fishing, wind.

Norns or Nornir: The Norse Fates. Urðr (what has become or happened, destiny, or spiritual purpose—also one of the etymological roots of wyrd), Verðandi (becoming), and Skuld (should, debt, what ought to happen, or a karmic debt that must be paid). They live at the base of, and tend, the World-Tree, Yggdrasil.

Odin: (Oðinn, Woden, Wotan) God of the Aesir tribe associated with ecstasy, poetry, war, magic, and the obsessive self-sacrificial search for wisdom.

Ørlög: Old Norse concept associated with fate; translates to "primal layers," "first law," or "that which has been laid down first."

Ratatöskr: The squirrel who lives in the World-Tree who delivers messages and insults between the eagle on the top and Nídhöggr in the roots.

Seiðr: A type of Nature-magic practiced by the ancient Norse and modern heathens that works directly with the Web of Wyrd.

Seiðrjallr: The ceremonial high seat used by the völva or spákona while engaging in oracular seiðr.

Seiðrkona: Translates to "seiðr-woman." Female practitioner of the magical practice seiðr.

Seiðrmaðr: Translates to "seiðr-man." Male practitioner of the magical practice seiðr.

Spákona: Translates to "prophecy woman."

Surtr: Giant whose flaming sword destroys Bifrost, kills the god Freyr, and brings about the incineration of the World-Tree and nine-worlds.

Thing: Periodic communal gatherings used for settling community affairs: trading, judicial proceedings, contests, entertainment, oracular seiðr, forging alliances, planning raids, and so on.

Thor: Warrior and protector god of the Aesir tribe associated with battle, war, protection, jovial gatherings, drinking, feasting, and thunderstorms.

Tyr: Aesir god associated with war and heroism.

Urðrbrunnr: The Well of Urðr (the Well of Wyrd). Located at the base of the World-Tree, Yggdrasil. The meeting place of the gods when in council.

Utiseta: Translates to "out-sitting." A magical practice associated with seiðr in which the practitioner spends the night atop burial mounds, in the wilderness, or at a crossroads to practice magic and commune with ancestors, land-spirits, and other living and dead beings.

Valhalla: The Norse God Odin's great hall and afterlife for fallen warriors, where half of those slain in battle go after death to feast, fight, die, and return day after day until the coming of Ragnarök.

Valkyries: Female warriors who collect the slain and transport half of them to Odin's hall, Valhalla, and the other half to Freyja's hall, Folkvangr.

Vanir: Norse gods and goddesses (including Freyr, Freyja, Njord) who live in the realm Vanaheim. Associated with the nature, fertility, abundance, agriculture.

Vitki: Old Norse word that translates to "witch." Practitioner of seiðr.

Völva: Old Norse word that translates to "seeress." Practitioner of seiðr.

Wyrd consciousness: Modern heathen term (coined by Valarie Wright as far as I know). A form of consciousness that has awakened to the Nature of Wyrd; also referred to as web consciousness, ecological consciousness, magical consciousness, or spiritual consciousness.

Yggdrasil: The World-Tree of Norse mythology. The body of the nine-worlds—the entirety of the cosmos.

Resources and Organizations

- Explore your astrological birth chart: https://astro.cafeastrology.com /natal.php or www.astro.com

- Explore your Enneagram Type: https://www.eclecticenergies.com /enneagram/test

- Explore your Human Design Chart: https://www.myhumandesign .com/get-your-chart/

- Find a therapist (search by location, fee, orientation, etc.): www.psychologytoday.com

- Fireside Project (Psychedelic Peer Support Line): 62-FIRESIDE (623-473-7433), https://firesideproject.org/

- MAPS: Multidisciplinary Association for Psychedelics Studies: www.maps.org

- The Troth (Heathen organization): https://www.thetroth.org

- The Asatru Community (Heathen organization) https://www .theasatrucommunity.org/shieldwall

- Reclaiming (Eclectic witchcraft organization): https://reclaiming collective.wordpress.com/

- ADF (Ár Ndraíocht Féin—Druidic organization): https://www.adf .org

- OBOD (the Order of Ovates, Bards, and Druids): https://druidry.org
- The Fellowship of Northern Traditions (Heathen organization): https://www.northerntraditions.org/
- Heathen Soul Lore (Heathen resource): http://heathensoullore.net
- Temple of Witchcraft (Modern magickal tradition): https://templeofwitchcraft.org/
- Bill Plotkin's Soulcraft (ecotherapy resource): https://www.animas.org/books/soulcraft/
- Joanna Macy's The Work That Reconnects Network (ecotherapy resource): https://workthatreconnects.org/
- Craig Chalquist's Terrapsychology (ecotherapy resource): https://www.chalquist.com/terrapsyche

Bibliography

Almaas, A. H. *Spacecruiser Inquiry*. Boston: Shambhala Press, 2002.

Andrews, T. *Animal Speak: The Spiritual & Magical Powers of Creatures Great and Small*. Woodbury, MN: Llewellyn Publications, 1993.

Beck, Renee, and Sydney Barbara Metrick. *The Art of Ritual: Creating and Performing Ceremonies for Growth and Change*. Berkeley, CA: The Apocryphile Press, 2012.

Bennett, Andrew, and Marc Théry. "Avian Color Vision and Coloration: Multidisciplinary Evolutionary Biology." *American Naturalist* 169, no. 1 (January, 2007): S1–S6. https://doi.org/10.1086/510163.

Blavatsky, Helena. *The Voice of the Silence*. Pasadena, CA: Theosophical University Press, 1976.

Byrd, Louis. "Native American Spider Mythology: 0024-Our Voices-Ehep Legend." Native Languages of the Americas: Preserving and Promoting American Indian Languages. 1998–2020. http://www.native-languages.org/legends-spider.htm#google_vignette.

Campbell, Joseph. *The Hero with a Thousand Faces*. Princeton, NJ: Princeton University Press, 1973.

Capra, Fritjof. *The Tao of Physics: An Exploration of the Parallels Between Modern Physics and Eastern Mysticism*. Boulder, CO: Shambhala, 2010.

————. *The Web of Life: A New Scientific Understanding of Living Systems.* New York: Anchor Books, 1996.

Cashford, Jules. *The Moon: Myth and Image.* London: Cassell Illustrated, 2003.

Courlander, Harold. *Fourth World of the Hopis.* New York: Crown Publishers, 1970.

Ehrenreich, Barbara, and Deirdre English. *Witches, Midwives and Nurses: A History of Women Healers.* New York: The Feminist Press, 2010.

Erdoes, Richard, and Alfonso Ortiz. *American Indian Trickster Tales.* New York: Penguin Books, 1999.

Gaiman, Neil. *Anansi Boys.* New York: Morrow, 2005.

Gangaji. *You Are That.* Louisville, CO: Sounds True, 2007.

Gendlin, Eugene. *Focusing.* New York: Bantam Dell, 1981.

Greene, Liz. *The Astrology of Fate.* York Beach, ME: Samuel Weiser, 1984.

Harper, D. "Weird." Online Etymology Dictionary. Retrieved August 2019. https://www.etymonline.com/word/weird#etymonline_v_4898.

Hassler, Lynn. *The Raven: Soaring Through History, Legend & Lore.* Tucson, AZ: Rio Nuevo Publishers, 2008.

Henderson, Josepf. "Ancient Myths and Modern Man." In *Man and His Symbols.* Edited by C. G. Jung. London: Dell, 1978.

Herbert, Frank. *Dune.* New York: ACE, 2005. First published 1965 by Chilton Books.

Hesse, Hermann. *Demian.* Translated by Thomas Mann. New York: Bantam, 1970. First published 1919 by Fischer Verlag.

Hillman, James. *The Dream and the Underworld.* New York: Harper & Row, 1979.

Johnson, Robert. *Ecstasy: Understanding the Psychology of Joy.* New York: Harper Collins, 1987.

———. *Owning Your Own Shadow: Understanding the Dark Side of the Psyche*. San Francisco, CA: HarperSanFrancisco, 1994.

Judith, Anodea. *Wheels of Life: A User's Guide to the Chakra System*. Woodbury, MN: Llewellyn Publications, 2009.

Jung, Carl G. *Aion: Researches into the Phenomenology of the Self*. 2nd ed. Princeton, NJ: Princeton University Press, 1959.

Jung, Carl G., Marie L. von Franz, Joseph L. Henderson, Jolande Jacobi, and Aniela Jaffé. *Man and His Symbols*. New York: Dell, 1968.

Kinsley, David. *Tantric Visions of the Divine Feminine: The Ten Mahavidyas*. Berkeley, CA: University of California Press, 1997.

Levine, Peter. *Waking the Tiger: Healing Trauma*. Berkeley, CA: North Atlantic Books, 1997.

Lonie, Alexander Charles Oughter. "Animism." In *Encyclopædia Britannica*. Edited by T. S. Baynes. Vol. 2, 9th ed. New York: Charles Scribner's Sons, 1878.

Louv, Richard. *Last Child in the Woods: Saving Our Children from Nature-Deficit Disorder*. Chapel Hill, NC: Algonquin Books, 2009.

Maharshi, Ramana. *The Spiritual Teachings of Ramana Maharshi*. Boulder, CO: Shambhala, 2004.

Margolin, Malcolm. *The Ohlone Way: Indian Life in the San Francisco-Monterey Bay Area*. Berkeley, CA: HeyDay, 1978.

May, Rollo. *The Courage to Create*. W. W. Norton & Company, 1994.

———. *Freedom and Destiny*. New York: W. W. Norton & Company, 1999.

———. *Love and Will*. New York: Dell, 1969.

Mencagli, Marco, and Marco Nieri. *The Secret Therapy of Trees: Harness the Healing Energy of Forest Bathing and Natural Landscapes*. Emmaus, PA: Rodale Books, 2019.

Metzner, Ralph. *Green Psychology: Transforming Our Relationship to the Earth*. Rochester, VT: Park Street Press, 1999.

Moore, Robert. *The Magician and the Analyst: The Archetype of the Magus in Occult Spirituality and Jungian Analysis.* Philadelphia, PA: Xlibris Corporation, 2002.

Moore, Robert, and Douglas Gillette. *King, Warrior, Magician, Lover: Rediscovering the Archetypes of the Mature Masculine.* New York: Harper Collins, 1991.

Moore, Thomas. *Care of the Soul: A Guide for Cultivating Depth and Sacredness in Everyday Life.* New York: Harper Collins, 1992.

———. *Soul Mates: Honoring the Mysteries of Love and Relationship.* New York: Harper Perennial, 2016.

Morgenstern, Erin. *The Starless Sea: A Novel.* New York: Knopf Doubleday Publishing Group, 2019.

Nichols, Sallie. *Jung and Tarot: An Archetypal Journey.* Newburyport, MA: Weiser, 1980.

O'Donohue, John. *Anam Cara: A Book of Celtic Wisdom.* New York: Harper Collins Publishers, 1997.

Ogden, Pat. *Trauma and the Body: A Sensorimotor Approach to Psychotherapy.* New York: W. W. Norton & Company, 2006.

Patterson-Rudolf, Carol. *On the Trail of Spider Woman: Petroglyphs, Pictographs, and Myths of the Southwest.* Santa Fe, NM: Ancient City Press, 1997.

Perls, Fritz. *The Gestalt Approach & Eyewitness to Therapy.* Mountain View, CA: Science and Behavior Books, 1973.

———. *Gestalt Therapy Verbatim.* Lafayette, CA: Real People Press, 1969.

Perls, Fritz, Ralph Hefferline, and Paul Goodman. *Gestalt Therapy: Excitement and Growth in the Human Personality.* London: Souvenir Press, 1972.

Pinkson, Tom. *The Shamanic Wisdom of the Huichol: Medicine Teachings for Modern Times.* Rochester, VT: Destiny Books, 2010.

Plotkin, Bill. *Soulcraft: Crossing in the Mysteries of Nature and Psyche.* Novato, CA: New World Library, 2003.

———. *Wild Mind: A Field Guide to the Human Psyche:* Novato, CA: New World Library, 2013.

Poe, Edgar Allan. *The Poetry of Edgar Allan Poe.* London: Arcturus Publishing, 2020.

Spira, Rupert. *The Nature of Consciousness: Essays on the Unity of Mind and Matter.* Oxford, UK: Sahaja, 2017.

Stokes, John and Kanawahienton. *Thanksgiving Address: Greetings to the Natural World—Ohén:ton Karihwatéhkwen: Words Before All Else.* Onchiota, NY and Corrales, NM: Six Nations Indian Museum & the Tracking Project, 1993.

Tolkien, J. R. R. *The Fellowship of the Ring.* Boston: Mariner Books, 2012. First published 1954 by George Allen & Unwin.

Tzu, Lao. *Tao Te Ching.* Translated by J. C. H. Wu. Boulder, CO: Shambhala, 1990.

Walker, Brian. *Hua Hu Ching: The Unknown Teachings of Lao Tzu.* New York: Harper Collins, 1992.

Wanless, James. *Voyager Tarot: The Way of the Great Oracle.* Carmel, CA: Merrill-West, 1989.

Weber, Larry. *Spiders of the North Woods: A Handy Field Reference to Our Most Common Northern Spiders.* Duluth, MN: Kollath-Stensaas Publishing, 2003.

Weigle, Marta. *Spiders & Spinsters: Women and Mythology.* Albuquerque, NM: University of New Mexico Press, 1982.

Whitfield, Charles L. *Healing the Child Within: Discovery and Recovery for Adult Children of Dysfunctional Families.* Deerfield Beach, FL: Health Communications, 1987.

Whiting, Bartlett Jere, and Helen Wescott Whiting. *Proverbs, Sentences, and Proverbial Phrases: From English Writings Mainly Before 1500*. Cambridge, MA: Belknap Press, 1968.

On Heathenism and Paganism

Acher, Frater. *Holy Daimon*. London: Scarlet Imprint, Bibliothèque Rouge, 2018.

Albertsson, Alaric. *Saxon Sorcery and Magick: Wyrdworking, Rune Craft, Divination & Wortcunning*. Woodbury, MN: Llewellyn Publications, 2017.

———. *Travels Through Middle Earth: The Path of a Saxon Pagan*. Woodbury, MN: Llewellyn Publications, 2009.

Bates, Brian. *The Real Middle-Earth*. London: Palgrave Macmillan, 2002.

———. *The Way of Wyrd: Tales of an Anglo-Saxon Sorcerer*. Carlsbad, CA: Hay House, 1983.

———. *Wisdom of the Wyrd: Teachings for Today from Our Ancient Past*. London: Rider Books, 1996.

Budapest, Zsuzsanna E. *Summoning the Fates: A Guide to Destiny and Sacred Transformation*. Woodbury, MN: Llewellyn Publications, 2007.

Byatt, A. S. *Ragnarok: The End of the Gods*. New York: Grove Press, 2011.

Crawford, Jackson. *The Poetic Edda: Stories of the Norse Gods and Heroes*. Indianapolis, IN: Hackett Publishing Company, 2015.

———. *The Wanderer's Havamal*. Indianapolis, IN: Hackett Publishing Company, 2019.

Crowley, Aleister. *The Book of the Law: Liber Al Vel Legis*. Boston: Red Wheel/Weiser, 2004.

———. *The Equinox: Volume III, Number 10*. Edited by Hymenaeus Beta X. Newburyport, MA: Weiser, 1991.

Dashú, Max. *Witches and Pagans: Women in European Folk Religion, 700–1100*. Richmond, CA: Veleda Press, 2016.

Defenestrate-Bascule, Orryelle. *Time, Fate and Spider Magic: A Brief Hirstory of Time*. London: Avalonia, 2014.

Fries, Jan. *Helrunar: A Manual of Rune Magick*. Oxford: Mandrake of Oxford, 2006.

Gerrard, Katie. *Odin's Gateways: A Practical Guide to the Wisdom of the Runes, Through Galdr, Sigils and Casting*. London: Avalonia, 2009.

Green, Marian. *The Elements of Natural Magic*. Rockport, MA: Element Books Limited, 1989.

Hughes, Kristoffer. *The Book of Celtic Magic: Transformative Teachings from the Cauldron of Awen*. Woodbury, MN: Llewellyn Publications, 2017.

Hyde, Lewis. *Trickster Makes This World: Mischief, Myth and Art*. Albany, CA: North Point Press, 1999.

Lafayllve, Patricia M. *Freyja, Lady, Vanadis: An Introduction to the Goddess*. Denver, CO: Outskirts Press, 2006.

Metzner, Ralph. *The Well of Remembrance: Rediscovering the Earth Wisdom Myths of Northern Europe*. Boulder, CO: Shambhala, 1994.

Paxson, Diana L. *Essential Asatru: A Modern Guide to Norse Paganism*. New York: Citadel Press, 2021.

———. *Odin: Ecstasy, Runes and Norse Magic*. Newburyport, MA: Weiser, 2017.

Peake, Anthony. *The Daemon: A Guide to Your Extraordinary Secret Self*. London: Arcturus Publishing Limited, 2008.

Rose, Winifred Hodge. *Heathen Soul Lore Foundations: Ancient and Modern Germanic Concepts of the Souls*. Urbana, IL: Wordfruma Press, 2021.

Svendsen, Lea. *Loki and Sigyn: Lessons on Chaos, Laughter & Loyalty from the Norse Gods*. Woodbury, MN: Llewellyn Publications, 2022.

Thomas, Kirk S. *Sacred Gifts: Reciprocity and the Gods*. Tucson, AZ: ADF Publishing, 2015.

Three Initiates. *The Kybalion*. London: Penguin Group, 2008.

On Seiðr

Aswynn, Freya. *Northern Mysteries & Magick: Runes & Feminine Powers.* Woodbury, MN: Llewellyn Publications, 1990.

Blain, Jenny. *Nine Worlds of Seid-Magic: Ecstacy and Neo-Shamanism in Northern European Paganism.* London: Routledge, 2002.

Desmond, Yngona. *Völuspá: Seiðr as Wyrd Consciousness.* Self-published, 2006.

Gerrard, Katie. *Seidr: The Gate is Open.* London: Avalonia, 2011.

Heath, Cat. *Elves, Witches & Gods: Spinning Old Heathen Magic in the Modern Day.* Woodbury, MN: Llewellyn Publications, 2021.

Hoogstraat, Kurt. *On Contemporary Seidr: A Guide to Norse Trance Work.* Self-published, 2019.

Paxson, Diana L. *The Way of the Oracle: Recovering the Practices of the Past to Find Answers for Today.* San Francisco, CA: Red Wheel/Weiser, 2012.

Price, Neil. "The Archaeology of Seiðr: Circumpolar Traditions in Viking Pre-Christian Religion." *University of Uppsala Brathair* 4, no. 2 (2004): 109–126. https://ppg.revistas.uema.br/index.php/brathair/article/download/616/535/1730.

Rysdyk, Evelyn. *The Norse Shaman: Ancient Spiritual Practices of the Northern Tradition.* Rochester, VT: Destiny Books, 2016.

Thorsson, Edred. *Witchdom of the True: A Study of the Vana-Troth and the Roots of Seiðr.* Bastrop, TX: Runestar, 2018.

E-Sources

Alliterative. "Weird: Fate, Shakespeare, & Turning Worms." YouTube. April 19, 2016. https://www.youtube.com/watch?v=CYPoTrHTXVQ&t=7s.

Crawford, Patrick. "The Norns, 'Wyrd,' and Fate." YouTube. August 2, 2017. https://www.youtube.com/watch?v=vcaG19-leJA.

Härger, Arith. "Wyrd and Ørlög—The Norse Destiny." YouTube. August 18, 2018. https://www.youtube.com/watch?v=NFJ2UVmpRmM.

Japyassú, Hilton F., and Kevin N. Laland. "Extended Spider Cognition." *Animal Cognition* 20 (February 7, 2017): 375–395. https://doi.org/10.1007/s10071-017-1069-7.

Macrae, Yolanda. "Tarot & the Web of Wyrd." YouTube. August 12, 2018. https://www.youtube.com/watch?v=kAdb99c3_BM&t=507s.

McKenna, Terence. "The World Is Far Weirder Than the Maddest Among Us Suppose (1994, Maui, Hawaii)." YouTube. February 6, 2018. https://www.youtube.com/watch?v=flh7O182YlU.

Multidisciplinary Association for Psychedelic Studies. "Explore Our Research." May 7, 2022. https://maps.org/our-research/.

Paxson, Diana L. "Hrafnar: Thirty Years of Re-Inventing Heathenry." Hrafnar. May 7, 2022. https://hrafnar.org/.

————. "The Return of the Völva: Recovering the Practice of Seiðr." Originally published in *Mountain Thunder*, 1993. https://seidh.org/articles/seidh/.

Index

A

H

M

Q

qigong, 135, 143, 146

queer, 73, 212

queerness, 212

R

racism, 75

Ragnarök, 117–120, 122, 123, 259

Ratatöskr, 179

relational, 8, 20, 30, 35, 52, 53, 64–70, 74, 75, 78, 90, 95, 112, 113, 116, 130, 137, 160, 161, 163, 182, 217, 218, 220, 221, 259

re-membering, 62, 182, 226, 264

repression, 112, 171, 172

revelation, 4, 8–10, 95, 96, 98, 106, 115, 118, 119, 121, 127, 129, 135, 152, 155, 159, 161, 176, 192, 196, 230, 231, 243, 256, 259

revolution, 90, 118

rites of passage, 81, 183

ritual, 3, 5, 28, 31, 32, 54, 71, 78, 96, 97, 128, 129, 144–146, 152, 154, 155, 159, 167, 169, 173, 177, 184, 211, 214, 216–218, 223, 228, 232, 233, 260, 261, 263, 264

runes, 26, 156, 164, 165, 174–176, 239, 249

S

sacred reciprocity, 137–141, 144, 147, 152, 183, 186, 193, 197, 203, 213, 231, 261

sacred place, 78, 79, 102, 223, 240, 243

sacred space, 78, 79, 154, 232, 265

sacrifice, 87, 105, 109, 133, 137, 152, 153, 155, 159, 183, 203, 207, 228, 261, 264

Saule, 29

science, 7, 15, 35–37, 49, 81, 82, 128, 182, 231

Notes

Notes

Notes

To Write to the Author

If you wish to contact the author or would like more information about this book, please write to the author in care of Llewellyn Worldwide Ltd. and we will forward your request. Both the author and the publisher appreciate hearing from you and learning of your enjoyment of this book and how it has helped you. Llewellyn Worldwide Ltd. cannot guarantee that every letter written to the author can be answered, but all will be forwarded. Please write to:

Matthew Ash McKernan
℅ Llewellyn Worldwide
2143 Wooddale Drive
Woodbury, MN 55125-2989

Please enclose a self-addressed stamped envelope for reply,
or $1.00 to cover costs. If outside the U.S.A., enclose
an international postal reply coupon.

Many of Llewellyn's authors have websites with additional
information and resources. For more information,
please visit our website at http://www.llewellyn.com.